To jim Renwick

From Ettie Frank & Family

LOYAL
The TODD BLACKADDER Story

LOYAL
The TODD BLACKADDER Story

PHIL GIFFORD

Hodder Moa Beckett

ISBN 1-86958-892-4

© 2001 Original text — Todd Blackadder
The moral rights of the author have been asserted

© 2001 Design and format — Hodder Moa Beckett Publishers Ltd

Published in 2001 by Hodder Moa Beckett Publishers Ltd
[a member of the Hodder Headline Group],
4 Whetu Place, Mairangi Bay, Auckland, New Zealand

Designed and produced by Hodder Moa Beckett Publishers Ltd
Film and colour separations by Microdot, Auckland
Printed by Toppan Printing Co., Hong Kong

This book is dedicated to my family, my friends, and all the people I've been lucky enough to meet in the great game of rugby. To every person who has touched me by going to the trouble to offer support, whether in a letter or fax, or with a kind word down at the park, a genuine thank you. A special thank you to the children who have sent letters or drawn pictures for me. You've always brightened my day. To every player who has dreams, hold on to them.

If you really believe, anything is possible.

Todd Blackadder, August 2001

CONTENTS

ACKNOWLEDGEMENTS

The author, writer and publisher wish to thank Simon Baker, of Pro Sport Photos, Christchurch, Andrew Cornaga, of Photosport, Auckland and the *Nelson Mail* for the illustrations, and Jan Gifford for the transcribing.

Foreword

How many All Black coaches have been asked to write the foreword to a book about the captain he's just dropped? But, then again, that's Todd Blackadder. To him, nothing gets in the way of friendship. You meet a lot of good blokes in rugby. Then you meet a few really good blokes. Todd Blackadder is an outstanding bloke.

He really is a leader of men. He wasn't made captain of the Crusaders and the All Blacks because he was the most popular, or the best player, but he won the total respect of rugby people long ago through his actions.

The American basketball icon, Larry Bird, once said: "Leadership is getting the players to believe in you. Players will see right through a phoney. They can tell when you're not giving it all you've got. Leadership is diving for the loose ball, putting your body on the line. That's the only way you're going to get respect from the players."

Todd doesn't just dive on the odd loose ball, or work hard once in a while. He gives it all, consistently. There are no off days for him. He comes to win, every time.

Todd doesn't just lead by example, he also has the ability to talk to the team. He has great wisdom for a young man. He doesn't waste words. He knows what to say, and when to say it.

Todd isn't a yeller or a screamer. He retains great composure in the face of adversity. The Crusaders were playing the Waratahs in 1999, in a game we just had to win.

The referee became increasingly upset at our ability to slow the ball down in the tackle. He called Todd over and told him that the next player who infringed would be sin-binned.

Todd was told to warn his team. He gathered his troops round him, and said: "You're doing bloody well. Keep smashing them, and don't let them score."

Todd still has rugby to play, and his own mountains to climb. When he's no longer playing the game people will still talk about him in the clubs and bars of New Zealand. That he could transcend parochialism and be revered as All Black captain throughout the country speaks for itself.

As the man himself might say, "When deeds speak, words are nothing."

And when it is all over he will be spoken of thus: Todd Blackadder, loyal, humble, committed, proud. All Black. Cantabrian. New Zealander to the core.

Wayne Smith
Christchurch, August 2001

1. A good guy to lead you out

"He's 100 per cent genuine,
completely honest, and totally
loyal to the All Blacks"

There's a voice next to Todd Blackadder's ear, and it's screaming. There are 109,878 people packed into Stadium Australia in Sydney and they're all screaming too. But this voice cuts through the noise with ease. It's George Gregan, the pesky, yappy, but very talented Wallabies halfback. "We're back Toddy, we're back!" Joe Roff has just scored in Blackadder's tackle, and the Aussies have clawed their way from 24–0 down to 24–all in the first Tri-Nations test of 2000.

"I made the tackle just as Roff crossed the line," says Blackadder, "and then George screamed in my ear. Before I could tell him, 'Look mate, I'm not deaf,' he'd already gone."

There are still 50 minutes to go in what many believe is the most amazing test ever played by the All Blacks, and at the heart of the maelstrom is the man whose All Black career had looked over and finished two years before this July night in Sydney.

Subbed off at Eden Park in 1998, banished to the relative wilderness of captaining the New Zealand A team, not within shouting distance of the squad of 31 players for the 1999 World Cup, Blackadder became not only the people's choice, but the selectors' choice in 2000.

He'd had some pretty high-powered support for captaincy. The great Colin Meads suggested in 1999 that "Todd's a leader. He gets up and gets into it, and it's very much a case of 'Follow me.' He's a perfect gentleman off the field, and with the experience he's developed he'd be an ideal man to lead New Zealand." Wayne Shelford thought he should be the captain too.

After the debacle at the '99 World Cup it was obvious some things had to change. John Hart resigned before he was sacked, and new coach Wayne Smith, whose association with Blackadder and the Crusaders had been warm and successful, decided on a new captain.

Was it a hard decision choosing Blackadder to lead the All Blacks?

"No," says Smith, "it wasn't really. First, because I'd had him operating for me for three years in the Crusaders, and we had a great relationship. I knew I could trust him. When you are going to a new job you have to have people around you who you can trust and there was just no doubt about Toddy.

"Secondly, he was also playing well enough. He'd played extremely well for the Crusaders that whole season and led his men really well.

"His lineout work internationally had limitations physically in that he's not 6ft 9in. He had to work hard, and we had to use smoke and mirrors at times, and use variations. But they worked well.

"We felt it was one part of the game, and he was so good in all other areas. Defensively, his leadership, his grunt in the scrum, and grunt around the track, that as long as he was performing well in those areas he was the man for us.

"Captaining New Zealand is different from captaining the Crusaders, but he didn't have to make any adjustments at that point. We had a good relationship and we'd talked about it. There is a Maori saying when all the different tribes come together they are all different coloured threads, but when they go through the eye of a needle they are all Maori.

"We used that analogy, that everyone coming into the All Blacks comes from different NPC and Super 12 teams, they're all different coloured threads, but when they come out of the eye of the needle it comes out All Black.

"He bought into that totally and he believed in the attitudes we were trying to instil, the education about the legacy. He believed that we had a responsibility to try to make the jersey better and make people proud of it. He believed in all that, it was right down his alley.

"But more than that, he had people who wanted to follow him out of the tunnel, so he had credibility and he had men who were going to follow him."

It certainly took all that good feeling in the team to get the better of the Wallabies in Sydney, the '99 World Cup champions, the Bledisloe Cup holders, the masters, if you believed people like Chris Handy and Peter FitzSimons of the rugby universe.

FitzSimons had a favourite story at the start of 2000. "Ooh look, I'm opening the trophy cupboard at the New Zealand Rugby Union headquarters in Wellington. Let's look inside. Nothing here. Let's look in this one. Nothing there either. Awww, that's right, I almost forgot. WE'VE GOT THEM ALL IN AUSTRALIA!"

The Wallabies were favourites for the first Tri-Nations game of 2000, which was only fair.

Five minutes into the game, played in front of a world-record crowd, it was hard to see why anyone might have thought so.

Blackadder laughs at the memory. "There's never been a game like it at that level, which is just so 'pow, pow, pow' it was unbelievable. I was almost too scared to touch the ball, because I don't think I had at all, and here we were 21–0 up. They were freakish tries."

In the first minute Tana Umaga scored, in the third minute Pita Alatini, in the fifth minute Christian Cullen. Andrew Mehrtens converted all three. Three minutes after Cullen's try Mehrtens kicked a penalty. Eight minutes, 24–0.

In the crowd there was almost silence from the Australian fans. But their men on the track weren't finished. They flung themselves back at the

All Blacks. "They kept on coming," says Blackadder. "I just remember tackle after tackle after tackle. By halftime they'd clawed their way back to 24–all. The intensity, and the ferocity was unbelievable."

The game had felt special, even before kickoff. The massive stadium, finished for the Olympic Games, which were just three months away, awed the All Blacks.

"When you're driving in there, and you see the hordes of people at the stadium," says Blackadder, "you think you've played at some amazing places, but they were all topped that night.

"You start to think how those people are there to watch your team play rugby. I really felt how special it was."

Waves of sound crashed onto the field when the Wallabies were scoring their tries, but the All Black captain heard just a dull roar.

"I know at Jade Stadium when the crowd's calling 'Canterbury' you know what they're saying. But when the game's going, at any stadium in the world, I've never listened to the crowd, you're that focused on what you're doing, you're just there to play rugby. The shutters go down, and you go into game mode."

Blackadder knew that the All Blacks didn't have the rock-solid confidence great teams of the past had commanded so easily. After the first golden eight minutes he was thinking, "We're going to win this. We've got to convince ourselves we're going to win."

This time there was control from the players. They slugged back at the Australians, and two minutes from fulltime a slick pass from Taine Randell gave Jonah Lomu just enough room to pick his way down the sideline for the winning try. The All Blacks won, 39–35.

"Really it was a bit of brilliance at the end by Taine and Jonah that won it for us," says Blackadder. "Who else but Jonah would have scored that try?

"The most enjoyable thing for me was it felt like we were erasing bad memories, that we could foot it with the world champions. We were a young team, and we were going to go for it, and we'd done it."

Building up the confidence of the players was a key element during Blackadder's long year as All Black leader. After the 1999 World Cup coach

Hart was vilified, and the indignities he suffered have been well documented.

What's almost been lost in the attention focused on how badly Hart was hurt by personal attacks is that the players were slated too. "Gutless" was one of the kinder phrases bandied about after the losses to France and South Africa. One former All Black suggested the All Blacks, who took a break in the south of France during the World Cup campaign, "couldn't make up their minds if they were playing footy or on a piss trip."

Wayne Smith was the back coach at the World Cup and he says that while he "can't speak for the players who were at the World Cup, I know that I've lost a lot of respect for some former All Blacks. I just could not believe that men who had worn the jersey could be so vitriolic in their criticism.

"Some of them had been through tough times themselves as All Blacks. They'd lost some games, let their guard down at times. I would say a lot of the '99 All Blacks were pretty confused by it all.

"It did really hurt. You saw some fallout with some of the players. I would say it's possibly hastened some of them going overseas. Jeff Wilson had a year off, and while the criticism wasn't the reason, it didn't help.

"I still feel like that personally. I've just got no respect for some of the former All Blacks who still make statements in the papers that are unbelievably ill-informed and harsh.

"If you spoke to a Stu Cron, or an Ian Kirkpatrick, or a Graham Williams who has been in the current environment, they'd tell you wearing the jersey means exactly the same to today's players as it did in our day.

"I don't think the All Blacks now are overpaid wowsers at all. They get paid, and some things are different. There's probably a better, more professional preparation, but the jersey still means exactly the same to the players, and there's been a lot of assumptions made by their critics.

"I think Toddy was really important to the All Blacks in that transitional period following the World Cup. He has that ability to override parochialism, because he characterises everything that's good about the Kiwi bloke.

"He's humble, he's not sophisticated, but he's wise in a No. 8 wire sort

15

of way, and he was the ideal person to help unify things.

"I don't know that it will ever be unified the way it was. Lindsay Knight's got a book out on 25 years of the NPC, and I thought, 'What the hell did we do before that?' We used to have a Ranfurly Shield, and a few friendly games.

"It's just so totally different, and you can't relate today to yesterday except for what the All Black jersey still means.

"That's the thing that I've wanted from my job with the All Blacks, and I'm sure Toddy would say the same, that from when we came in to when we left there was a growth in the standing of the jersey, in what people said about it, the commitment the players give to it, how they put their bodies on the line.

"I'm certain Todd got a long way down the track with that last year.

"Inside the team he was totally respected. Tana Umaga said that he was just a good guy to run out behind. There was that feeling in the squad.

"Externally, even the Andy Hadens who have their own agendas, even Andy admitted Toddy was a good man in the All Black jersey, a good leader. He might not rate him as a lineout forward, but even he admitted he had a good heart, which he gave to the cause.

"I think a lot of people around the country feel well towards him, and he was really important in Anton Oliver's development as well. I'm sure that Anton, having a year under Toddy's captaincy, will have taken a lot out of it."

For Oliver the arrival of Blackadder, and coaches Smith and Tony Gilbert in 2000 was almost manna from heaven.

"What Toddy and Smithy and Tony put together I could really identify with, as opposed to the All Black regime under John Hart," says Oliver. "It was more who I am. It was kind of less corporate.

"It was more about playing for your friends, and your mates, rather than getting things distorted. There was no playing off between people. It was just, 'Okay, we're all a team, whoever is playing, whoever isn't, let's just all bloody get in there and do our best.' If you don't get the nod then give your mate all that you can to help him play well.

"That's definitely part of who Todd is. He is a team man through and through. He'd die for the Crusaders and Canterbury and the All Blacks. Those were the qualities I really identified with.

"I struggled with my first few years in the All Blacks. I came in at a bad time, around WRC, and my ideals over what an All Black was kind of got blown right out of the window from day one. I guess I was left floundering a bit. I had all these superstars, my idols, and I came in and they were bickering about money, and wanting to flag the All Blacks, and go and play overseas. I was just, 'What the hell's going on?'

"It took me a long time to get centred, and that was what Todd and Smithy and Tony did last year.

"The key to winning is that you have the same ideals of playing for your mates you have in a club team. Look at the Crusaders, every year, they were still written off. They had that intangible quality of people caring about each other, and caring about what they were playing for. If anything, that should be more heightened in the All Blacks.

"My first few years in the All Blacks were a bit like playing with people who were quite disconnected. It was just about 15 individuals. Even if we lost a test, some of them, I felt, as long as they played a good game, and their powder was dry, they didn't give a shit. It was terrible."

If some of his boyhood heroes weren't quite what Oliver expected, Blackadder the private figure inside the All Blacks, certainly was.

"First and foremost Toddy is such an honest person. What you see as a member of the general public is what he's actually like.

"The media can often paint a picture of someone that they're actually not. But Todd's everything that he appears to be. He's 100 per cent genuine, completely honest, completely loyal to whatever he's put his heart into, and that was definitely the All Blacks in 2000."

As an Otago stalwart there was already respect from Oliver for Blackadder as an opponent in the NPC and Super 12. "We always felt that he was the heart and soul of the Canterbury forward pack. They all look up to him, and he hasn't missed a game for goodness knows how long.

"We felt if we could get into him, because he was such an unyielding guy, that was the first part of trying to erode the Canterbury pack, especially when they were sort of unstoppable."

What does Oliver hope to emulate from the Blackadder way as captain?

"He doesn't get flustered by a lot of things, things don't seem to affect him that much, he takes things in his stride, and he's quite well balanced.

"He accepted his lot that he was the captain, and had to do a lot of the media stuff, which both he and I aren't that comfortable with. Watching how he dealt with all that was really enlightening for me.

"On the field he's one of those guys who knows what to do in the hard, dark places. I mean that you know he's there, you don't have to look around, you know he's breathing down your neck for when things hit the fan. They're the kind of people you want as your mates and on your team.

"I've been told often that I'm quite hard to get to know. I guess it takes a while for me to really open up when I trust someone, and Todd and I were getting to that stage at the end of the year. I was lining up to do a lot more dirty work for him this year, because I don't think I fulfilled that role for him last year.

"As a senior member I just stuck to doing my own job, and wanting to be in the All Blacks as a starting member. That's quite a selfish view, and I wanted to do more to help his captaincy out by dealing with all the off-field stuff that goes on."

* * *

The recall to the All Blacks in 2000 for Blackadder was hardly unexpected, but it was certainly not leaked in advance. Smith and his assistant coach, Gilbert, said they would not talk individually to players during the Super 12 season, and they kept their word.

There was no nod or wink, much less a whisper, from them for Blackadder to let him know he was about to become the captain.

The Crusaders, says Blackadder, flew into Christchurch airport after their Super 12 win in Canberra "all pretty tired and hung over. We hardly slept on the plane, and then when we got back to Christchurch Andy Dalton (the president of the New Zealand Rugby Union) came on the plane and read out the All Black team there.

"We'd been through the emotional roller coaster, and nobody had been told who was in the team.

"It was great, but it was also hard in some ways. When you go through everything together as a team, and then an All Black team is named, some guys are in, and you feel happy for them, but the guys who are left out, there's a certain amount of sorrow.

"It's very hard to hide your emotions, whether it's good news, or bad news. You can never deny your true emotions, and that's where it was bloody hard.

"You don't know whether to yell for joy, or feel the pain for someone who's given the Crusaders so much, who's helped win our third title, and has then missed out.

"I know it's par for the course, you can't pick the whole team, but you go through everything as a team. It had been a tough final, and we'd had a lot to celebrate. Three years of hard work, and three trophies.

"My wife, Priscilla, and the kids, and my Mum were at the airport, which was great, but before you hardly say hello and congratulate everyone, you've got cameras in your face, being interviewed on television while you're feeling a little bit the worse for wear.

"It's not easy when you're sweating some of the fluids from the party out. It's a bit of a testing time, but you get through that, and then there's everyone at the airport for another amazing reception for the Crusaders.

"I was absolutely shattered after that. We got into a bus, went back to the Christchurch Casino, and had a bit of a feed with the kids and all the partners, but we were absolutely stuffed."

There would be just four days at home before the All Blacks assembled at the adidas Institute of Rugby in Palmerston North.

For Blackadder the time at home was broken by what had become almost an institution in Christchurch, the Super 12 victory parade through the heart of the city, which for three years at the start of winter was always blessed with perfect weather and a massive crowd estimated at close to 100,000. Says Blackadder, "Every year you think it's going to get smaller, but it doesn't."

It was Blackadder's first visit to the institute in Palmerston North, although through the winter all the All Blacks would become very familiar with it.

"It's a great facility," he says. "They've got it indoor/outdoor, and it's totally geared up for rugby.

"Being the way we were, a new team, a new captain, a new manager, a new trainer, a new physio, just lots of new faces, we needed an environment where we could spend time together.

"You live on the campus, which you quickly realise is very much a rugby campus. The whole building is the shape of a fern, there's an All Black rugby jersey on the doors with the numbers on them. There's no question about it being a rugby camp.

"There's everything there, a gym, a training field, an indoor area about the size of two tennis courts to train under cover.

"Palmerston North is a nice place to have it, because it's out of the way a bit, and it's not overly commercialised. The institute is on the outskirts of town, part of the Massey campus, but self-contained.

"There was a little bit of criticism at the time, because I think some people thought we should have been out in the public more. But really we needed every minute of every day.

"It was intensive, tiring work. Smithy and Tony Gilbert wanted a new game plan, and we had to lay our values and protocols out, and try to build a team culture in a very limited period of time.

"The thing with Super 12 is that usually you've got months to prepare. But when you're selected as an All Black you have about four days, if you're in the Super 12 finals, to get up to the national camp, and usually you're shagged, mentally and physically drained from Super 12.

"If you get into the All Blacks, it's such an honour, and you're ready to go again, playing for the pride in your country. But the coaches do have such a short period of time that it's really a pressure-cooker situation."

In 2000 the All Blacks stayed in Palmerston North, and left for test venues very close to the game, usually not arriving in test cities like Auckland and Dunedin until Wednesday night.

It was a bit, says Blackadder, like being on tour in your own country. All Blacks joked, usually in a good-natured way, about being allowed good behaviour passes to spend time at home.

Things were done differently in 2001, with the All Blacks spending most of the week where the tests would be played. It's a move Blackadder agrees with. "If you go to the test venue, you're just that little bit more settled in that environment. As it happens none of us actually lived in Palmerston North so nobody spent a lot of time at home. In New Zealand in 2000 with the All Blacks we were away off and on for 12 weeks. In that time I was only home for 11 days."

What did work well was a training timetable for the week, which was based on what the Brisbane Broncos do. "We trained on the Monday, Tuesday, and Wednesday, had Thursday off, trained at a captain's run on the Friday, and played Saturday. We had one full day off a week and it worked really well."

Blackadder's captaincy of the All Blacks started on a Friday night, June 16, at North Harbour Stadium, against Tonga.

"I was primed for the first test. You look for motivation, and the All Black jersey is motivation enough." He laughs. "Being a new captain you certainly want to start off absolutely on the right note.

"Tonga the previous year had played really well against the All Blacks at the World Cup, and their coach kept referring to that all week, that they were going to get stuck into us. He kept baiting us, with a bit of gamesmanship.

"Players and coaches look for anything for a bit of extra motivation. I believe personally in never ever giving anything for your opponent to grab hold of. The game's hard enough without trying to inspire someone to play well against you."

In slippery conditions the All Blacks were clinical against the Tongans, piling on 102 points without a reply. It wasn't, Blackadder swears, as easy as it looked.

"It was actually hard footy. People might feel that with a score of 102–0 the game itself might be easy, but it was played at such intensity for the full 80 minutes it was physically exhausting.

"That was my first test after being dropped, so you do think, 'Am I up to it?', 'Can I do this?' There's so much pressure on yourself that you just want to get out there and rip people apart. You just want to get your hands on the ball, and enjoy it."

Next up came Scotland, with two tests, one at Carisbrook, the second at Eden Park. Both were won convincingly, 69–20 in Dunedin, 48–14 in Auckland.

"We'd done our homework, and we'd really been working on our game plans," says Blackadder. "We did a lot of snaking, driving guys over the advantage line, and they were good performances.

"In Auckland, things had been pretty intense, and we hadn't taken the foot off in training. The games were part of our conditioning for Tri-Nations, so we were probably a little bit flat at Eden Park, to be honest. We talked about it after the game, that it was probably time to do a bit of freshening up."

By now Blackadder was enjoying the games, without the jitters that came before his first test as leader, but he knew the real tests were on the horizon.

Still, heading for Sydney for the Stadium Australia thriller, the game Murray Mexted would rate as the best test of all time, was something Blackadder looked forward to, and not just for the rugby.

For a start his determined, non-flashy style of play probably wins more accolades in Australia than it does here. Justin Marshall recalls that during the 2000 Super 12 competition "players in Australia would say, 'Do you think Toddy's going to be the All Black captain? He should get it.'"

And while bagging the Aussies is almost a national sport in New Zealand, the reality for players like Blackadder is that the Australian rugby players "are all good buggers, ferocious on the field, but good guys off it.'"

In fact he admires their attitudes a lot. "Their culture over there is different. They just seem a little bit more balanced than our guys. They dress well, they speak well, they come across really well.

"There's a real intelligence going on there, with the core attitude that they want to win. You'll get the odd one who's a bit smart, but good footballers like Tim Horan don't have to say anything.

"It's really amazing how low-key it is in Australia at an after-match function. You get to know players well enough to say there's a common bond there, even if you're not close mates.

"Over the years I would have actually met most of their parents. Stephen Larkham's Dad always comes up and says g'day. You meet Mums and Dads and brothers and sisters.

"A guy like Steve Larkham is a very talented football player, and when you listen to him talk, the way he handles himself, he's a very mature guy as well. They all are, right across the board. They're very intelligent guys.

"I feel there's a mutual respect between John Eales and myself. He's a good fellow.

"The Aussie after-matches are a lot more informal than ours. Over there it's basically just a beer and a yarn. In New Zealand, you get there, and before anyone can really delve into a great conversation there are speeches, and then it's all over, and the teams go their separate ways.

"In Australia it's more low-key, and a lot more relaxed. In the Crusaders in 2001 we took that philosophy into the way we did things. We didn't get into No. 1s. We put on a nice track suit, and had a beer and a yarn.

"After a game most of the recovery is done in your changing room. You go in there and get a heap of fluid into you, and step into an ice bath up to your neck, to help with the recovery. Then you can catch up with the other team."

From Sydney it was back to Palmerston North, then down to Hanmer Springs, the thermal resort town to the north of Christchurch. The All Blacks stayed at the gleaming new Heritage hotel, trained at the local rugby club, and soaked in the hot pools.

It seemed like a good idea at the time when it was decided that on the way by bus to Christchurch for a Jade Stadium test against the Springboks that the team would stop off at Rangiora, Blackadder's hometown. The town, so proud of Todd there have been times when the sign on the outskirts has been officially changed to Blackadderville, went wild. Kids, parents and grandparents swamped the town centre.

"We stopped in the main street, and we only signed autographs for five minutes, then got back on the bus. With hindsight we really should have got on the back of a truck, driven through the main street and waved.

There was a bit of bad feedback, because a lot of kids missed out. It really was just a flying visit."

If the fleeting visit home wasn't entirely a roaring success the test against the Springboks, in Blackadder's memory "an old-style, old-fashioned, bruising, hard battle" was a much more complete effort, the All Blacks winning 25–12.

"It was a proud moment to be able to lead out the All Blacks against the Springboks at Jade Stadium. It felt a bit funny because only a year or two before I'd been in the stand myself watching and having a beer."

Two excellent tries by Christian Cullen showed the way, but there wasn't much left in the tank for celebrations later.

"They had an after-match back at the Convention Centre in town, and by the time you go in there and do your speech, you're gone really."

By now the 2000 season was looking like a dream come true. Five tests, five wins. At the top of the Tri-Nations table and heading to a game in Wellington against Australia where a win will mean not only the Tri-Nations title, but bringing the Bledisloe Cup home too.

Oops. It came so terribly close. A few minutes from the end of the test, with the score 23–21 to the All Blacks, coach Smith and his assistant Tony Gilbert actually got up from their seats in the glassed-in coaching box, and started to pick their way down to the players' tunnel.

As they walked down the steps a wave of applause broke out. It was probably only their inborn Kiwi reticence that stopped them from waving and blowing kisses to the crowd.

But then the tide started to turn on the field, with a penalty awarded to Australia, and Wallabies captain Eales lining up a last-gasp kick.

"By the time we got down to the bottom of the steps," says Smith, "it had all turned to crap. It was unbelievable."

Eales' penalty followed a lineout on the All Blacks' 22. At the time it seemed Blackadder and veteran Auckland prop Craig Dowd might have been arguing, before hooker Mark Hammett threw to the line.

That wasn't the case, although the lineout was a problem. At halftime in the test the All Blacks had changed their calls. With hindsight Blackadder thinks that was a real blunder.

"We'd come up with a series of lineouts, and they worked bloody well against them. We made the mistake of changing the calls. As the events unfolded we got reserves on who thought the calls were the original calls.

"It's not the reserves' fault. The calls should never have been changed. It was a huge mistake."

So when Hammett prepared to throw the ball in, Dowd asked Blackadder what the call was. "We weren't fighting at all," says Blackadder. "I was saying, 'Have you got the call? The call's been changed.'

"Mark Hammett was waiting for the throw. The call was to catch one right on the five metres. You're probably 30 seconds away from everything. It was terrible.

"We lost the lineout, but that didn't matter. We really lost the game about two minutes before that. We were under their posts, and all we had to do was keep possession. All we had to do was hold the ball.

"It was something that had been drilled into us, and into us, and into us, that we needed composure, but when the pressure came on us, we didn't keep our composure.

"We had the game in the bag, it should never have come down to that one lineout, and penalty. When you look at the video there were holes everywhere, we just made some dumb options with the ball.

"Eales hadn't been doing the kicking, and then the bugger comes on, slots it over, and our hopes of winning the Bledisloe are gone."

There were some pretty ugly scenes at the end of the test, the first played in the magnificent new Westpac Trust Stadium. South African referee Jonathan Kaplan added an extraordinary amount of injury time to the game, and disgruntled spectators started to pelt him with cans at the end of the test. It was All Black lock Norm Maxwell who came to his rescue, wrapping a big arm around the minute referee's shoulder, and hurrying him off the field.

He was a slightly unusual guardian angel. On the field Maxwell had given the referee a bit of a verbal touch-up as the clock ran and ran and ran.

"I think it was something like seven minutes over," says Blackadder. "It was like, 'Look pal, just blow the whistle.' He said after the game he'd been adding the time when we'd been wasting our time at the lineouts. When I look back on the video we didn't waste time at any point in the lineouts.

"I'd never heard of adding time for lineouts and he didn't say a word to me during the game. I certainly couldn't work it out. When he said that I was miffed. It would have been different if he'd said injuries."

There was also the question of substitutions, some made with less than 15 minutes to play.

"All these things are critical. I firmly believe that if you're a reserve you need 20 minutes, you just can't get into the game so quickly. You can't totally absorb the pressure in five minutes, and be up to the speed of the game, you just can't.

"Look at most reserve forwards. In the first five minutes when they come on they always give penalties away. They're a little bit fresher, they're hungry to get on, they're a little bit over-anxious I suppose.

"They do give penalties away. By the time they've run that little edge off, they're into a groove.

"Take a new front rower coming on. Invariably the scrums are upset for a wee while aren't they? They're so keen, and they want to make a mark on the game, they can actually be a disruption at times. You've got to take those little things into account.

"But all in all we had the game, and we should have nailed it under the posts. Instead it went all the way down to a bloody lineout, and John Eales nailing the penalty, which ruined our hopes of winning the Bledisloe and sealing the Tri-Nations.

"We did square the series with Australia, who had been the world champions the year before, but it was still a bitter pill to swallow.

"On the other hand, what made me proud to be a part of it was that people said it was the best Tri-Nations they'd ever seen. It certainly was a different brand of rugby. It was like Super 12 at an international setting, fast, open, running rugby.

"Overall I thought our guys played bloody well that day in Wellington. It was a great game to play in.

"We were pretty well primed, and the boys were on fire for most of the game. It had the feeling early on that it could have been a walkover, when the Aussies went out to 12–0 early on. We were throwing our lives into it, and while they were playing really well, we were getting the ball in hand and having a go at them.

"There were some fantastic tries. I was still proud of the players, although it was bloody gut-wrenching. It was so close, and I'll never get a chance to be that close again."

As it happens the Wellington test would not be the game that was Blackadder's biggest regret in 2000. There was still a chance for the All Blacks to clinch the Tri-Nations at Ellis Park in Johannesburg, but their performance just wasn't up to scratch.

"The South African test, and the second test in France, would be the two most disappointing games for me. With a bit more effort we could have won the game in Marseilles, and we could have won the game at Ellis Park. If everyone in the team had put in another 5 per cent we could have won it.

"It's very hard to put your finger on what was missing. We were trying to build three years into one, but really we were a one-year side building towards something. It showed in that game."

Coach Smith says that, "We still nearly won the test in Africa, despite letting our standards down.

"Tony and I found it really difficult getting the guys up again after the loss to Australia. You could see it in their eyes, even Toddy. You could see the disappointment, the bewildered sort of looks, because they had the Wellington game won and lost it."

Personal tragedy would strike assistant coach Tony Gilbert while the team were in South Africa. His mother became very ill and died, and he flew back to attend her funeral.

The All Blacks stayed in Durban at sea level before flying into Johannesburg the day before the test. With Ellis Park at an altitude of 1800 metres teams try many methods to overcome perceived performance problems in the thinner air.

"There's no substantive evidence," says Smith, "that any one way is better than any other way, when time is short. To fully acclimatise to altitude you need a decent period, more than 10 days sort of thing.

"If you're not going to acclimatise you're better to go and play within a 48-hour period of being exposed to altitude. We chose that route for the All Blacks. With the Crusaders we have also done it the other way, spending several days at altitude, and we've won both ways.

"I feel that altitude was irrelevant [for the All Blacks in 2000]. It was an accumulation of factors, such as fracturing the squad, when some players not in the playing 15 were left in New Zealand to play an NPC game, the loss to Australia, and being unable to get over that disappointment, the hostility of the environment. What we missed out on was the intensity and hostility that was building in Jo'burg, so that came as a bit of a surprise.

"I think there were a lot of factors. We managed them quite badly as far as the cumulative approach.

"We weren't able to get onto Ellis Park and do any kicking. For some reason the park was locked and we couldn't get on.

"You expect a lot of those things to happen, and I just think we didn't handle them all that well, down to the team, really, being affected by it all, and for some reason we just didn't front."

Blackadder is just as blunt. "Altitude had nothing to do with it. They were at altitude as well. It's perhaps whether you really want to put someone away or not. They did play well, but we could have played a lot better.

"When you look at that game, there was so much riding on it. I thought we had an ideal preparation, and it was something like four missed tackles which made the difference.

"You learn tackling when you're five, and I know you're playing against bloody good players, but when you're a captain, the heat's on you. You're responsible. It was just so frustrating.

"The way the Boks started it looked like they were going to put 100 points on us. It was like, 'Hang on, we're in the best nick of our lives, we've had an ideal preparation, we're keen, we want to win, but, shit, we're 30 points down, what's going on boys?' We looked like we were going to get one put right up us. It was the worst performance by the All Blacks, and we were playing catch-up the whole way.

"The score, 46–40, shows you that both teams defensively weren't on their game. It does show they were a little bit better than us. That result hurt the most.

"It isn't easy losing, but you have to accept your losses. But after a game like that you have to go to the after-match, get up and speak and then suck lemons all night. Then you have to suck lemons all the way home on the plane. You can never take it back.

"We went back to Sydney and stayed at a hotel in Manly, and did a two-day debrief with the coaches, and the trainers, one on one. They told us where we were and where we had to go. We'd put something like 15 weeks into the campaign, and to come so close and fall away was devastating.

"It's bullshit for anyone to say it doesn't hurt when we lose. People can say what they like, but I'd like to think what people look for in our teams is that we're giving it our guts.

"Most people want to see your team firing, and playing like they would if you were giving them five minutes in the jersey. The most disappointing thing in Tri-Nations was that I think they saw it up until the last game.

"This is where you have to be in the situation, where you have to look back, and although I'm not a great man for reflection, you think, 'We've made a lot of sacrifices here. I've tackled my arse off at all the defensive drills.' People only see you on telly or at the games, but there's a lot of hard work behind the scenes.

"That's what's so disappointing. The hours that you work through, the hard work you do. I'm not disappointed in how people perceived us. I'm disappointed in how we performed, that was bloody hard.

"Going through the whole season we went through everything in one season. We made every mistake, and learnt every hard lesson in one year."

Smith still has no concrete answers to what happened at Ellis Park. "Sometimes it's just not there. You can do everything dead right, and it's not there. Sometimes the feeling in the team is so good you can do everything wrong in the lead-up and still win.

"I'd liken it to being on railway tracks, and once you're on them it's bloody hard to get off. That's the roll that we got on with Crusaders teams, where I knew that if we were going to lose it was going to take a really extraordinary effort from the other team, regardless of what I did as a coach.

"We had a bit of that feeling in the 2000 All Blacks, up until when we lost to Australia, and I think we'd just shot our bolt really. We struggled from there.

"We still should have won that Springbok game, despite giving away 30 points. But afterwards I said that it wouldn't have been enjoyable for me even if we'd won, because we just let our standards slip. It was shocking defence."

After the Tri-Nations the knives started to come out for Blackadder. Until he was made All Black captain the only person really slamming him in the media was Andy Haden, a former Auckland and All Black lock, and close friend and supporter of John Hart. A failed candidate for the All Black manager's job with the 2000 All Blacks, Haden was relentless, but he was usually a lone voice.

But with the disappointments of Wellington and Johannesburg, the ugly opinion started to emerge that Blackadder wasn't as good a captain as many had thought. In the magazine *Rugby World*, for example, it's now become almost a matter of faith that Blackadder somehow changed from a proven, successful captain of Canterbury and the Crusaders to a mediocre leader in the All Blacks.

A year later Wayne Smith looks back and says, "He's the best captain I have ever been involved with as a coach. He retains his composure. You talk to the referees, they would say in world rugby he is probably the best captain to deal with, which says to me he is cool and calm and can process things under pressure without getting het up.

"If you look back on the lineout against the Wallabies in Wellington, the calls had changed. It wasn't indecision, on Toddy's part. He never seemed to get really flustered. He knew what he wanted there, and it just didn't work out. The rest is history.

"As an All Black captain on the field he had tactical awareness and nous a lot of players don't have. It's difficult at times for a tight forward, as it will be difficult for Anton Oliver at times, because of the nature of what they are doing and the way they see the game.

"You have to have lieutenants and other people that will feed information, who you'd expect will do things right under pressure.

"Toddy can get men to follow him. He might not be a John Dawes tactically, or a Graham Mourie tactically, but not many people are, and he's not in a position, as a tight forward, to be. I certainly don't buy into the idea that he was tactically poor.

"I would have his sort of captain any day."

2. Great years to come

"Toddy was a massive influence in turning the All Blacks around"

At halftime in the 2000 Armistice Day test in Paris, All Black coach Wayne Smith bent down and picked up a bit of soil from the playing surface at Stade de France. Rubbing the dirt between his fingers he said to his players, "This is Kiwi blood and bone here."

Smith could see he'd touched a nerve with his young team. "We'd talked about how many Kiwis had died in France, and we really felt the occasion. At that point you could see it in the guys, they were going out to lay waste to the French. It was fantastic."

In the past Armistice Day, November 11, has always been an occasion where French teams have played with all their fire and passion. Until 2000 the All Blacks had never won on the anniversary of the end of World War I.

But this time the history behind the date meant as much, or more, to the All Blacks as it did to the French.

A vivid memory of the end of season tour for Todd Blackadder was the time spent visiting — and learning about — military sites in France that are special to New Zealanders.

The test in Paris was played for the Dave Gallaher Trophy, honouring the man who led the 1905–06 All Black tour of Britain and France, who would die of wounds received in the battle of Passchendaele in 1917.

Before the team left New Zealand they met Gallaher's family, and when they visited the memorials and the battlefields the week before the first French test they were accompanied by military historians Chris Pugsley and Ian McGibbon.

"The war historians were brilliant. They didn't just give their version, they answered all our questions, whatever you liked. There are always one or two questions you would really like to know, and often they're brushed over. That didn't happen in France," says Blackadder.

"As far as being a New Zealander goes it was a wonderful experience, to learn about our history, and to be able to stand on New Zealand sovereign ground in France.

"It was really very moving. I planted a wreath at the memorial at Nine Elms, where the New Zealand war graves are, and then planted a rose at Dave Gallaher's grave. His family had given us the Lest We Forget rose and we took it over there and planted it at his graveside.

"We were able to see the graves of all the New Zealanders who had given their lives in the war. You don't learn about these things at school in New Zealand."

After the ceremony at Nine Elms the All Blacks were joined by the New Zealand A players at the town of Le Quesnoy, the scene of a remarkable military action by New Zealanders in November 1918.

New Zealander soldiers climbed the ancient walls of the town to liberate it street by street from German troops, rather than bombarding it, with the subsequent loss of life and buildings.

"We walked around the town," says Blackadder, "and we laid a wreath there. I was standing next to a Frenchman who had tears streaming down his face. He was moved by the generosity of the New Zealanders all those years ago. It's something you don't understand when you're in New Zealand.

"They had a pretty lavish reception at the civic centre. But Justin

Marshall and I went into the bar and had a beer, which we felt the old soldiers would have done."

When the time came to play against France the All Blacks made a point of not mentioning the 1999 loss to France at the World Cup.

The official line was that this was not a test aimed at seeking revenge for the semi-final upset. Not every player thought the same privately. Justin Marshall says, "I wanted a bit of payback. My main motivation for the test was that the year before I'd had to sit on the sideline and watch my World Cup dreams get destroyed."

To Blackadder there was a different monkey to get off the All Blacks' back. "The French had never lost on Armistice Day. I wasn't involved in the '99 test, so that test didn't enter my mind. To me it isn't what you've done as a team in the past, it's what you do now.

"We were pretty fired up for the game in Paris, and it went by so quickly. It wasn't a really forward-oriented game. It was a game with a lot of movement, a real backs' game."

There had been a flood of complaints from the All Blacks after the semi in '99 that the French had put in a lot of filth, with hints of everything from squeezed scrotums to slippered heads.

There was no dirt in Paris, says Blackadder. "I didn't experience one bit of it. I thought they were just a good side playing footy like us. Sure there were times it was a little bit hard. I actually quite like some guys putting a little bit in. I mean you are trying to win a test for your country. But I certainly never thought they were filthy or anything like it."

* * *

The test had kicked off at 8.45pm, so by the time the All Blacks and the French rolled up for the after-match pleasantries, speeches, toasts, and, as Andrew Mehrtens remembers it, "heaps and heaps of cheese, crackers, and red wine," it was a quiet night for Blackadder and the team. "By the time we finished it had been a long, big day."

In the lead-up to the next test, in Marseilles, an abiding memory for Blackadder is exhaustion.

"After we won the first test on the Monday, we had a bloody hard workout, and on the Tuesday we trained at night, another hard training, and we trained again on the Wednesday.

"I remember sitting on the bus, because we travelled on the Thursday. I'd never been so shagged in my whole life. I think I moaned to Anton the whole way. Absolutely shattered. After a long year I think the wheels were about to fall off. We were absolutely exhausted.

"In hindsight I think we should have gone back and looked at the whole schedule and probably, if anything, done things a little bit lighter. I believe we made the mistake of going too hard. Sometimes less is better.

"It's hard for the players to say, 'Look we're a bit stuffed here.' You feel like a sook, because during the whole season everyone is looking for a hard edge."

Once in Marseilles, there was a very odd prelude to the test. "On the day before the game we're usually allowed to have a walk over the ground. We got to the ground in Marseilles, and there was no bloody way they were going to let us on the field.

"When you turn up to a venue you like to look in the changing room just to familiarise yourself with it. But come hell and high water, not that day."

In the end the weird compromise of allowing the All Blacks to look in the changing room in groups of six was agreed to. Out on the ground Andrew Mehrtens, a competent French speaker, was sniping at a French rugby official, claiming he was allowing himself to be pushed around by people from the Marseilles soccer club, which actually owned the ground.

If there were fiery moments off the field, coach Smith still remains unsure about whether the lead-up for the All Blacks had enough passion in it. "In Marseilles we perhaps assumed that the factor of Armistice Day, the tradition, the Gallaher factor, was still going to be there.

"That's not necessarily the case. You still have to build every occasion and perhaps we didn't build that well enough."

The game started badly for the All Blacks. "The French were really fired up and they started with a hiss and a roar, 14–nil after seven minutes. I was thinking, 'Shit, here we go boys.'

"But then we came back, and got ahead. Prior to that tour, after we'd played Tri-Nations, we talked about the lessons we'd learnt. Then in Marseilles we went out there and we clawed our way back into the game, and just when we needed our composure and ruthlessness we did it again. It's pull your hair out stuff.

"At Marseilles a sign to me that we were stuffed was that after the game when we got back to the hotel I didn't see one guy go out. They just lay around knackered, collapsed."

* * *

To Blackadder, the 42–33 loss after the All Blacks had been ahead 30–26 with 20 minutes to go was another case of the All Blacks players, when they were really under pressure, starting to do their own thing.

"Eventually, on the French tour we came up with a call 'plus nine' which I think the Auckland Blues had been using. When we were in trouble, we'd just hang onto the ball for nine phases. And we'd been talking about it, calling, practising it, and when it came down to a pressure moment against France, when we'd clawed our way back into the game, we still couldn't do it.

"You're talking about some of the most experienced All Blacks, who couldn't do it. Building that composure is not something that happens overnight, it takes time. I know from my experience with the Crusaders that it took time there.

"In the All Blacks we went through it, where everyone wants to score the winning try, to get through that gap, and then it closes, and there's no support. You just need to hold onto the ball, and keep attacking, and keep grinding away.

"If the worst comes to the worst, as it did in the Wallabies test in Wellington, you might come down to the need for a penalty in front to decide the game.

"In a big game when it comes down to the wire, you need every man on deck. It's such a crucial stage of the game."

For Smith "The French played very well early on, and we over-committed to a couple of rucks, with the numbers. They freed up the ball, and scored very good tries.

"We came back and played some great rugby that day. But then they brought on some heavy artillery in the second half, and staved us off.

"Probably the two disappointments for me in 2000 were the game with the Boks in Jo'burg and, to a lesser degree, the test in Marseilles. I don't think we let our standards slip in Marseilles the way we did against South Africa, but it was still a real disappointment."

Nobody felt the disappointment of the loss to the French more than the All Blacks themselves. "We had a debrief from hell," says Blackadder, "to try to nail down what went wrong. We were talking about some grey areas, because no one ever likes to admit that, 'Hell, I let the team down and that's why we lost.'

"But it came down to a case of where we really had to find out. It's a psychological thing because when you are under pressure you start reverting.

"The Marseilles test was a game where we'd been down and absorbed the pressure, we'd showed we had the fight to come back and win the game. But instead of nailing the game, once again we let the foot off, and once again we are sucking lemons.

"It must be bloody frustrating for the coaches. They do their best to prepare the side and they're left with a bitter taste in their mouths like everyone else.

"The guys under pressure are really the leaders. After a game the coaches get it in the neck, followed by the captain. It is part of the responsibility that you accept.

"I take responsibility for those games. I look at it as if I hadn't done my job. We'd talked about those things, but when it came down to a crunch thing they didn't happen, so perhaps we didn't put enough effort into nailing them.

"We'd had a separate meeting early in the tour, just the players, led by Justin Marshall, and we'd talked about dealing with pressure. Yet when it came down to the game, it was, 'Hang on, we've been here before, we talked about learning our lesson, and we've just had another one put up us.' Here we were back in the same boat.

"I look back on it as perhaps being mental tiredness. It had been a huge season, but your body is your body, you can make it do anything. The problem is your brain needs to be as mentally sharp as your body is physically sharp.

"Physically we were up there with the best sides in the world, if not better. The guys were strong and fast enough. It's more the top two inches, and we are possibly diluting that with the amount of footy that's being played, because your body won't function if it's not in tune with your mind.

"The difference can be minimal. I mean, in Marseilles we were on our heels instead of our toes right from the start, so perhaps it's a little bit of fatigue, but it's a little bit of mental toughness as well. It shows what a tough side we were to claw our way back to get in the lead and just when we had the foot on the back of the neck and nailed it, it went again.

"It's a bitter pill to swallow. I don't blame anyone. Shit, the whole team went through it. It doesn't matter how well you perform personally, if the team loses, you all lose.

"I've never had any satisfaction in running out there and playing well when we've lost, because what does it matter? The team is always going to be more important than the individual."

There was one game left on the tour, and it was against an Italian team, now coached by former All Black Brad Johnstone, in Genoa.

A loss in Italy was unthinkable for a team still smarting from the brutal honesty that followed the French loss.

"We'd been told and it was highlighted, that we were lacking mental toughness," says Blackadder. "As a New Zealander, and an All Black, that's pretty cutting, and certainly motivation enough to play well in the last game.

"You know, I don't care who they are, whether it's Italy or Tonga, people may say they're not as good as Australia, or South Africa, but I've never played an easy game. There is no such thing as an easy game at provincial or, especially, international level. The only time you might get away with it is now and again at club level."

The All Black team struck early, with a very good try from Bruce Reihana, and dominated the match, winning 56–19. The game featured one of the more unusual scuffles in test rugby, when Filo Tiatia was suddenly attacked, without warning or reason, after scoring a try in a perfectly straightforward way.

"It was all just a bit of push and shove really," says Blackadder, "but it was good to see the whole team in there to help out. That to me was a great sign."

Justin Marshall recalls how he and Troy Flavell, the only two All Blacks not involved in the ruckus, raced each other from halfway to the goal-line to lend a hand, but found it was all over before they arrived.

Blackadder has nothing but fond memories of the time in Italy. Genoa was the sort of town he can relate to the most. "It was a great place to visit. Gordon Slater and I went for a walk once, and we got lost in the middle of nowhere, asking for directions as you do in little towns. It certainly was exciting.

"Dad came over for that test too. My very last test. I was pleased with the way we played, and it was good to finish on the right note. Of course, it would have been so much better to have finished with the two French tests won as well."

Blackadder looks back on the 2000 season without a single regret. "It could have been a golden season for the All Blacks, it was so close. When you look at where the team was and where they are going now I'd like to think it was a step forward.

"At the start of 2000, led by Wayne Smith and Tony Gilbert, the whole management, we talked about traditions, and how we wanted to be perceived, and who we are.

"We talked about how much the All Black jersey meant to New Zealanders, just to get those core values ingrained into the side.

"Smithy had interviewed a lot of All Blacks and it was part of a video presentation to the team, not a motivation tape, just to remind you who you are and your goals. We played it at certain times of the season, at crucial stages to remind everyone of who they were.

"I felt all the way through that we had played with guts and pride and I don't think you can ask for any more than that. I never heard that being questioned.

"Guys did their very best to do all the right things by the All Blacks.

It was about enhancing the jersey and I think we did that for most of the season.

"I see 2000 as the first season of some great years to come. Hopefully people will look back and see that some great things started in that season.

"By the time the World Cup comes in 2003 it will be perfect timing. If you look at the All Black team now, apart from a couple of changes, that team could be together for another five years.

"A lot of those guys have played a lot of footy but they have been through some glorious years and some hard years and now they are starting to consolidate.

"They have a management who have their feet firmly on the ground and there's a little bit of normality about who the All Blacks are and how they are perceived.

"I got sick and tired of the whole corporate thing that was getting bandied around, how people perceived that they were a corporatised team. You certainly couldn't say that about the 2000 team.

"Under the regime they have now that will never happen again. These guys' feet will never leave the ground and nor could they afford to have that happen.

"Things have changed in international rugby, and there is no way the All Blacks could now say they were always guaranteed of a win. One thing professionalism has done is draw everyone a lot closer. Every test is a potential challenge.

"I believe things are firmly on track. It was so close to being one of the golden years in All Black history. I learnt a whole lot in one season, and I have no regrets about any of it."

* * *

The news that his time as All Black captain was over came for Blackadder on a Friday in Rangiora, in late May 2001, when Wayne Smith and Tony Gilbert got out of their car at Todd and Priscilla Blackadder's home.

"I felt I had a responsibility to do what I thought was right," says Smith. "But that didn't make it any easier. All I could focus on was getting the process right, and being up-front with Todd.

"We hopped out of the car, and I just blurted it out. I thought, 'There's no use beating about the bush.' I said, 'Look Toddy, it's not good news.' I thought that was the best way, and then, if he wanted to kick us off the property, so be it. Then he tried to make us feel good about it."

When Smith is interviewed a month later, his eyes glisten as he recalls sitting inside with Blackadder and Gilbert, the three men drinking cups of tea.

"It's always 10 times worse for the person than it is for the coach. That's the bottom line. If you think too much about it, it'd drive you crazy, if you start thinking about what it's done to the guy, and his family.

"I think the measure of Toddy is that as soon as we let [New Zealand Rugby Union chief executive] David Rutherford know, and the second we let Anton Oliver know, he flew in, hired a car, and drove out there. As David Rutherford was leaving, Anton pulled up. I don't know that too many captains in history have had that support. It's a measure of Todd."

As the Crusaders struggled in the 2001 Super 12, there had been media pressure for Blackadder to lose his captaincy, some of it reasoned, some of it unpleasant and unfounded.

As he had when he appointed Blackadder captain, Smith floated no media stories himself, and in the end he says the decision was largely made because he believed "Todd was buggered, and his form had dropped off."

Smith recalls that in 2000 Blackadder himself had raised the question of being dropped from the team. "I'd been speaking with Todd after we lost in South Africa, and he felt he'd let us down, which he hadn't, but that's the mark of him, and he said, 'Smithy, if I'm not up to it, you drop me. All I want is this team to win.'

"That night I thought, 'Drop Toddy?' It had never even entered my head. I thought that I would love to be able to go through, do my time, and him still be there. At that point I would have said it was just about not worth coaching the All Blacks to have to make that decision."

What changed his mind? Smith says that he believed there were signs of tiredness in Blackadder's play during Super 12, and that Blackadder's aerial skills needed improvement.

"We only made the move because Todd was buggered, together with the fact we think that Anton will be there at the World Cup."

Blackadder's Super 12 coach, Robbie Deans, himself a former All Black, says, "There's no question that Toddy did a superb job as a leader in 2000. When we look back in time that will emerge as quite a pivotal point for the All Blacks.

"They came out of the World Cup campaign in a reasonable state of disarray. The reaction of the leadership in that time was pretty critical, and hence they turned to Toddy.

"He's the one guy who is all pervading. Right across the board he links with people. He's a big reason for the turnaround in the camp.

"But year by year the pressure of being All Black captain grows, unless it's carefully managed, and the player gets the support he needs, and he's allowed to do what he's appointed to do. Not be Prime Minister, and Governor-General, and NZRU public relations person. Just let the guy get on and do his job.

"There's no question that side of it took its toll on Toddy. I would suggest that when they appointed him to the position, they intended to have him continue for longer than one year. I believe that no matter what reasons you give for dropping him, at the end of the day it's a very hard call on Toddy.

"He gave everything, and he had to take an interest in areas that were much wider than they should have been. For the year he was there he really was the face of New Zealand rugby.

"He was the vehicle that they used to turn the public attitude around. When you look at it in that light it was a pretty harsh call on a guy who had given so much emotionally to it, to then suggest he wasn't even in the top 30.

"Toddy's a guy who, regardless of whether he was captain or not, he's not going to inhibit, or in any way erode the next captain."

But Deans says it's worth remembering one great thing. "Toddy did get the opportunity to be All Black captain, and he had a massive influence in turning the All Blacks around, and in turning the New Zealand public's perception of the All Blacks around. It's better that he had that opportunity than he never had it.

"While he finished unfulfilled, if you ask any rugby player, we all finish unfulfilled. When John Kirwan finished in 1994 he was our most-capped test player, with 63 tests, but the day he stopped he was unfulfilled. You never get enough.

"The great thing was that Toddy got that opportunity, and he deserved it fully."

There are some who would argue that Blackadder's form in 2001 wasn't a great deal different from the previous year, and Blackadder himself would have loved one more crack at the Tri-Nations. He had no desire to tour again at the end of the year, and would happily have handed over the leadership mantle.

But there would still be one more task, not a pleasant one, that Blackadder was asked to perform for the All Blacks. On the Sunday the team was announced in Dunedin at lunchtime he had been asked to go to Rugby Park in Christchurch late in the afternoon for a press conference.

"I guess I should do it," he mused the day before, "but I'm certainly not looking forward to it."

With an almost theatrical red sunset behind him Blackadder faced the cameras and tape recorders, and spoke with a dignity few people could have mustered in the circumstances.

Yes, he would have liked one more year, but his rugby career wasn't over. "I'm still a young man, and I'm looking forward to trying to make the Canterbury NPC squad and play for my province later in the year. I've still got a lot of things I want to do.

"I'll just take a brief break after what's been a hard couple of years, and make sure I get back and pull on that red and black jersey with pride."

Would he be supporting Anton Oliver and the All Blacks in 2001?

"I think we all should be getting in behind Anton and the team. I know I will be."

3. He slept with his boots on

"It always ended the same way, with another screaming match"

The scene is as much a part of a New Zealand rural childhood as calf club day or lining up for the school bus. At Woodend, just north of Christchurch, the Blackadder boys are standing in their brand-new footy boots, signing in for the first game of the new season.

They've travelled to the game in Mum's big straight-eight Buick, excited about the rough and tumble ahead with their mates.

Scott, the darker-haired one, is seven. His brother Todd has barely turned six. Bill Dodds, the coach of the under-eight team, looks over Scott.

"Okay son, you're okay. Go over with the other boys." Todd, a little bloke with a substantial pair of feet, steps up to the mark.

The coach checks out his age, looks at him again to size him up. He doesn't hesitate for long. "No. I'm sorry, but you're too young to play this year."

His mother, Carolyn, remembers clearly what happened next. "Todd just went ballistic. In the end he was in the back of the car screaming through the whole game. That night he wore his boots to bed, and we went through that drama every Saturday until the end of the season.

"Every Saturday morning he'd come out with his boots all ready to give it another crack, and every Saturday it ended the same way, with another screaming match."

Scott, who still plays in the front row for the Woodend club, got used to the banshee background to his first year of rugby, but with hindsight believes that "We would have been better off letting him go on. Who knows? He might have been better than us."

Being left out while Scott played rugby wasn't something Todd ever took lying down. "Once he was old enough to play, he wanted to be there," says Carolyn, "I can remember one day when he smashed his head on a window edge and cut his head open. It was like a fountain, the blood spraying way up above his head. Naturally, I wouldn't let him go to rugby. He screamed all day, not because his head hurt, but because he couldn't go to rugby."

It'd be nice to suggest, with Todd Blackadder and rugby now so closely associated in the public mind, that a burning, all-consuming passion for the game drove a wee boy to such violent protest, but that's not exactly how his mother and brother, or Todd himself, say it was.

"Back then I did want to play footy. But there were a lot of things I enjoyed," says Todd. "Bullrush, rugby, soccer, but nothing that I can remember thinking, 'I really want to play this.' That's when I was first at school, it was just cruisy. Once I was a bit older, playing at my club was when I got quite keen."

Scott and his twin sister, Megan, were the first children born to Ross and Carolyn Blackadder, in February 1970. Tragically, Megan would be a victim of cot death when only 11 weeks old.

Todd Julian was born in Rangiora on September 20 the following year. He was 7lb 7oz at birth, "not a great big boy," says Carolyn. "Probably because Scott was the first he was the gentle one, and then when the second one came along he was an absolute little terror as a child. He was screaming, throwing tantrums, holding on to me for maybe four years."

The youngest boy, Dean, was born in October 1973. When Carolyn brought him home, Scott and Todd looked at the new baby. Todd, only two, trotted off and came back with a book.

An early sign of the caring, gentle nature so many people remark on in the adult Todd? To be honest, no. "I thought he was going to read to him," says Carolyn. "Instead he smacked him over the head with it.

"I had Dean out in the sun one day, with the little net over the top of the pram, and Todd went and tipped him out.

"Todd did grow out of the tantrum throwing, smashing his head on the floor stage and he became much quieter. Then Dean became the terror.

"Dean was the one who set the fires under the bed — if anyone did anything it was Dean. I do remember a time though when Dean got a hiding for something that Todd did, when he set fire to the neighbour's toi toi bush and nearly burnt their house down."

Scott recalls that "Dean was more cunning. If Todd or I gave him one during the day then when Mum came home from work, as soon as Mum pulled up the driveway, he'd give a wee smile, and then he'd start crying.

"He was quite a fast wee runner, faster than all of us. I can remember Dean running backwards, laughing at Todd, and Todd would be that angry, but he'd stay just far enough away from him all the way round the house."

Dean was dyslexic, but it wasn't a problem that embittered him in any way. He was a person who didn't need to be shown anything more than once, and he was especially astute with money.

By the time he was a teenager he was growing into the biggest of the three boys, at 17 just a fraction shorter than Todd, with huge hands that gave the promise of more growth to come. Rugby wasn't a consuming interest for him, but Dean made an impact in other ways.

"He was a loud, life of the party guy, who was great with kids," says Carolyn. "He wasn't bad, but he spoke his mind. Out of the three boys he was the one who would have walked up to a coach he felt wasn't being fair to Todd, and said exactly what he thought of him without batting an eyelid."

In May 1991, Dean would die in a car accident, a dark, devastating time during which Carolyn recalls Todd as the anchor for her and Scott. When the boys were still young their parents had separated, and the bond between mother and sons grew close and strong during the years that followed.

Todd's earliest childhood memories are the boys and Carolyn "living on Granddad's farm in Gressons Rd in Waikuku. Granddad had a stud farm of Holstein friesians. He was right up there in the breeders' game. I remember antagonising the herd testers, watching the old-fashioned walk-through cow sheds, all that sort of stuff."

Three boys who loved the outdoors found the farm a big playground. "We went eeling together, trying to whack the eels with sticks in the stream right down at the bottom of the farm."

The stream, an irrigation ditch, almost spelt disaster for Scott. "There was a time when Scott nearly drowned in the creek," says Carolyn. "There was a big paddock out the back of the farm, and the boys had wandered off.

"I looked out the window and here's Todd and Dean both running round the paddock, arms out, doing aeroplanes. I thought, 'Where the hell is Scott?' I went roaring down there and asked. They said, 'Aw, we forgot. We were coming up to tell you, he's in the creek.'

"I raced down there and there was a piece of barbed wire going across the creek, and here's Scott, hanging on for dear life, with the water up to his chest.

"He was in there for ages, and Todd had forgotten to tell me. He got sidetracked on the way back home."

And while Dean was quick, Todd had his moments too. "I can remember a time when they were never allowed to play in the hayshed," says Carolyn, "and they had sneaked up there. Their Granddad saw them, playing on top of a big pile of bales, about three metres off the ground.

"Dad sneaked up. Scott saw him and he just stopped. But Todd took off, shot out his legs in front of him, aimed for and landed on top of a single bale of hay that was on the ground, landed his bum on it, and was gone."

Todd remembers "walking to school right down Gressons Rd, and that's a long road. I went to Waikuku School. Doug Bruce was a teacher there and there was a lady teacher. I really enjoyed it.

"I knew Doug was with the Canterbury rugby team, and that he'd been an All Black. At the time I never really thought much of it apart from that.

"We were at Waikuku for two years, and then we moved to

Woodend, and we had different friends there.

"Terry Mehrtens [a former Junior All Black, and father of Andrew] was one of my teachers at Woodend School, and quite strict in those days too I might add. School for me was a great opportunity to go along and play. I enjoyed my sport, and did my schoolwork, just got along."

As a boy, his mother recalls, Todd suffered a lot from growing pains, and was often lethargic.

"We used to have a big fire place at Woodend, and nobody else was allowed near it. He was like a big dog that just lay there and snarled at anyone who got in his way."

All Black coach Wayne Smith, in those days travelling for the Europa petrol company in North Canterbury, knew the family. "Toddy was a skinny kid, with big feet, and I taught him how to drop kick. We'd use the clothesline like a goalpost, and try to dropkick it over. Just a bit of fun.

"I knew the boys were into rugby, and playing for Woodend. If you'd looked at them at the time and tried to pick who was going to be a great footballer, you would probably have said Dean. Dean was a real sparky kid, a livewire. Even though he was just a little fella he was racing everywhere."

Smith was a brilliant first-five then for Canterbury and the All Blacks, and when Todd began playing rugby for Woodend it was at first-five or fullback.

"I can remember being told I'd get a dollar a try," Todd says. "I think I scored 52 tries and never got a dollar. I wouldn't have liked to be playing outside me back then.

"One year we made the final for Woodend. I can remember being up on the back of the old Frews stock truck to receive your certificate. I remember playing for North Canterbury but I could never make the full Canterbury Country side. I wasn't despondent about it, I just thought I wasn't good enough to make the next step."

But when he was 12, and playing flanker for the Belfast club in town, he got a taste of bigger things in rugby. "I made the Canterbury under-13 team. I think we played a curtain raiser in a shield game against Bay of Plenty. We ran out on to Lancaster Park, played the game, and I remember getting the Fresh-Up can of juice, and a pie at halftime in the main game.

It was my first taste of the whole thing, your name in the programme and wearing the red and black hoops.

"Having a connection with Belfast back in my early days, we knew Les McFadden, who was the manager of Canterbury at the time Grizz was coaching. As a kid I was down at Lancaster Park watching all those Ranfurly Shield games. I knew who was who in Canterbury, and somebody like Grizz Wyllie was someone you don't forget.

"When I went to Lancaster Park as a kid, I dreamed of playing for Canterbury. I wanted nothing better than to be the guy who runs out first. I wanted to be the captain of Canterbury one day. That's why I say that I'm living my dreams."

Scott remembers watching that first, and, as it turned out, only age group game Todd played for Canterbury and "he scored a try out on the wing. He stepped this guy and scored in the corner. A guy beside us said, 'Who's that?' The man next to him said, 'Todd Blackadder, he's a flanker.' I thought, 'Hell, he'll be stuck on the wing now.' He wasn't actually playing wing, but he was standing out there."

When he entered Rangiora High School Todd wasn't a boy who stood out in a crowd. "I wasn't a rebellious sort of child. I was in a bit of trouble here and there, but never enough to be bad or nasty. I was very average-sized when I started school. I shot up when I was about 16 or 17, and out of school. I was a bit of a late developer."

Despite his representative selection while he was at intermediate school, Todd didn't set the rugby fields of Rangiora High School alight. "I didn't play any First XV rugby at all. I had a trial for the team when I was in the third form. I don't think that back then rugby meant as much to Rangiora as it did to the likes of St Bede's, and those sort of schools.

"When I didn't play rugby at high school I played for the Woodend club. Apart from the first trial, when I didn't have a dog's show, I never heard anything. I wasn't terribly worried, and no one would be able to remember it either. I just saw out my school years, and never had an inkling about first XVs. I left school when I was 16."

One essay that would have been worth reading from Todd's schooldays would be the traditional "What I Did In My Holidays" effort, after the summer break he had when he was 15.

Through family connections he and good mate Darren Atkins went to the Chatham Islands, the remote farming and fishing settlement to the east of the South Island. "It was a bit of an eye-opener. We went out on the crayfish boats. It was an amazing place, really raw and rugged. It was a part of New Zealand most people don't get to see.

"There is really only a pub there so there's not much to do really, because I was too young. The things I did see were pretty amazing, like the Moriori carvings and the trees and wildlife."

After working with the rugged men on the Chathams, going back to Rangiora High just confirmed his time was up at school. He went to work in a factory for Hamilton Perry. He enjoyed the work, but he was working long hours, sometimes from 10 am until 12 at night, which meant he always felt tired.

"I looked for another job and I liked engineering, so I went to Nelson to do a polytech fitting and welding course for a year.

"I had very little money, and got through by the skin of my teeth. I just had my Hillman Hunter car and had to stay at the hostel. Dad helped me out a bit, but I didn't have any spending money to play with."

The course had started at the end of winter, and Todd played a few games for a Nelson town club, Rival Old Boys, at the end of the 1987 season.

Scott McKay, whose sister, Priscilla, would one day be Todd's wife, was doing the same fitter welder course with Todd, and he played for the Collingwood club. "Scott asked me to play the last game of the season with them, and I did that. I met Scott through the course, and I started going back to Collingwood with him for the odd weekend.

"That was how I came to meet Priscilla. At that time Priscilla was in Nelson working as a hairdresser."

Collingwood, a former gold mining town nestled in one of the most beautiful parts of New Zealand, Golden Bay, is remote. To get there, you drive 112km north-west from Nelson, then climb the winding road over the massive Takaka Hill.

Barely 300 people live permanently in Collingwood, and a city boy might have been bored to distraction by the basic pleasures it offered. But the little town, the people, and the surrounding countryside suited a teenage Todd Blackadder to the ground.

"It's a great place. There's fishing and hunting, and the outdoor life in the district is fantastic. The people up there sort of welcome you with open arms. I started playing pre-season rugby, and they wanted me to stay, and I kept playing and took a job I was offered working on Priscilla's parents' factory supply dairy farm."

In Collingwood, Priscilla's parents were "very good to me. They took me under their wing and fed me up. That was where I had my growth spurt I think.

"The whole thing about Collingwood is that it was just a good experience. The lifestyle, the rural atmosphere, the good people. As a young fella going through the years there, it was a great time."

In a place like Collingwood everybody pitches in. "It's like the rugby team, where you've got 15-year-olds playing with 40-year-olds. In a small town everyone treats everyone pretty well equally. I remember early on there going to a stag do, trying to drink a heap of rum, and then being loaded into a friend's car and taken home. You all look after each other."

Rugby was as natural a part of life as the hunting, the fishing, and the farming. "Everyone turns up for the games, and people are quietly encouraging. When you play, it's like you're all brothers. You sort of die for each other.

"We had a good coach, Speed Robinson, who trained us hard with the fitness work. Five laps of the paddock, then another five laps of sprinting the 22s. I don't think we'd ever been so fit. We started as senior thirds, and then fought our way into the senior B competition.

"I never really thought about age group teams. The only team they had in Collingwood was the senior B team. When you look back at it, the biggest game of the year was Golden Bays playing the Buccaneers, who were players from the Nelson area who weren't in their top team.

"The trips we had coming back from Nelson, whether it was a win or a loss, they were memories I'll never forget. Listening to a bit of Meatloaf, talking a bit of shit, and having a good old singalong. Stopping at all the pubs along the way, having a feed of pork bones. It was just great times."

The impact he made is clearly remembered by former team-mates. Garth Strange was 17 years older than him when they played for Collingwood, and he says, "You know it's strange, but although I'd been playing for donkey years, when we played together I felt like I was following him. For his age he was just streets ahead of anyone else.

"He could inspire everybody else with what he did. I can remember him cutting wingers off with a tackle in the corner, and it didn't seem possible that he could actually do it. For a teenager he was just so committed to the team.

"He got better and better so quick, that while there were some other good players in the team, he was basically the difference between us and the other teams in the end. By the time he left here he was pretty damned good. The other teams were getting pretty worried about him.

"There was something there on and off the field even when he was a teenager. He never ever talks about himself. Everybody else, if you do something bloody good in the game you spend the rest of the night trying to tell everybody so no one forgets it, don't you?

"He never ever said anything like, 'Did you see me do that?' That's why people respect him. Even now, if he rings up, he might have just captained the All Blacks, but he wants to know what's happening up here. He's more worried about every other bugger, and it's hard to find out what he's doing.

"Guys that played with him are still so proud that they ever managed to be here at that particular time when he was playing."

In 1989 Blackadder made the Nelson Bays under-18s. "I was probably pretty lucky to be there. I can remember turning up to play on occasions with a bit of a hangover. Nelson Bays games were all in Motueka or Nelson, the day after a Collingwood game, so it was a big trip really.

"Then we went down to Southland and won the South Island under-18s tournament. We beat all the top teams to get the title. We beat Otago, Southland, the West Coast, and then we beat Canterbury in the final. It was quite ironic, because I'd never thought I was good enough for that level."

The impact he made at that tournament was noticed back in Christchurch, by Wayne Smith. "I'd changed jobs and I was working at the Canterbury Sports Depot. I'd been reading the paper about this rampaging, raw boned No. 8 who had just smashed the Canterbury team in the under-18 tournament.

"I was interested because I was playing for Canterbury at the time. That week Carolyn came in to the shop and said 'Smithy I need some boots for Todd.'

"I said, 'Yeah, no problem.' She said, 'No, it is a problem, because you're not going to have any big enough.' For a start I said, 'Where is Todd?' Carolyn said he was up in Nelson Bays, and he plays for Nelson Bays.

"I said, 'What's his surname?' She said 'Blackadder.' It just clicked, because by then she was Carolyn Humm, her maiden name. I just knew Todd as Todd, not Todd Blackadder, and this was the kid who had torn apart the South Island tournament.

"He'd come from nowhere. Nobody knew him. He hadn't played for a first XV or anything like that.

"Then it became apparent that we weren't going to find any boots big enough. So I went to see the boss, Murray Smith, and he said, why don't we get in touch with Morne du Plessis [the Springbok No. 8 and captain in the 1970s] in Africa. He had a sports shop there, and those Afrikaner forwards have big feet.

"So we called him, and he said, 'Yep, we can send some out.' Carolyn bought two pairs, which were quite expensive. Then these huge boats arrived, about size 16, and she sent them up to Todd."

Outfitted in his South African boots, in 1990 Blackadder went to the New Zealand under-19 trials. "There were national technical coaches there, like Grizz Wyllie. Then they named the New Zealand under-19 squad. I was lucky enough to make that."

Nobody would have given the kid from Collingwood a bolter's show before the trials. At first, neither did Todd. But the old campaigners who had pulled on the Collingwood jersey with him had other ideas.

"The people up in the Collingwood area really believed in me so much, that I started believing them. [Veteran Collingwood prop] Don McKnight said, 'You're going to make that side.' Garth Strange said, 'You're going to make it into that team.'

"I remember marking Karl Todd, from Counties, in the under-19 trial, and being told, 'If you can beat him, you're in the team.' It wasn't just for me, it was for all the people in Collingwood. I went out and made them pick me really. Back then one kid from Nelson Bays was neither here nor there. I was pretty proud of who I was representing, and they gave me a lot."

Evan McLellan, a Collingwood dairy farmer, was the No. 7 to Blackadder's No. 8 in the club side, and their friendship was so strong that they would be best man at each other's wedding.

The growth in Blackadder as a rugby player, from a high-schooler who didn't play in teams where he had the benefit of expert coaching, or specialist skills training, to an 18-year-old good enough to play at national level is one of the most remarkable periods in his career.

McLellan offers some clues to how Blackadder's game was tempered. "When Todd first came here he was a good player, a guy you would have wanted in your team, but he grew from that enormously, until he was taking us with him.

"When he was playing for Collingwood he was playing against men, rather than with boys in age group teams. We got bruised up through the grades moving up from third grade, which was very social — if you turned up you got a game — to senior B. We got hammered at first, until we realised we were as good as they were. I think after what he went through playing against some older guys who were as hard as nails, nothing was ever going to scare him.

"He put a tremendous amount of time into his rugby then, and I think he might have wagged a few milkings. Sometimes he'd head over to Nelson for training at night after he'd worked all day, so he put a hell of a lot into it. He deserves everything he's got."

Brother Scott was an eye-witness to what playing with and against grown-ups in Collingwood had done to Todd.

"He hardened up so much up there. When I'd played with him before he was pretty laidback, just played the normal game.

"Then he came back and went to Belfast, and I went with him, for a pre-season game. Todd was in front of me in the lineout, and I was the openside flanker. He was marking Rob Penney, who was a Canterbury star. I was

'Whoa... he's marking Rob Penney. We're playing against Rob Penney.'

"In those days you didn't get lifted, and the ball came down the back of the line. Todd didn't go for the ball. He elbowed Rob Penney right in the side of the head. I was, 'What are you DOING? We're in trouble now.' But he just took it to him, and had a stormer of a game. Rob Penney didn't do anything all game. It was like Todd was saying, 'I'm here.' I was stunned."

For the 18-year-old Todd there would be some big rugby moments in 1990. The New Zealand under-19 team made a brief tour of Australia, coached by Ross Cooper, later an All Black selector and Chiefs coach.

Future All Blacks in the team, Marc Ellis, Mark Cooksley, Jason O'Halloran and Gordon Slater, were joined by a man who would later pull on red and black jerseys in many key games with Blackadder, Angus Gardiner.

At the time Gardiner thought it was the first time the two had met, or played football together. Years later he would find out he was wrong. "It was quite interesting," says Gardiner. "I'd asked him how he ended up in Collingwood and he said, 'Go and look at your photos. We were in the Canterbury under-13s together.' And sure enough, there was a skinny Todd Blackadder standing in the background.

"At the time it just passed over me but in later years it touched me, and I realised the red and black jersey was important to him even then.

"In Canterbury I think he got sick of not being selected, and even at 13 and 14 it meant a lot to him. He was a country boy through and through, and it's an easier road for a town player. In town you get selected and it's bloody difficult to get out of it for the next five years. You get some old guy who's the age-grade selector, who has seen you play once and thinks you're the bee's knees, and your place is set in concrete.

"It's still great when you're a town kid to play on Lancaster Park, but maybe for some of us as schoolkids it didn't mean so much as it did to a kid who, through circumstances, rarely got the chance, like Todd."

Gardiner and Blackadder roomed together in Brisbane. "We played three matches in Queensland, and in that era you always got billeted out. The family stands there, and if you're like me and Todd, a bit shy, you're hiding at the back of the room.

"It's like a dating service and the names get read out, and they called 'Todd Blackadder and Angus Gardiner.' I thought, 'Thank God I'm with someone, not staying with strangers on my own.'

"I'd been to Australia maybe twice before, and it was Todd's first trip out of New Zealand. Being the city slicker, and considering myself quite worldly, we got a taxi from the suburbs where we were staying to meet the team at a bar, because the drinking age over there was 18.

"In the taxi I was looking out, thinking, 'Isn't Brisbane great? Look at the size of this city.' I said so to Todd and this gruff old country boy beside me says, 'No, the place gives me a guts ache. I can't wait to get home. It's just a concrete jungle out there.'"

Gardiner is actually understating the case when he suggests Blackadder had never been out of New Zealand before. Todd had never even been to the North Island, much less Australia. He chuckles now at the memory. "I was a bit green really."

As a traveller that may well have been the case, but as a player the Blackadder characteristics were already fully formed. Former All Black captain and coach Sir Brian Lochore once said that Blackadder was "one of those guys that you would have hated having to mark. There are players like him who are all knees, and elbows and hip bones, and when you look at him in a lineout, you just know you're in for a hell of an afternoon."

Gardiner says in the under-19 team that, while Blackadder was "a lot skinnier then, he was all knees and legs and getting stuck in. He was into everything, and probably why he excelled at even that young age was that he didn't have any reservations, no matter who he was marking.

"You can get caught up and be in awe of a name player, but for Toddy, living in Collingwood, in his own tight-knit community he was doing something he enjoyed when he played rugby, and it didn't matter if it was a top-rated team or player, he'd just go out and get stuck in. He knew no other way. In that respect he was no different to what he is now."

So Blackadder was never a player who had the yellow-brick road laid out for him? "No. A guy like Todd you can pretty much guarantee any rep side he made, he played his way in. He would never have been singled out at the age of 15 or 16 saying he is going to be the next All Black captain.

"People do tag players in that way but I'd bet it never happened with Toddy. What he did have from the time I first met him was something special inside him that must have come from that time playing in Collingwood. If every player in New Zealand had it, the All Blacks would never be beaten. I'm sure a lot of that attitude came from playing in a team with older guys, where you grow up pretty quickly."

Fresh from the trip in May to Australia came a taste of international rugby against the touring Scots. Led by the legendary prop David Sole, the 1990 Scotland team would run the All Blacks close in their second, and final test, at Eden Park. Not long after that muddy battle the nation would be thrown into uproar when All Black captain Buck Shelford was dropped.

Still wide-eyed and slightly amazed at how quickly things were moving for him, Blackadder found himself named in the combined Nelson Bays-Marlborough team to play Scotland in the third game of their tour.

"I was amazed at how well I was received," says Blackadder. "I was shy, and I didn't know anyone. There were a lot more Marlborough players than there were Nelson players, and I didn't really know the Nelson players either.

"I remember getting on in that game. I went that bloody hard, although I can't remember whether I touched the ball. I do know I couldn't catch my breath, and I coughed for about an hour after the game. But just to say that I once had 20 minutes against the Scotland team in 1990 was a great experience."

His debut season for Nelson Bays was confirmation that the start he'd made at age group level was no fluke. He'd play every game for the team in the third division that year, either at openside or blindside flanker, and be named the province's player of the year. The *Rugby Almanack* authors would say that he "made an impressive debut in first-class rugby and must be destined for higher honours soon. He was the team's outstanding player."

At the end of that season his form was rewarded with selection in the New Zealand Divisional team, who early in 1991 would tour Australia, playing five games.

All Black selector Lane Penn, at the time becoming the reluctant meat in the sandwich formed by the national panel feud between Grizz Wyllie and John Hart, was the coach, and the captain was Kevin Schuler, later an All Black at the 1995 World Cup. Other future All Blacks were Norm Hewitt, then playing for Hawke's Bay, and King Country prop Phil Coffin.

"It was a tough tour," says Blackadder. "We didn't have a doctor, or a physio, and the whole tour was marred by injuries. If you look back you'll see that Kevin Schuler, the captain, had a stress fracture in his foot.

"I was rooming with Frank Marfell, the lock from Marlborough, and he took me under his wing the whole tour. We've always got on bloody well.

"After the game against New South Wales Country at Batemans Bay, I had what felt like a little bite in my shin. As you do, you sort of carry on, but by that night I couldn't even put the weight of a blanket on my leg.

"I spent the whole night writhing in pain. Frank was looking after me, and he was concerned, but not having a doctor, everyone thought it was a bruise.

"It was just a red spot, but the pain was excruciating. You would have thought someone was jabbing a hot poker in your leg. I was out of action, and it just got worse and worse. We were travelling by bus, and it was going on for about six or seven days, and it grew into a big black thing like a tennis ball on my shin. I could smell it. It smelt like it was rotting.

"Finally we got to Adelaide, and I threw my bag on my bed and said, 'You've got to get me a doctor.' They finally got one, and I was rushed to hospital where they had surgery on my leg that night.

"Something had got into my leg after a whack on it, and it wasn't far off being gangrene. I've still got the scar, a good two inches long.

"They left me there because they had to keep playing. They left me with one pair of underpants, a shirt, and a pair of pants in a little carry-bag. But they forgot my shoes.

"One of the local liaison guys took me to the airport from the hospital, and I had to hobble out to the plane with bare feet. The air hostess felt so sorry for me she put me up into business class.

"I went home to Mum. I wasn't well. The thing on my leg took months to heal. I'd lost a lot of weight from fever. I was skin and bone. It knocked me to bits. I just lay in the sun and let it heal."

Even before the horrific end to his Divisional team tour Blackadder had decided to leave Collingwood and come back home to Canterbury. "I'd been working at Graham Smith's farm, and he was really good to me. When I was playing for Nelson Bays that was three long trips a week, so there are a lot of sacrifices to be made by both parties. They gave me that opportunity to take the time off to play rugby, which a lot of people don't have the chance to do."

He would return to Canterbury with a distinctive facial feature, the scar on his left cheek team-mates suggest facetiously was a tribute to Canterbury sponsor Nike. It was actually from a car accident in Collingwood. "I had an old green Valiant, it was hosing with rain, and I was trying to change a ZZ Top tape. I ran straight into a concrete bridge abutment and the rear vision mirror ripped into my face. It was pretty nasty at the time.

"I decided that if I was going to give rugby a crack, I'd come back to Canterbury in 1991. I played for Belfast for two seasons, and I made the New Zealand Colts in 1991, under John Hart."

The Colts played four games in the South Island, with Blackadder playing in every match. Future All Blacks Glen Osborne, Marc Ellis, Lee Stensness, Liam Barry, Steve Surridge, Mark Cooksley, and Gordon Slater were in the side, and the short tour went out in a blaze of glory with a 61–9 victory at Rugby Park in Christchurch against the Australian under-21 side.

At the time coach Hart said it was "as close as I have seen to the perfect game of rugby. A few passes went to ground, but that was only because the players were trying new things."

4. You could point out your family

"No matter what, you got the feeling he loved you anyway"

Andy Earl was pretty much the epitome of the hard-bitten Canterbury rugby forward. A farmer, on the football field he was all angles, elbows and hard work. His All Black mates called him "Wurzel" because his hair tended to sprout in different directions, like the television scarecrow.

One of the famous Baby Blacks in 1986, his last test was in 1992 when, as he described it, "with my bum hanging on the ground," he never stopped running against the Wallabies on a fiercely hot Brisbane afternoon.

The performance was even more astonishing than the team management knew at the time. For the previous month, before he got a late-night phone call to fly to Australia to help out the injury-struck All Blacks, he'd actually played no rugby. Instead he had helped neighbours in North Canterbury drag stock from the massive snow drifts left by the Big Chill of '92 in the province.

Earl had no time for anyone who wouldn't put his body right on the line for his team, and he had even less time for flowery public sentiment.

So it was a huge vote of confidence when, on his retirement from the Canterbury team in '92, he said, "This young joker Todd Blackadder's got plenty of guts."

Blackadder actually used to get a lift to Canterbury training with Earl. "I was living with Mum in Woodend and Andy used to come through from his farm and pick me up. The first time I was bloody nervous. You hear these stories. But Andy used to really push me and encourage me. He even said he wouldn't mind sitting in the reserves for me."

Blackadder's debut game for Canterbury came in 1991 after his return from Collingwood. "I had a game for the Canterbury Colts and then I was drafted into the Canterbury B team. Wayne Smith and John Mills were the coaches. I'd known Smithy for a long time through family connections. So to play under him was good.

"I didn't really know anybody in the side, but everybody made you feel really welcome. I've still got a lot of friends from that team. Guys like Hamish Murray, who played for Glenmark, Alan Lindsay, Steve Hansen, who was the captain; they were great days."

Coach Smith recalls that "Auckland B had been the top B team for years. But we'd beaten them the last two years, and they were coming down for revenge at Lancaster Park. Our fullback, Richard Connell, kicked 11 out of 11 and we won 63–3.

"Toddy was blindside flanker. I went into the changing room afterwards, and it was my last game as coach. I said, 'I think there are a couple of All Blacks in this room.' Todd was one, along with Steve Cleave and Dion Kerr. They all had the talent. But Todd had the attitude as well.

"I remember saying to him when he was first in the team that he had to change his contact style. He used to go in with his head first, and guys would back off him. He was just so much more committed than most B players.

"He was just a raw-boned windmill of a kid, and I said that at B level it would work, but I thought that when he got up into the A team he could have problems with technique. What he soon proved was that even at that level he could still out-commit people, and he did improve his technique.

"At the time I thought he was a kid who was 19, going on 29. He's always had wisdom, even as a young fellow. He's always been caring, but known where he wanted to go, and had the hard-nosed attitude to get there. There aren't many around like that.

"I remember talking once to John Mills, who was my assistant with the team. We had some concerns at openside that year. He just pointed to Todd and said, 'Look at him mate, we don't need an openside, he does both jobs.' Todd used to run all over the show and take a lot on his shoulders, even as a kid."

Blackadder remembers most the camaraderie in the B side. "It was the good old days of touring. We toured around that year, and I think the only side we lost to were Manawatu. It was a great experience.

"I was playing mostly blindside, and when we had that big win in the game at Lancaster Park against Auckland B, it was the curtainraiser to the Canterbury-Auckland NPC game. Canterbury got cleaned up by Auckland (42–14), and people wanted changes. Because of that I got the call-up."

Coaching the Canterbury team in 1991 was John Phillips, famous himself as a tough, dynamic flanker for Canterbury in the 1970s and 80s, with 99 games for the province.

Phillips was a man who had no time for glamour boys. "At the end of the day," he once said, "you can have the fabulously skilled players who just won't take the crunch. When it comes to the real crunch tackle they're too worried about their pretty little faces. You must have some hard nuts, who don't mind jumping off that big fence and dying for the team."

It'd be fair to say that Phillips was in a filthy mood after the hiding from Auckland. On the Sunday after that game the Canterbury team had a famous training session, which survivors claim was one of the hardest runs there's ever been, more ruthless than anything even Grizz Wyllie dished out.

"I missed that one, thank goodness," says Blackadder, "but then I had the next week of training, and it was one of the toughest I've ever had in my life. The whole week was brutal. He hammered the side.

"When we went up to Bay of Plenty, for the game in Rotorua, we had a run the day before the game, and I recall that I said to John Phillips, 'I think I'm too buggered to play.'"

Blackadder debuted that day with Aaron Flynn, the Sydenham halfback, with whom he'd share many Canterbury memories, and a 1998 Super 12 win. "In the shed before the game in Rotorua, with us new guys I can remember John saying, 'When you're man enough, come and get your jersey.' I said, 'I'll have mine right now thanks.' He presented us with our jerseys, which was certainly something special.

"I think in the first scrum there was a huge punch-up. So straight away it was right in there. It was just a great experience, and it was certainly a step up from the level I'd been playing at. I got player of the day that day, which rounded off a very good day.

"I'd only ever wanted to play for Canterbury, so to get that chance was bloody magnificent.

"I actually think the court session after the game was harder than the game for a young fella."

So, at the end of 1991 Blackadder, just turned 20, could look back with some satisfaction on his Canterbury debut and was "as keen as mustard for the following year."

The Bay of Plenty game, which Canterbury lost 28–13, was the last of the season, and it would prove to be Phillips' last game as Canterbury coach. Despite mediocre games at the tail-end of the NPC, Canterbury actually finished fourth in the competition. But that wasn't enough to keep Phillips in the coaching position, and he was replaced by Alister Hopkinson, the former All Black prop.

The late Hopkinson, who was just 58 when he died in 1999, holds a special place in Blackadder's memories. "Hoppy" to everyone he met, there was a decency and spark about Hopkinson impossible to resist. His humour was typified by the suggestion, possibly true, that as coach he kept track of possible candidates for Canterbury by writing their names on the wall of his woolshed. It would prove to be a brutal season for Canterbury in 1992, but somehow Hopkinson kept his famous good nature intact.

"To me Hoppy was a great coach," says Blackadder. "After every game we'd have a few beers at the pub and he'd pull us in together. If it had been anybody else I think things could have got pretty nasty. But he was a top man, and he kept that team together through pretty trying circumstances. You sort of got the feeling that no matter what the results were, he loved you anyway. You had undying respect for him. You just loved him.

"He was great for me. He treated his players like they were his sons. A few years ago, after Hoppy had stopped coaching Canterbury, I was playing for Glenmark against Oxford. His son Rob plays for Oxford. Hoppy called me over, and he had a bottle of whiskey in the car, with the cups. By the time I staggered into the after-match I was about three-quarters of the way gone."

Hopkinson, who in 1989 and 1990 had acted as an assistant coach to his brother-in-law, Frank Jack, reversed the roles in '92, calling in Jack to help him with the backs.

"When you look back on it now," says Blackadder, "1992 was nearly the year Canterbury were relegated. We were staring down the barrel of second division."

The season proper began with the Super Six series, an early season forerunner to Super 12. Canterbury, Wellington, and Auckland were the New Zealand teams, up against New South Wales, Queensland, and Fiji.

Before Super Six began there was a memorable pre-season game against Queensland on a sweltering March day in Brisbane. "I was playing openside flanker and it was about 38 degrees," says Blackadder. "There was no air conditioning in the changing room, and we were all just about dying.

"Frank Jack came up to me and said, 'Do you love the heat, Toddy?' That became our joke. I said, 'Yeah, yeah, I love the heat.'"

In Super Six, Queensland played Canterbury at Lancaster Park, and the weather was so cold several Queenslanders were treated for hypothermia.

Jack, a man who liked his humour dead-pan came up to Blackadder that day too. "He said, 'Do you love the cold Toddy?' I said, 'Yeah, I love the cold.' He said, 'What? Do you love the hot AND the cold?' He had such a serious look on his face, like he believed it. Hamish Murray and I were sitting next to each other, and we just about pissed ourselves."

Carolyn and little Toddy, when the lighter streaks in his hair were blond.

Todd's first day at school, with brothers Dean (left) and Scott (right).

The Blackadder boys ready for mischief on the farm. Scott, with the dog, Todd and Dean.

Blackadder Collection

The biggest boy in the back row of the Woodend under-11 team is Todd, no longer too young to wear the boots.

Blackadder Collection

In 1986 the Woodend under-15 team were North Canterbury champions. Todd is second from left, middle row.

All Collingwood cheered. In 1990 Todd's first starting game for Nelson Bays was against Buller. This apparent try was disallowed.

The 1991 New Zealand Colts team, coached by John Hart. Todd is the last player on the right, middle row.

Wedding bells for Priscilla McKay and Todd Blackadder in Collingwood.

Laurie Mains drove them hard but Todd loved the experience of playing for the 1995 All Blacks in France.

Locking the Boland fullback in the truck headlights. On tour in South Africa, 1996.

Happiness is being the winning captain of Canterbury in the 1997 Air New Zealand
NPC final at Lancaster Park.

Climatic extremes were the order of the day in Super Six. When Fiji beat Canterbury 38–17 in Suva, Blackadder recalls that "It was monsoon weather, mud round your ankles, with frogs actually leaping out of the mud. The Fijians were running on top of the mud like it was a hard, fast track. That day in Suva, nobody would have beaten them.

"When the ball was kicked it would just stick in the mud where it landed. They were then running through the mud and scooping it up at full pace. There was no way we even looked like being in the game."

The year marked one of the few times when Canterbury fans, usually so fanatical in their support, virtually turned their back on the team. Even the lure of free drink and food at after-match functions wasn't enough to fill the Lancaster Park social room, where old players and officials actually hissed "gutless" at the current team as they shuffled in after yet another loss. It was just as lonely on the park.

"We were getting crowds of about 2000 to a game," says Blackadder. "You could run out there and point out your family. You could see your Mum and Dad and your brothers.

"In some ways I was oblivious to it all. I just wanted to play for Canterbury, and here I was doing it. The people that really mattered to me were at the games.

"It wouldn't have worried me how big the crowd was. I knew that Mum was there, and my family was watching, so that meant more to me than anything.

"But it was a trying year. The only NPC games we won were Hawke's Bay and North Harbour. The game against King Country [lost 24–20] was Andy Earl's last game, and losing to them at Lancaster Park was definitely not one of the highlights of my life. It was a bloody terrible performance.

"In '92 it was also the worst, most shitty weather we'd ever had. One game was almost snowed out, and it just went on.

"Against Queensland and North Harbour the ground announcer said that everyone could go into the stand. So a handful of people were huddled up together, trying to keep warm.

"Every single home game the weather was crappy, sleet and rain.

People didn't turn up, and we played wet weather rugby, badly. I have to say that was also a factor in how the season went."

Halfway through the winter there was a Ranfurly Shield challenge against an Auckland team showing signs of wear, who would actually not make the final of that year's NPC. Canterbury lost their game at Eden Park, 47–38, and Blackadder lasted just a couple of minutes, off with a bad finger injury.

"There were a few little divisions inside the team that year," says Blackadder. "Some of the side were experienced, and had played a lot together, and a reasonable-sized group of younger guys had just come in. When things aren't going too well on the field the shit hits the fan a bit.

"There weren't major things. Just little things, groups who sometimes did their own thing, that aren't conducive to team work."

Greg Coffey, in 1992 an old campaigner at first-five for Canterbury, still has vivid memories of how, at a training run when many of the players were moaning about how the season was going, the quiet kid on the side of the scrum suddenly spoke up.

"I couldn't quote the exact words," says Coffey, "but out of the blue he said that we should stop pointing the finger at other people, and just get on with it ourselves. Here was the new boy on the block, standing up when he had to.

"It was pretty impressive, and it certainly made me think that he would be destined for leadership. The way he worked on the field, but usually stayed quiet off it, said a lot about the guy. Right from the start on the paddock he had everything going, and he was physically hard, you might say hard-boned, and a few opponents found out about that."

Despite the miserable results, there were plenty of lessons learned by Blackadder in 1992. "I remember lining up against Waikato in a lineout, and John Mitchell just turned round and gave me a good whack straight in the side of the head, and said 'Welcome to the first division, son', or something like that. He didn't drop me, and I didn't do a thing. I just said, 'Thanks pal.'

"It was, I suppose, a way of earning respect. It was a time when, if you were an arsehole, you got sorted out by the opposition.

"Guys lying over the ball in those days were never penalised. Referees would actually encourage you to get rid of them. You'd look at a guy like [Waikato flanker] Duane Monkley, who was always lying on the ball.

"He'd come off with his back ripped and torn and bare. He thoroughly deserved it, and he never blinked an eyelid. If you get players like that now, it's more out of frustration that fights start, or punches are thrown, because you can't actually sort out a player who's constantly infringing with rucking these days. In those days, in your own way, you could sort a player out in one game."

Player enforcement in the professional era can be a very costly business. Players who are banned for, say a week, don't have a week taken out of a year's salary, even though they're paid by the week over a full year. The 'cost' is based on how many games they miss from the competition involved, which will be a lot more than the weekly wage. "It's a nasty business," says Blackadder.

With the experiences of 1992 stored away another year with Canterbury loomed, with new coaches Vance Stewart and his assistant, Brian "Aussie" McLean.

The rugby season of 1993 would provide the answer to a great trivia question: In what year did Todd Blackadder play at a World Cup? For Blackadder it will also be remembered as a tough time, when he "probably bit off more than he could chew."

It all began with sevens rugby. "I'd played in the South Island sevens champs the year before, and in 1993 we won it. And then there was a New Zealand B team under Gordon Tietjens. I'd gone with them to Fiji for the Fijian sevens, and it was bloody tough. They were all provincial sides, and some of them were better than their national side.

"I ran myself ragged basically, and I got a really bad case of food poisoning in Fiji. When I was on the plane coming home I was shivering and sweating.

"Then I got home, and I was selected to play against Western Province under Vance Stewart. I turned up at the training, trained, and the next day I went downhill. I just lay on a mattress at my aunty's place in Waikuku. I couldn't go to bed, because I was sweating so much. I lost so much weight. I was lucky to make 98kg then, so I had no condition on me. I lay on the mattress and listened to the game.

"Then, two weeks later, I was called up by Peter Thorburn, for the very first sevens Rugby World Cup, when Marc Ellis was injured. We played it in Edinburgh. I went up to Auckland and played in trials, and Peter asked me to go to the World Cup."

One of Blackadder's team-mates was Eric Rush, who remembers an occasion when "we got a sports psychologist down to talk to the boys about mental imagery. After the session Peter Thorburn asked the boys what they thought, and everyone was saying it was great until Thorbs got to Todd. 'It's just bullshit mate. You just run, tackle, run and tackle some more.'"

To Blackadder, just being at the tournament was almost unbelievable. "I'm sure I just got there by the skin of my teeth as a reserve forward and then, in the very first game, Pat Lam injured himself, so apart from the first game I played every game. I just loved every minute of it.

"I can remember warming up, and the whole *Black Adder* TV programme was at its height. Every time I went out these people would sing the words to the Blackadder song.

"I was out there playing against the likes of David Campese, and we had All Blacks in our side. It was amazing."

New Zealand went through the pool play unbeaten, but stumbled in the quarter-final pool, where they were joined by England (who would eventually win the tournament), Australia, and South Africa.

The game with England was a disaster, with New Zealand down 21–0 by halftime. Tries by Glen Osborne and Blackadder brought them back to 21–12 at fulltime, and a 42–0 thrashing of Australia meant a win over South Africa would have put New Zealand into the semi-finals. New Zealand really found form against Australia, whose captain Michael Lynagh swears that in the second half his team didn't touch the ball once. But the clash with South Africa was another nightmare, eventually lost 31–14.

Coach Thorburn says that Blackadder was picked for the sevens team because of the way he filled the role Buck Shelford had played in the very successful New Zealand sevens sides of the 1980s.

"Toddy was extremely fast, and strong on the break through, which allowed other players to run off him. In sevens all the things we love about his play in recent years were on display.

"His workrate, hardness, aggressive tackling, and, in my view, very underestimated ball skills and agility were the reasons he was a very good sevens player.

"Although our lack of total success was a disappointment, the extreme cold and wet and injuries to a couple of key players were to blame. It certainly wasn't due to any lack of Toddy's well-known qualities.

"I have a memory of one try he scored, in particular, against a star-studded Australian team, where he ran over 60 metres to touch down. The win that day was one of the best two or three efforts I've ever seen by a New Zealand sevens side.

"With the way that he played, he became a much sought-after star of the tournament. I clearly recall groups of people singing the *Black Adder* theme song as they clamoured for his attention and autograph.

"The other picture that I have in my mind is of Toddy at a fence at Murrayfield, signing innumerable autographs for people of all ages, poking programmes and autograph books through the fence. Typical of the man he continued signing and chatting until he had to move on and join the team."

Blackadder returned to New Zealand in tatters. "I was absolutely burnt out. I played against the Lions for Canterbury and I think I'd spent two weeks in bed. To get up and play I was living on aspirins.

"I was injured, I'd done both AC joints, and I was in a hell of a mess. I think my rugby suffered because of it, but I was still in the side.

"Then I was dropped for a wee while, which probably did me a lot of good, because it gave me a chance to regroup.

"I had Priscilla and Mum to look after me, and to get the old energy levels up a bit. I was still quite young, and I was working as a drainlayer as well. There wasn't a lot of meat on the bones. It was tough going.

"It certainly was a bloody hard time. We were living down at Woodend Beach, and the house was cold. You go through those things as a young fella. I'd probably just gone too hard.

"I played against Southland, and the British Isles. I can remember running out against Southland, and after about 10 minutes I was ready to walk off, but there was no way I was going to. I played the whole game absolutely crook as a dog. I was absolutely buggered.

"Vance may have found out a bit about what was happening to me behind the scenes. He rang up and asked me to come to training, then I was back in the team for the last two games of the NPC, and I've never missed a game for Canterbury since then. I can remember saying to Vance before his last game as Crusaders coach [in 1996] how much I respected him. But I did say that I hadn't forgotten how he dropped me!"

Vance Stewart is, to a degree, the forgotten man in the renaissance of Canterbury rugby in the 1990s.

Blackadder certainly credits him with laying vital foundations, and introducing some vital players to the red and blacks.

It was Stewart who introduced Mark Mayerhofler to Canterbury from North Harbour, going to the trouble of organising cross-credits for training college to make sure Mayerhofler didn't suffer academically when he shifted. He encouraged Justin Marshall to rehabilitate a niggling groin injury in Canterbury, rather than Southland. He elevated Andrew Mehrtens, Tabai Matson, Daryl Gibson and Angus Gardiner from local club competitions. "If you look at the last five years," says Blackadder, "these guys have been some of the best players Canterbury has ever had."

If you'd never met Stewart, it would be easy to form a mental image of a man who locked the scrum in the 1970s for Canterbury, and the All Blacks, and who now runs a business trading in metals as a hairy-fisted, bull-necked ruffian.

Nothing could be further from the truth. Softly spoken, well read, and an immaculate dresser, Stewart was a revelation to Blackadder, and the Canterbury team.

"When I was first in the team I didn't really know him, or know how to take him," says Blackadder. "Now I really like the guy. He's a top man. I often go round to his work, and we get on like a house on fire.

"He introduced a lot of things that have happened in professional rugby. He set goals, which we'd never done before. If someone had asked what a goal was we would have said it was something you kicked between the posts.

"He brought a lot of intellect into our side. We had been pretty much just blood and guts, and we played more just on emotions. I think I played the first few years on pure emotion. We didn't really devise game plans.

"I can remember his team talks before the games distinctly. He'd recite, for example, something out of Charles Upham's book. He'd obviously done a lot of reading, and there were things in certain books that he picked up on. I found his talks inspirational."

Stewart says the most striking thing about Blackadder in his early days was the way he ran. "He wasn't compact at all. The shoulders rolled, he was all shoulders and knees going all the time. It was a striking sight, and I don't think the draw and pass was an option in those days. He came from the hard country school of rugby, where the forwards dominated, and if the ball went to the first-five it was pretty expansive play.

"More than anything his rugged approach was in contrast to his pretty quiet demeanour in those days. He was just establishing himself in the team in '92, although with so many young players coming into the side, by 1994 he was a bit of a veteran!

"His commitment was huge. You never had to question Toddy, or pump him up at training. During the games it was full-on Toddy, and I don't think he ever played the game any differently.

"It was at a stage where some of the others in the team were lacking in confidence. In some cases it was possibly because they didn't have the ability to adapt to the change of pace from club rugby to provincial rugby. In some cases they had been in provincial rugby, had tried different things, found they hadn't worked, and went into their shells.

"So the team was pretty constricted at that stage. But Toddy wasn't. He was a blood and guts man, it was a case of 'Give me the ball and I'll smash it up the field.' He was aggressive around the rucks and mauls, as you'd expect a country forward to be like.

"He came through from an era where country forwards had been dominating the Canterbury team, going right back to when Alex Wyllie was playing. It was the way that country boys had to be, that hard school of provincial players for Canterbury."

As well as Stewart, Mike Brewer would be another powerful figure during what would prove to be a brief spell in Christchurch. The captain of Otago for seven years from the time he was 20, Brewer would have been Laurie Mains' All Black captain from 1992, except for his appalling luck with injuries, which had already kept him out of the 1987 and 1991 World Cups.

Work for the Canterbury International clothing company brought him to Canterbury in 1993, and although he played just three games for the province in that year, in 1994 he was, coach Stewart says, "an obvious choice to captain Canterbury. Players would follow him off a cliff."

Blackadder felt the same. "Mike Brewer was absolutely outstanding, after what we'd been through. He was the first guy that gave us real direction. He brought intelligence into the side and we started to do things for a reason.

"He also started pointing the finger at guys and putting pressure on the guys to perform for the team."

"I thought he was the breath of fresh air we'd been lacking. Until then there was too much of an attitude that it was good enough just to be in the side.

"Under Mike there was no place for complacency. I'm not sure if he had a say in selection but the guys who did the work certainly got rewarded for it."

Stewart and Brewer even went to the lengths of having a signed covenant for the team. "The covenant was something of a flow-through from the previous years, when things hadn't been going well," says Stewart. "I wouldn't say there was dissent within the team, but within the Canterbury rugby community there was dissent over who was being selected, and who wasn't being selected.

"Some of the reserves were going to their club representatives on the union, and they were having a go there. Things were being slipped to the media that should have been kept in-house. So, to a degree, we were beating ourselves to death.

"So we sat down and talked about something, that I think Benjamin Franklin said when signing the American Declaration of Independence,

'We shall all hang together, lest we all hang separately.'

"We looked at the whole season, and set our goals. Decided what we needed in place with the manager to make everything tick over smoothly, what were the coach's responsibilities, the assistant coach's duties, the masseur's role. We put all that in place.

"Then we decided that we'd be loyal to each other. That no matter what happened we wouldn't go sniping at each other in public, through the media. That formed the basis of the covenant.

"We had a meeting of the senior players, and they all had their ideas. I put it in writing, Mike [Brewer] read it, and agreed with what was said. Then we all signed it. It was actually a secret document. Even some officials of the Canterbury union haven't read it. It was a personal thing within the team.

"If people didn't sign it, then they weren't in the team. They were either with us, or against us. It was really good, because we committed to each other."

Brewer, a hard taskmaster, with a personal taste for hard training that even Laurie Mains would say "bordered on the masochistic," showed Blackadder another side too, the importance of team building.

"I learnt more from Mike than I had at any other time. He did back then what we do now with players, make them feel welcome, help them out, and give them as much help as you can to make them part of the environment. To basically treat them as you would want to be treated yourself. Mike was a lot like that.

"In previous years I'd felt just a wee bit like an outsider. Perhaps you only notice those things if you're sensitive to them.

"But with Mike I certainly enjoyed it, playing with an experienced All Black, with a guy who was so forthcoming, and who took the time for me. He was really an inspiration for me.

"In the past we hadn't had a great deal of direction, and because he is quite a domineering force in any side, he basically took over the side.

"I think Vance, Aussie McLean, and Mike had a lot of meetings, but Mike was out there in the front. He certainly gave us a lot of direction.

"He was always talking about putting the heat on the tight five, and having your nose on the ball. If your nose is not on the ball you're not in the game. All these little things that I think really turned us around."

Canterbury would end the '94 season with the Ranfurly Shield, but what might have been a golden, and now extremely rare, chance to be a provincial team who beat South Africa slipped by.

The previous week Otago had beaten the Boks. It's claimed that the Otago coach of the time, Gordon Hunter, walked into the changing shed before the game with a hammer and nail, hammered the nail in the wall at the height you'd mount a trophy Springbok head, and walked out again.

But Canterbury lost, 20–10, and Blackadder agrees with his captain Brewer, who said at the time it was only a lack of self-belief that held Canterbury back from a famous victory.

Blackadder marked Rudolph Strauli that day, and the Boks were captained by François Pienaar. "The South Africans had just come back into world rugby, and they were a little different, they were huge physically. When you looked at Pienaar and Strauli, they were massive.

"There may have still been a bit of a lack of skill among the South Africans then, but if that was the case, they still took the All Blacks very close that year, and they seemed to have come solely just to play the All Blacks."

There wasn't a great deal of social contact after the game. "Springbok sides were renowned for not talking to the opposition. I think they've opened up a bit more now, but back at the start of Super 12 at Lancaster Park after one game the South Africans sort of stood in one corner and we stood in another, and I don't think anyone exchanged one word."

What was a happy memory from the '94 game was how Blackadder came to keep his game jersey. "They brought out special jerseys, that had Canterbury versus South Africa with the date on them. They auctioned the jerseys off for charity. The Glenmark club bought my jersey, and Stu Loe's jersey, and then presented them to us at the club, which meant a lot to us."

There were two massive highlights still to come in 1994. The first was on September 3, when Canterbury had a Ranfurly Shield challenge against Waikato in Hamilton, who had won it from Auckland the previous season.

The Canterbury preparation was thorough, and took one turn that was perfect for men like Blackadder, who had grown up in the rabid red and black shield era of the 1980s. "Those players were my heroes. I used to deliver *The Star* with full-page posters of people like Robbie Deans, which kids my age all wanted."

In the week before Canterbury went to Hamilton they had one of those heroes, the 1980s captain, Donny Hayes, in to talk about the game.

Mike Brewer recalls that "he came in on the Thursday night. He began by saying that he wasn't very good at delivering a talk, then pulled out a few notes on a bit of paper.

"He was good. When he speaks he doesn't mince any words, and when he talks you can see he's reliving what it had been like. The hair on the back of the neck started to stand.

"He talked about the build-up, winning the shield, and defending it.

"Vance and I could have gone on for hours about some of the points Don made, but the sincerity of the man, and hearing it from someone who had done it, was a real boost for the team."

Blackadder also recalls that having Belfast club stalwart Les McFadden as one of the officials with the team was a good omen.

"He'd been with Alex Wyllie, and he knew all the ins and outs, the do's and don'ts. We flew up on the Friday, and I was rooming with Graham Bachop, in a motel near Rugby Park.

"We took the whole squad up. The guys who weren't going to be on the bench went out that night and had a few beers. Some pricks were outside ringing the cow bells trying to keep us awake. I think a certain Rob Penney and Scotty England were coming home at the same time, and I think there was a bit of a sort out. The cow bells stopped anyway.

"We played our hearts out in that game. I know I did. I think we played beyond ourselves really."

Playing at No. 8, with Brewer on the blindside and Angus Gardiner on the openside, Blackadder was outstanding. Coach Stewart used to rate his players on the scale of 10. That afternoon he marked Blackadder as a nine.

"Waikato had a very good team. Their pack was full of All Blacks — Mark Cooksley, Steve Gordon, Warren Gatland, and John Mitchell.

"But when Vance came in he had a new vision for us. He wanted to play 15-man rugby and to run it. We played it that day and saw some great tries from Mike Brewer, Bubs Mayerhofler, Paula Bale, and Simon Forrest. We played out of our skins. We'd gone away from the old, and even a whole new strip with our names over the back for the first time, it was just a new feeling.

"They started to come back in the second half, but we held on and although the final score was close, 29–26, we'd always been in front. I remember right on full time they kicked to the 22. My old mate Stu Loe had the pill and, being a sensible prop, Stu put leather to leather, and kicked it out to finish the game."

The next day the team flew home to Christchurch. When they arrived at the airport one of the players saw people lined up at the top of the terminal and said, "It's like the Pope's arriving." Another remarked that there was a bigger crowd at the airport than they'd been getting at Lancaster Park.

"It was unbelievable," says Blackadder. "Shield fever is a huge thing in Canterbury. In the 1990s supporters still had fond memories of past eras and still talked about them. In the years we didn't do so well it was, 'You useless bastards, we are not coming down to see you.'

"For us to win and say we were a worthy side meant a lot to me. To see great games and to be part of that team, it was very special. Rugby was well and alive in Canterbury again.

"When we got the shield home we were surprised to find it was ripped and dented, and almost in two. Chris England, who's a wood turner, did a lot for the shield and New Zealand rugby in restoring the Log. We didn't only win it, but reconditioned it as well."

The first challenge at Lancaster Park came from Counties, coached by future All Black selector Ross Cooper.

"There was an unbelievable crowd of 30,000 people," says Blackadder, "and Counties were a side who had been going bloody well. They'd never won the Ranfurly Shield, and they targeted that game as the first time they were going to bring the Shield back to Pukekohe.

"That was where Bruiser's [Mike Brewer's] leadership really came through. It was the first time the team had got a bit of self-belief.

"I can remember Vance saying, 'We're not going to defend the shield, we're going to win it.' That just changed the focus a bit.

"Then to get out there and be playing in that game, it was an awesome occasion. In that game we had one of the best tries we've ever seen from Andrew Mehrtens, where he ran 45 metres right round the outside of the defence, and scored in the corner." Blackadder himself joined in the 42–16 scoring spree, with a bullocking run for a try.

"We were a side full of potential, but we'd never really delivered until we won the shield. Now we had our hands on the shield, and here were Counties, ready to take it off us. Suddenly there was a big crowd there, and there was red and black fever.

"In '94 the weather was absolutely beautiful, and we had the backs and forwards playing dry-weather rugby. It was a great day against Waikato in Hamilton, and then we had two beautiful Canterbury days against Counties and Otago.

"Our backline was full of running, free of injuries. It was the start of a good era for Canterbury."

The last home game of 1994, on October 1, would be one of the best ever played for the Ranfurly Shield.

This was one of the great local derby games. There was outrage in Otago when the Canterbury union allowed just 10,000 of the 42,000 tickets to be sold in Dunedin. In 1993, at the Lancaster Park sports museum, they had sold just one Canterbury jersey. In the week before the Otago challenge they sold 800.

A lot of the build-up focused on the stars in the Otago team — John Timu, who was about to switch to league, Jeff Wilson, Marc Ellis, Steve Bachop, Arran Pene, Jamie Joseph, and Josh Kronfeld.

The hype became so intense that, after a Christchurch radio station produced a song with nonsensical lyrics teasing the Otago players, Wilson appeared on television with the incredible caption on screen: "Jeff Wilson — accused of having a small ding-a-ling." Wilson snarled that words wouldn't hurt him.

Otago coach Gordon Hunter would say that in hindsight the media build-up was allowed to be mismanaged, and become a major issue.

On the other hand, it was inspirational stuff for Canterbury. "I don't know if it was true," says Blackadder, "but through the media we'd heard that in Dunedin they'd already ordered the scones and pikelets for the celebration, and booked the road for the parade back home through town."

After five senior Canterbury team members spoke at the captain's meeting on Friday night there was electricity in the air, and that was topped off by a magnificent pre-game speech from coach Stewart.

"He delivered one of his all-time best speeches," says Blackadder. "It was absolutely inspiring, about how there are times in your life when you've got to make a stand."

Brewer says that when Canterbury left the changing room after Stewart's speech he "wasn't the only one choking back a tear. After that talk we were rock solid."

Despite the emotion, it was Otago who scored first. "Basically the talk had been about how the game would be a case of what they were going to do us, and sure enough, they scored a try in the first couple of minutes," says Blackadder.

"Jamie Joseph went over right between the sticks. I can remember being behind the posts thinking, 'Shit.' I had that tingling feeling that someone was walking over my grave, and here we were in front of a full house.

"We just dug it in and held on. I saw a video five years later, and when I look back on that game, we were just kids really. I think we just got through on sheer emotion and enthusiasm. Having our crowd too made it good. We pulled out one of those performances."

Into the final minutes Canterbury trailed by one point. Referee Colin Hawke says that "I looked at my watch with, I think, about eight minutes to go, and I thought 'This is pretty tight.' So I thought, 'Let's not have a situation where I call a penalty that's pretty nondescript, which can have a major influence on the match.' In other words, let the players decide the outcome. I was conscious of not doing anything that was 50–50. That was my mind-set at that stage.

"There was something just before the penalty that I recall I could possibly have penalised Otago for. But I didn't do anything about it. Then this ruck developed, and it was for a Mehrtens dropped goal. I couldn't really believe what then happened."

David Latta, the Otago captain and hooker, dived through on a loose ball, clearly offside. "There wasn't any point in playing advantage," says Hawke, "because the ball had been killed. It was really quite clear."

Mehrtens kicked the goal, and the shield stayed in Christchurch, with Canterbury winning, 22–20.

"We'd held that shield, which was an amazing effort when you look back on it," says Blackadder. "Those games go so quickly. You're absolutely shitting yourself. You've got all the nerves and expectations, and you're playing against what is probably a better side.

"The game itself was just ferocious. Absolutely ferocious. It went so hell for leather it was a fleeting memory.

"We were magnificently led by Mike. He worked on a pressure game, of putting pressure on other sides. When we got the penalty at the end he was working on the theory of assert pressure, assert pressure, be patient and the penalty will come.

"He gave us real leadership, and a lot of direction. He was that well respected that we did as we were told basically, and we learnt a lot from him.

"When that final whistle went in the Otago game the crowd swarmed onto the field. Having all the kids run on was something special. To me it's a shame that it's something that we're now missing out on.

"For a kid just to be able to walk onto Jade Stadium I think is something special. They started canning kids running on the field a few years ago. I know there might be worries about crowd safety, or player safety, but if I was a kid I'd want to be able to run on, and touch your stars.

"There's a lot of night rugby now, which doesn't help it, but what's wrong with patting your hero on the back? It's a great feeling if you're a kid running out there to get an autograph.

"What worries me is that players run inside, and they eat a banana for recovery and all that, and the Andrew Mehrtens of tomorrow are waiting in line and they can't get a signature these days."

The division one final in the NPC in 1994 saw emotions boil right over when Auckland beat North Harbour 22–16 at the Onewa Domain. Robin Brooke and Eric Rush were both sent off, after Brooke and Mark

Weedon were sin-binned in the first 10 minutes.

Canterbury had a chance to be in that final, travelling to Takapuna to play North Harbour in one semi-final.

There were moments to remember from the game for Canterbury, but only moments, as they lost 59–27. Their centre, Tabai Matson, fended off All Black centre Frank Bunce, not once, but twice, in one stirring run. Nobody else in world rugby, much less New Zealand rugby, had ever managed to do the same.

"Tabai Matson was knocked by a lot of people," says Blackadder. "I think that may have been because, with the long strides he took when he ran, he looked slow, but he certainly wasn't slow.

"He had a great ability that he was strong enough to stay on his feet, he was balanced, and he was extremely skilful. He created space for his wingers. What more could you want out of a world-class centre?

"To go up and play Harbour, in the semi, we were no less focused, but we were never in the same ballpark. Our season had really ended after that Otago shield game. We'd put all our emotions, all our energies into that game, and with a young side, we'd given it our all, and there was nothing left."

5. Pushing the limits

"It's surprising what you'll do"

Stories about how hard Laurie Mains trained his teams had become folklore in Otago long before he became All Black coach. Mains, a former All Black fullback, was an almost brutally hard taskmaster who says that from the time he first coached a senior team, with the Southern club in Dunedin, he concentrated on the forwards.

"One of the great things [legendary Otago coach] Vic Cavanagh, and after him [Otago and All Black coach] Eric Watson impressed on me was that if you don't have your forwards doing it dead right, your backs are no bloody good."

His commitment to getting forwards doing it "dead right" was legendary, and backs weren't spared the lash at training either.

Nobody ever actually died after a Mains' training session, but when Otago suffered a feeble one-point loss to Wairarapa-Bush in 1985, the Tuesday run was so brutal an Otago inside back actually landed up in hospital being checked for a heart murmur.

When Todd Blackadder was selected for the All Blacks for the 1995 tour of Italy and France, in a team coached by Mains, he'd already had a taste of how fit Mains wanted his players.

"The level of fitness in the 1995 World Cup All Blacks was exceptional. The guys that year worked their guts out.

"Early in the year I was called down to train with the World Cup squad in Christchurch, which was pretty exciting, and my job was to stand there and tackle them. They'd have a No. 8 running and I'd have to tackle the runner off him, and then they'd clean that ruck out.

"I blew both AC joints. When one shoulder was buggered and I couldn't move my arm I'd tackle with the other shoulder.

"I was lucky enough to then be called in, for a game on the West Coast, the day after, which was basically an All Black trial. I think I had cortisone in both shoulders so I could play.

"Then I had to go back to my work on the Monday, which was a courier contract, and I'll tell you, it wasn't easy running round delivering parcels with two stuffed AC joints."

If the training for the World Cup was demanding, Blackadder had heard how Mains was keen on an old school All Black tradition of seeing how much pressure a new man in the team could take.

Taine Randell and Blackadder were the new forwards who came under the hammer in Takapuna, when the All Blacks assembled.

"I don't know if he drove us as hard as he did some other guys," says Blackadder, "but it was pretty tough. There was me and Taine, and we had to just keep hitting these two ruck machines around a flag, and then we had to do down and ups with the team watching us.

"He pushed us through 150s, because we were both loose forwards, and if the locks beat us we had to do it again.

"It was certainly one mean, hard training, and you might think it was demoralising to see young guys doing that, but in some ways with Laurie it was a way of earning respect in the eyes of guys who had gone through the same amount of pain before you.

"The one valuable lesson I learnt out of it was that you would be surprised where you can push yourself. If you think about it as though you're stuck in a ditch, and only you can push yourself out, it's surprising what you'll do. You'll find enough grit and determination to claw your way out.

"When you know what a pain threshold is really like, I think that once you've been there, you can push yourself through it again. That was a big lesson I learnt from Laurie."

Mains was a controversial figure during his time as All Black coach, which began in 1992 and would finish at the end of '95. As Otago coach he'd always been suspicious of media people from outside the province, and before the World Cup would be almost constantly under attack, especially from northern critics who believed John Hart should have got his job.

At one stage, after some average play by the All Blacks in 1994 against France, he was grilled by Paul Holmes on national television to the point where it seemed he was being treated not so much as a rugby coach whose team had lost two games, but more like a convicted child molester.

It's a reflection more of personal animosity than reality that Keith Quinn, for example, in his autobiography suggested that he doubted the World Cup All Blacks "were affected too much in the playing of that epic final" by the vicious gastric illness that swept through the team.

To Quinn, Mains was best suited to the nickname "Laughing Laurie", a man who as a player had an astounding number of excuses, and as a coach was excessively paranoid.

Blackadder, like so many of the players Mains coached over the years, has a quite different view of the man.

"He was superb on that tour. He was a pleasure to play for, because he was straight up. He was hard, he demanded honesty, and the best from his players, but he was the sort of guy you'd bloody die for.

"When you see the likes of Zinzan and Robin Brooke lift him up after his last game in Paris I think that showed how much the players really admired him.

"He was a hard taskmaster, and he looked you in the eye and demanded the best out of you, and that's how he got it. He was awesome.

"I think as New Zealanders we're not into bullshitting around. Some of the best team talks I've ever heard have been the ones that have been straight up and very demanding.

"Laurie put the spotlight on you in a team environment, and when he put the heat on, it was straight on you.

"You knew with him that the team always came first, and whether he was right or wrong, or you didn't like something he did, it didn't matter, because the most important thing with Laurie was the team.

"Technically he was very good, and he wasn't afraid to kick you up the arse, because he just wanted the best from you, and he pointed you in the right direction.

"From '95, on to where we are now, he was the first to bring in a ruck machine, to start cleaning out, and when you look at it now, the Brumbies probably do it the best, and New Zealand may have gone away from it a little.

"Guys like John Mitchell are bringing it back, but as far as technical knowledge in a forward coach goes, Laurie would be one of the best in the world.

"He used a lot of repetition and hard work until things were right. The games were sometimes easier than the training."

Blackadder found out he was named in the All Blacks, while he and his wife, Priscilla, were at the Canterbury Supporters' Club end of year dinner at the Racecourse Hotel in Riccarton.

"I think it was Richard Loe, who told me, and Justin Marshall too, while we were all there together as a side. It was just awesome and kicked off a very good night.

"It was unbelievable, just pure excitement. There's no feeling like making a team for the first time, it was great.

"Professionalism was just around the corner, but this was the last of the amateur tours. I was a courier, working as a contractor, with a truck and a van. All the drivers looked after each other, and the truck kept going with a driver while I was away. Priscilla kept the van going. In 1994, when Canterbury had gone to England on a tour I couldn't go because I couldn't afford it.

"Working as a courier I was getting out of bed at five in the morning, and we were training at night.

"I'd finish work at 6pm, then go straight to training, and be home at nine. It was bloody hard going, because you're running round all day.

"In some ways it did keep me fit. Training was almost a break."

While there was no big pay cheque at the end of the All Black tour, that wasn't a downside to Blackadder. "To me it was a whirlwind, and it was exciting. It was an eye-opener. To me, to be playing in Sicily at Catania, for the All Blacks against Italy A, was amazing."

The manager of the All Blacks that year was Colin "Pinetree" Meads, one of the icons of the sport. Getting his first All Black jersey from Meads was something special, but what sticks in Blackadder's mind the most was "actually being out there on the field, with an All Black jersey on. It really hit home, 'Shit, I'm an All Black.'"

Blackadder, Marshall and Randell all played their first games for New Zealand that night, and right from the start things were very different from playing at Lancaster Park.

The Santa Maria Goretti stadium is usually used for soccer, and in a part of Italy that is famous for being the birthplace of the Mafia, the playing area is surrounded by a huge wire cage to keep the fans contained.

As the All Blacks were about to kick off, a local cameraman stood his ground on the field, right in front of the All Black forwards, as they pawed the turf, ready for the chase.

The media liaison man with the All Blacks was Ric Salizzo, now the host of Sky television's "Sports Café" show. As his name suggests Salizzo, while born in New Zealand, has Italian heritage, and speaks the language. But despite his ability to communicate, there were a volatile few moments before he could hustle the stubborn cameraman off the ground.

At last the match was under way, and for Blackadder it was an occasion with both happy and sad memories. On the bright side of the ledger there was a win for the All Blacks, 51–21, with Blackadder himself scoring two of the team's six tries. The sad touch was that Andrew Mehrtens suffered a strange knee injury, which ended his tour. Mehrtens was running from his goal-line, trying to make sure his kick wouldn't be charged down when, untouched by any opponent, he heard "an awful crunching, graunching sound" which proved to be a partial rupture of the anterior cruciate ligament.

Minute details of the game are hazy for Blackadder, who played at

No. 8. "It was almost too exciting to remember for me. You just want to play the game without making too many mistakes, and try to enjoy it. But it's not easy to do that in your first game, because you're so nervous, you're unproven, and really your coach is taking a chance with you.

"You want to reward him, but you just want to be an All Black. You go through all those emotions, but the reality is you've got to get out there and play."

The All Blacks won their test against Italy, in Bologna, 70–6, and then the tour moved to France, where the opening match, in Toulon, was against the French Barbarians.

In a New Zealand team that was near test strength Blackadder found himself on the blindside with Zinzan Brooke captaining the team at No. 8.

"The French Barbarians would be one of the better games I've ever played — it felt like another test match. I felt a little bit out of place, to be honest, finding myself playing with these guys against a Barbarians team who had players like John Eales at lock, mixed in with a shadow French test side.

"We knew it'd be hard, and a lot of the experienced players had told us how hard the French players would be, but I loved it."

Blackadder was one of a generation of players who had grown up with the infamous story of how Buck Shelford was kicked in the scrotum when the All Blacks lost a fierce test in Nantes in 1986. Shelford's fellow loose forward Mark Brooke-Cowden says he will never forget going to the All Blacks' changing room after the test and seeing Shelford sitting, staring with a steely gaze into the mid-distance while a French doctor crouched in front of him.

"I made the mistake," says Brooke-Cowden, "of looking to see what the doctor was doing. When I saw that he was sewing up Buck's scrotum, which was split up the middle, the room started to spin a bit, and I had to go and lie down in the showers so I wouldn't faint."

Blackadder was fascinated by the approach that the French took before games. "Watching the French team warm up, they'd be punching themselves, biting each other before kick-off. They were pretty fired up, but so were we really. As a young player you'd always heard stories about what these dogs had done to Buck.

"We went through the midweek games unbeaten, which was a pretty proud record, and we just lived for them."

The French tour, where the New Zealand union had denied Mains' request for a touring party of 30 players, limiting him to 26 players, would be the last time that All Black squads on tour would not divide into two clearly defined groups, a test team and a midweek side.

"Being in a midweek team from '96 onwards, never really felt the same as it did in '95," says Blackadder. "As a young All Black in '95, you had an opportunity to rub shoulders with the test players.

"You felt more like you were really part of it. In a midweek team you feel that you're not really involved in the whole picture.

"If you look at 1996, when we won the test series in South Africa for the first time, if you're in the midweek team you're there in Africa, and you're still really proud of the achievement in the series, but you don't really feel part of it.

"You might go and play your game, while the test team might stay at the hotel, so they're ready for the next game.

"In '95 we were all in together, and you roomed with guys like Olo Brown, and Alama Ieremia, the incumbent test players, and you spent a lot more time with them. Maybe playing chess, or doing things as a team.

"It's bloody tough being in a midweek team. The test is played on a Saturday, and you have to travel on the Sunday. You have to train on the Sunday afternoon, and your team only comes together then, because you have the Monday off, so you can play on the Tuesday night.

"You're expected to put pressure on test players, while the locals are looking to beat the shit out of you, because they regard you as an All Black team.

"On the Wednesday after your game you've got to wind down and have a few beers, then you're off to the test venue. Some of the guys in the midweek side are the test reserves, so you've got a mixed bag and you can't train as a side for the rest of the week. You just do fitness and skill training.

"On the Saturday you've got to support the test team. You're out of the hotel the morning of a test, and you go and do training, and stay out of the hotel during the day to let the test players get ready.

"Whereas in '95, with a smaller squad, you just felt so much more part of it. People were passing on their knowledge, and making you feel comfortable. It certainly was a different feeling.

"A midweek team can make their own fun, and still have a great time, but you don't really get a chance to train with the test side. In '95 I found the test players were all good guys. If you were rooming with someone they looked after you. Guys like Walter Little would look after anyone. The whole team got on bloody well."

For the first test of the '95 tour, in Toulouse, Blackadder was elevated to the test squad, as a reserve. His form on tour had been impressive, and in *Rugby News* Bob Howitt wrote that "Blackadder was one of the stars of the team. Trained like he played, at 100mph. He has the hard nosed, knock-'em-over attitude of players like Mark Shaw and Andy Earl."

To Blackadder it was "exciting to be in the test squad. I just wanted to get a run, but I think I might have been too nervous to do any good.

"Sitting on the sideline for the whole game, I was dying to get out there. On the other hand, there was a part of me that was almost scared about going on. It's a real mix of emotions. This is a test match. Your heart's in your mouth, and the adrenalin is pumping the whole game, just sitting on the sideline.

"It wasn't a good day for the All Blacks, and I can tell you, we got a real tonging-up after the game [lost 22–15], at the next place we went to after the test, Nancy."

Manager Meads had not only been our greatest All Black, as a fearsome lock forward, but he was also a successful coach with King Country, the Junior All Blacks, and had been an All Black selector. He made a real point to never step on Mains' coaching toes, but after the loss in Toulouse he asked if he could speak to the team.

"Pinetree has been there and done that, and he wasn't a guy who minced his words.

"We'd done a few things that weren't acceptable. We'd blocked off a corridor outside the changing room in Toulouse when we were warming up, and apparently we'd blocked off some high-placed French officials.

"Then we went out there and didn't play very well. Things were getting a little bit loose. There were some things that should have been ironed out right at the start, about what were the boundaries, what were the job descriptions. By the time we got to Nancy the team needed a kick up the arse, and we certainly got it.

"I don't think anybody went to the meeting expecting what they got. He gave us the talk of all talks, I can tell you that. No stone was left unturned. He meant every word he said and he was right on the mark in every respect. Looking back, it was appropriate, really. He's one of the few managers who could say the things he did, and he went through the whole team.

"In the context of the whole tour, we had a midweek game and a test to go. He certainly pulled things back into line."

The second-to-last game was against a French Selection, and there's not much Blackadder can remember about it.

"I got a good punch from someone. All my vision had gone. All I could see was the side of the ground.

"Mark Cooksley was playing, and this French guy came through and he tried to throw a punch at him, and Big Rigger hit this guy with one of the best punches I've ever seen in my life. He just swung this big arm, and collected the guy right on the jaw. It was as clean as a whistle, and they stretchered the French guy off.

"In the meeting Pinetree had called in Nancy, the test side had been told that everyone was fighting for a test spot, so how the team played in Nancy was important. Guys who weren't playing in the game were on tenterhooks."

Bob Howitt reported at the time that Blackadder was on the brink of selection for the second test, but Mains opted to go with Michael Jones and Liam Barry, in his test debut, on the side of the scrum, with Zinzan Brooke at No. 8. Justin Marshall would play his first test at halfback.

There was one unexpected bonus that came with non-selection. "The guys who weren't in the test squad, did our pilgrimage to Epernay, north of Paris, as guests of Moët, the champagne people. It was unbelievable. We caught a bus, and had dinner at the Chateau Saran.

"We'd never seen anything like that, drinking vintage champagne, being served pheasant by people with white gloves. It was like things were 200 years ago. Then we retired to the smoking room, and we all grabbed a cigar.

"We were given a huge bottle, which we thought we'd save for after the test, plus a magnum each as well. On the bus, and we started having a wee drink. We probably had the best champagne in the world, and we all just whacked the tops off them, and were sculling them on the bus, being good old Kiwis.

"We stopped the bus and Richard Fromont got out and did a nude down and up. The French police turned up, put us all back on the bus, and sent us on our way."

For the last test in Paris, Blackadder and his champagne mates had the job of scalping tickets. "We had to hop out of the hotel and sell all the tickets to make a few bob for the team kitty. It was an interesting change."

The test itself was a triumph, the All Blacks winning 37–12, in a dominant performance. "The All Blacks were awesome in that game. I was proud of them. It was Laurie's last game, and the boys chaired him off."

Some All Blacks stayed in Europe for private holidays. Blackadder wasn't one. "I came straight back home. After being away from Priscilla and the kids it's nice to get home. For me there's no place in the world like New Zealand.

* * *

For Canterbury the 1995 season began with Super 10. Any confusion with the professional approach to Super 12 as we know it now should be discounted immediately.

"We had one week before we played Queensland in Super 10 in Brisbane," says Blackadder. "That was our whole pre-session campaign, one training run before we played.

"We lost 24–6, but we actually didn't play too badly. It was the first time where, when we lost a front rower, someone else had to come off.

"We were standing around and, as captain, Mike Brewer had to decide who to send off and we were all looking around 'cos this was entirely new.

Old Scotty England, one of our locks, goes 'Oh, bloody hell, I s'pose its bloody me' and stormed off the field."

The next day a trip to the Gold Coast was planned, and most of the team expected a pleasant day at the beach.

"Ivan Morgan [Ziggy], and I had a big night out, with a fair number of drinks, and we were late for the bus. We thought we were just going down there for a bit of a swim.

"But, Mike had got a bee in his bonnet and put us through one of the hardest training runs I've ever suffered.

"Some of us had a feeling something wasn't right the way Bruiser was carrying on. Poor old Stu Loe jumps straight off the bus, saying 'Come on guys,' and runs down the beach, and dives into the salt water. As it turned out not many followed him and then, as training progressed, his chafing progressed as well, the poor bastard.

"Mike took us to this little park on the side of the road and, shit, we were doing down and ups, sprints, 20–50s, the lot. Because Ivan and I were late we had to do 20 per cent more than anyone else, and all those who had steak before the game had to do a couple of extra runs. This was all in a public park on the side of the road. He'd certainly learnt at the feet of Laurie Mains."

Next up in Super 10 was Auckland, the game played at the home of league's Warriors, Ericsson Stadium, lost by 27–22, but still the closest Canterbury had come to Auckland for some years.

At that point Richard Loe and Mike Brewer were the only players in the Canterbury team who had beaten Auckland, and Loe had done it playing for Waikato, Brewer playing for Otago.

"We were down and out at halftime, and Vance Stewart gave a few stern messages at halftime, and we came back and played very well."

A good win over Tonga at Rugby Park, 75–5, was followed with a loss to Free State, 42–35. Blackadder remembers vividly his first taste of rugby against a South African province.

"They were tough buggers, with some of the biggest forwards I'd ever seen in my life. From the kick-off their hooker, who was a real nutter, ran up and kneed me right in the back. The whole game was like that.

"Mehrts got injured too, and we went down, which was disappointing, but back then it was my first time to actually play a South African province, so it was pretty interesting really. You would think that you'd mingle but I don't think one player exchanged a word after the game."

Canterbury held the shield in '95, and after Super 10 finished defended it against Mid-Canterbury, on tour in Ashburton, and at home against Nelson Bays, Marlborough and South Canterbury.

Then it was into the NPC, drawing with North Harbour, and beating Southland, 27–22, at Lancaster Park.

"I went to the first lineout against North Harbour, and got either punched or kicked. I played the whole game in a daze. I basically didn't wake up until the court session that night, when I wondered where the hell I was. Until that game I had never really worn a mouth guard, but I certainly did after that.

"Then we gave Waikato a spanking, 58–30, which was probably one of the best games we played all season. In those days when we were on fire, we were really on fire.

"On the other hand we lost to Counties in the last minutes at Pukekohe, and when we played King Country at Te Kuiti they absolutely cleaned us out, 48–28. I remember [coach] Vance Stewart coming to me that week and saying you're not playing this weekend, he said he was going to give me a rest.

"So I wasn't on the field, but it wasn't pretty up in the stand I can tell you that. We were the shield holders, and the crowd gave Bruiser [Mike Brewer] shit, right through the game.

"We thought we were a better side than that, but we got cleaned out. We were still going through that potential tag where 'potentially' we were a good side. I don't like that word potential because it means you haven't actually done it. We were one of those teams that would win the tough games, then lose the games we shouldn't lose.

"I remember reading Grant Fox saying good teams win the games they should win. You lift yourself for the big ones, no matter who you are, but you must win the games you should win."

The night of the King Country disappointment there was a massive court session in the team's hotel, during which Andrew Mehrtens' career was nearly snuffed out by Richard Loe. For reasons that are almost certainly connected to the glasses he had already drunk, Mehrtens suddenly tipped a full glass of beer over Loe's head.

As Justin Marshall recalls it, "Loey jumped up roaring, and he grabbed Mehrts by the throat. All of a sudden Mehrts just slumped, out to it. Mehrts had thought it was so amusing tipping his beer over Loey's head, and he got the sleeper hold put on him. Eventually Mehrts came round, and he certainly never tipped beer on Loey again."

The Wellington Ranfurly Shield challenge the following week would again prove that Loe wasn't a man to trifle with.

Wellington had a massive Fijian prop, Bill Cavubati, who was never far from the newspaper headlines, whether it was trying to drop some of the 135kg he was reputed to weigh, or darting away for a futile attempt to rebuild his career in Sydney when he felt he was unappreciated in Wellington.

Before the challenge at Lancaster Park Cavubati was on television, and on newspaper front pages, grilling Canterbury lamb, which he suggested was what he'd do to the red and black front row.

"One thing about playing with a guy like Richard Loe was that he was so bloody aggressive," says Blackadder. "He lived for guys like Cavubati to come out and say stuff like that.

"All week we'd been hearing how the Capital was going to be chewing on Canterbury lamb during the game, and they were just going to walk all over us. They had a pretty good team back then too.

"They were confident, but I think they fuelled our fire. I know I'd never try to antagonise Richard if I came up against him. Really, by kick-off, Richard was just going to rip Cavubati apart."

Wellington were whipped, 66–17, and Loe brought Cavubati to his knees in the scrums. Mike Brewer would say after the game that when Cavubati met Loe, "We saw the difference between an international prop and a provincial prop."

During the season, says Blackadder, "We did a lot of innovative things. We were doing stuff off the back of the scrum, where I would pick it up and pass to Mark Mayerhofer at second-five. We were trying a lot of new stuff.

"We basically tried to play that style from 1994, but I think against Auckland, in our last game of the '95 season, when we lost the shield, that was actually our undoing.

"They were a big team with a lot of internationals and they really applied a lot of pressure on us. I had the ball once and I was running across to do a cut with Mark. I could see Zinzan Brooke coming, and before I could pass he hit me in a real good tackle. The ball spilled forward, and Eroni Clarke picked it up and scored a try.

"Those little things showed you we were a young side on the rise, but that we still lacked that little bit of experience, that big match temperament.

"That was the game when Carlos Spencer kept kicking it dead, and we just kept trying to play in our own half. Basically they just ground us down through pressure.

"They certainly targeted us, and they did their homework very well. With Graham Henry coaching them I think Auckland then were still a step ahead of everyone else.

"Our real experience started and stopped at Richard and Bruiser. Mehrts was young and still on the rise, it was Justin Marshall's first year, and while I'd been there three years we were all a bit green really.

"We lost 35–0, and had to hand the shield over to the Auckland team. It was before they had brought in that rule that if you kick the ball dead, you have to go back to the scrum where the kick is from. They kept kicking it and kicking it, and we had to drop out.

"It wasn't one of the prettiest games to watch, and certainly at the time a little bit of me felt they were bad sports or something. But they played the rules, and really they just played clever rugby.

"Every time we tried to run it they smashed us and forced a mistake and got field position.

"They just kept on pinning us and pinning us and for forwards running back all day it can be pretty demoralising. You can never get yourself back in the game in the right half.

"So basically they taught us one hell of a lesson. It highlighted where we were and where they were. We were basically playing on guts and pride, we hadn't fully worked out our tactics yet.

"We wanted to play an expansive game but when they shut us down we ran out of plans. We didn't have a plan B."

Canterbury finished fifth in the NPC. Ahead lay professionalism, and some bitter lessons.

6. Cash, contracts and captaincy

"Perhaps we should have known that the world was turning"

The great rugby issue of the mid-1990s wasn't who would coach the All Blacks, who should be the captain, or was there really a woman called Suzy who poisoned the All Blacks at the World Cup?

It was way bigger than all of those put together. It was, in simple terms, who would actually run the game by the end of the 20th century.

At a time of upheaval in the sport the biggest, and most lasting, would be the decision in 1995 by Australia, New Zealand and South Africa to make the game openly professional at the start of 1996.

South African rugby chief Louis Luyt, a beefy, aggressive, filthy rich man whose idea of a rational discussion was usually him laying down the law, and everyone around him agreeing, made the dramatic announcement at Ellis Park in Johannesburg on the Friday before the World Cup final.

Luyt had signed a deal he hammered out on behalf of the three Southern Hemisphere rugby powers in London earlier in the week, with an executive of billionaire Rupert Murdoch's News Corporation, Sam Chisholm. It's a very Luyt aside that when Luyt was called back to Chisholm's apartment to formally sign the papers he was, according to Peter FitzSimons in his book *The Rugby War*, reluctant to leave the giant meal of spare ribs he had only got halfway through.

For a total price of $US550 million, television rights to all domestic games in Australia, New Zealand and South Africa for the 10 years starting in 1996 were sold to News Corporation.

In itself that seemed staggering enough. The money boggled the mind. What was almost as astonishing was that a rival organisation, the World Rugby Corporation, linked to another Aussie media giant, Kerry Packer, was working behind the scenes to snatch away the very players Murdoch's outfit thought they had bought the unchallenged rights to.

The WRC was the brainchild of a quiet South African-born Sydney lawyer, Geoff Levy, in association with former Wallaby prop Ross "Mad Dog" Turnbull. They swooped in and signed up players all over the rugby world, and in New Zealand some of the most enthusiastic proponents of switching allegiances to the WRC were senior All Blacks.

In Canterbury the point man for WRC was Mike Brewer, their charismatic captain, whose contract was to be $US1 million a year for three years.

Todd Blackadder remembers clearly being at a Canterbury training when the WRC contracts were handed out by Brewer to a group of about nine or 10 players.

"The contracts weren't offered to all of the Canterbury players, just some of them. There were a lot of dropped lips, because a lot of guys didn't get contracts. We had to meet in a room, and I think my contract was $US100,000, which even to this day is very good money. Back in 1996 that was a hell of a lot of money.

"It was all a bit of a joke, and there were a lot of whispers everywhere, but at the end of the day the whole team were basically offered a WRC contract as a Canterbury team.

"Mike had convinced us that, if it was going to work, we should all stick together as a team. We had three or four meetings, and we held out.

I think the WRC had gone through the top players, like Mike and Sean Fitzpatrick, and sorted them out with very good contracts, and then the boys would follow."

Canterbury stayed staunch to the bitter end. Jock Hobbs, a former Canterbury and All Black captain, came to Christchurch as part of his exhausting travels round New Zealand to sign up players for the NZRU, but he was wasting his time. "We held out," says Blackadder. "We went through thick and thin together, and not one guy went the NZRU way. That was one of the biggest mistakes we ever made."

In the rest of the country players were having second thoughts, while at an international level, there were suggestions that a deal was being struck in the rarefied world that Murdoch and Packer moved in, which led to Packer withdrawing the money the WRC needed.

In Canterbury the story was all over *The Press* about how leading players like Otago All Blacks Josh Kronfeld and Jeff Wilson, and Counties captain Errol Brain, had signed with the NZRU.

"Obviously the guys who signed then were on very good contracts. We were probably the last team to hold out. By then it was all over, and when all our boys signed up I think everyone of us signed up on the $65,000 contract.

"I know that we were penalised as a side, because we hung together as a team to the bitter end. In one way that's commendable, but in another way perhaps we should have had the common sense to know that the world was turning.

"I believe all the guys like Bruiser got a payment of some description, but guys like myself came out empty-handed from the WRC.

"Even back in those days, the first year of professionalism, by the time you've taken tax off $65,000, it's not a massive amount of money.

"They were three-year contracts too, so for those three years from 1996, the majority of the Canterbury players, with the exception of the All Blacks, were on $65,000.

"For an up-and-coming player, smashing his body round for 12 months of the year, it's nothing really, not when you look at the amount of money these guys in their early 20s are bringing into the game.

"Certainly they're earning a living while they're playing, but gee, after five or six years you don't get another hamstring, you don't get another knee, you don't get another shoulder, and you can't take back those years.

"You can't build a business career while you're playing professional rugby. Only the big corporate companies could afford to pick up a player, and, to be honest, you're too committed to your football to be able to focus on something else.

"We've always had a battle to get our guys up to what I think is the going rate compared to all the other Super 12/NPC players. It's been a hell of a battle over the years.

"Like the rest of the guys, I didn't get any special deal in 1996, because they had us by the scruff of the neck. We've had a few problems with contracts. It hasn't been handled too well. We've been the low men on the totem pole.

"I'd been fighting for my contract, so after two years on the base rate, during which time I made the All Blacks and became Crusaders captain, I had my contract upped a bit, and they told me that was a top-line contract, comparable to any other player in my position.

"Then I heard that an Auckland player was on a lot more just for Super 12. It was a rumour, more than anything, but I had a hunch about it. So I got on the phone and I rang up a guy at the NZRU and said, 'You bloody lied to me. You told me I was on a top contract, and you bullshitted me. I know for a fact you've got a guy there in Auckland, who's on a lot more'.

"He wanted to know who I was talking about, and overnight they jumped my contract up, obviously to where he was. I was only going on a hunch, on a rumour."

When Super 12 arrived on the scene in 1996, it wasn't anything like the streamlined operation it is today. There wasn't any lack of will among the Crusaders, but nobody really knew how professional rugby should be run.

A big decision for coach Vance Stewart was who he would choose to captain the side with Mike Brewer heading to Ireland.

"Toddy was asked at the time Mike intended to shift overseas whether he could be considered as an option," says Stewart. "I had discussions with Mike at the time, and at the end of the day he felt Richard Loe should be given the first option, as far as the seniority side of it went.

"At the same time we had Todd saying that, no, he didn't really want to be captain, so it was obviously hard to get him to move into that role."

Hard work would the order of the day before Super 12 started, but country players like Blackadder, Richard Loe and Stu Loe had it easy, compared to the weights regime prescribed for the city boys.

"The country guys could do our weight training in Rangiora, but the guys in town like Norm Maxwell had to be at the gym at the university at some crazy time like 5 or 6 o'clock in the morning.

"We did a lot of fitness work, and I think we were the fittest team in New Zealand in Super 12, but we just didn't have the right balance.

"We'd just gone into a new era, and there were certainly a lot of demands, and as soon as the season started we knew what we were in for.

"We went through 35 players that season, and in many areas we were trying to be professional, but missing the mark a bit. You can see how much things have changed since '96 just by looking at our list of officials. Andrew Mehrtens, who was getting over his knee injury from the previous year's All Blacks tour, was our media liaison man."

In February the Crusaders got a real taste of the brave new world of Super 12, when they jetted off to South Africa for warm-up games with Northern Transvaal, lost 10–16, and Western Province, won 17–12.

It was Blackadder's first trip to South Africa, and he was fascinated by the whole experience. "My first game as captain was when we beat Western Province, which was certainly a highlight for me. You hear so much about South Africa to finally get over there to those big stadiums was unbelievable. It was a great time, certainly one of the great countries to tour. You have to get out and do a bit more and experience it to appreciate it.

"Playing in Africa was all new to most of us. Our first game at altitude was against Northern Transvaal in Pretoria. We didn't find it so bad. We had a night game, and there was a bit of dew on the grass, and we didn't notice a lot of difference.

"Over time we found the more we talked about altitude the worse we went. In games up on the veldt, as we got a bit puffed we'd think 'Oh, our legs are gone' and blame it on altitude.

"But then we never talked about it, and when we looked at the South African teams they were stuffed as well. I think it's more of a mental than a physical thing. You just can't get going at 100 per cent all the time — you go in bursts."

Back in New Zealand the first game of the Super 12 was in Hamilton against the Waikato Chiefs and the Crusaders got a taste of nightmares ahead. They were almost alone in the country in not falling in love with the game's new showpiece.

The immediate and massive impact Super 12 had in 1996 is now almost difficult to recall. Remember that in the lead-up to the competition there were actually plenty of people who sensed disaster.

Amalgamating provinces into regional groupings? That'll never work, there are too many jealousies and grudges from years past.

Giving the sides names, like the Crusaders and the Chiefs? American crap that Kiwis would be turned off by.

Had there been enough lead-up time? Even Peter Thorburn, who was given the title of Super 12 commissioner, and told to fix the nuts and bolts of the competition, confessed not long before kick-off that there were elements of the competition that would have to be worked out as they went along.

Come the first game, a night match at Palmerston North between the Hurricanes and the Blues, and all the doubts were swept aside. The game was a thriller, the Blues had to work hard to get home 36–28, and suddenly everyone in the country was sold on Super 12.

The Crusaders were less effusive after their first game, on a Sunday afternoon in Hamilton. Into the last minute they were leading 26–24, when a touch judge flagged Crusaders wing Adrian Tukaki, for a late charge on Eric Rush. Ian Foster kicked the penalty, and the Crusaders had lost 27–26.

"We were a new team trying to find our feet," says Blackadder. "We had a lot of injuries and as a side we really didn't know each other." Certainly there are some unexpected names in the Crusaders of 1996. Only a rugby quiz fanatic would know that Pita Alatini, Deon Muir, Pat

Lam, and Danny Love were all Crusaders in that year.

Richard Loe took his unyielding attitude as a player into the captaincy role. "He was driven," says Blackadder, "and you could see why he was feared. As a man who had played so many games for the All Blacks, defeat was not an option."

Whether he was the perfect man for a team with many players who struggled to play to the level needed for Super 12 was, thinks Blackadder, a moot point.

"When Mike Brewer was captain, Richard was great, he led from the front physically. But I think Richard only had one way and that's the aggressive way, and in today's game I don't think I can afford to tell you 'You're a useless beep beep.' Some guys just couldn't handle him, he was too aggressive."

After the close shave with the Chiefs the Auckland Blues cruised through the next Super 12 game, in Christchurch, cleaning out the Crusaders, 49–18. Coach Stewart, asked after the game what positives the Crusaders would take from it could only manage a sad shake of the head.

Adding to the woes was a fight that broke out on the sideline that saw Con Barrell and Mark Weedon, on loan from North Harbour, both suspended for two weeks.

"Con got banned for just chasing someone," says Blackadder. "It was a crappy incident really, but that was just what the day was like for us.

"Every team should have a guy like Con. He's a laugher and a joker, always cracking some sort of joke, or he's farting or there's something going on.

"It was in '96 in the changing room at New Plymouth, my first time as captain of the Crusaders, against the Hurricanes, and things were getting pretty fired up.

"I think I was getting a bit emotional, making sure we were ready to play. I was talking to Con saying, 'I want you to perform' and all that sort of stuff in those short, sharp, not-so-nice words you use in team talks, and Con starts sniffing.

"I looked at him and he goes, "Mmmmm, I can smell hot dogs." He could smell the hot dogs coming through the louvre windows, and it just threw me. I laughed, and said to Con, 'If we win today I'll buy you as many hot dogs as you like!'

"Con gives it everything on the field for the team, but he loves his meat pies, and his food in general. I went away with him once to his Mum and Dad's place in the Bay of Islands. I went up there at 106kgs and came back at 118kgs. My pre-season build up, and we went for one run and I can tell you, it was a struggle. Con is a real fisherman, who loves eating, fishing and drinking. It was one of the best holidays I've ever had."

In Super 12 the relentless pressure continued. The Crusaders flew to Brisbane to play the Queensland Reds. "It was 35 degrees and 76 per cent humidity and we ran out onto the field and honestly, our whole team started walking it was that hot.

"We got thumped and caned 52–16, and I guarantee it would happen today under the same circumstances. The conditions were unbelievable. We just weren't used to that heat and we were absolutely gone. The sweat pulsed out of your body in time with your heartbeat.

"We'd been unlucky, but we'd lost our opener, Auckland had slaughtered us, the pressure was on, and you run out in those conditions. It was that bad that guys slumped on the floor of the shower. I don't want to make excuses, but there was no way we could have survived."

Back in Christchurch the brutal realities were about to be faced, and, to the surprise of the Crusaders, the whole town would know about them.

Going to training, and waiting for the team for the next game to be named is one of the least enjoyable times for a rugby journalist. Unlike a game, there's usually no drama at training, and the ritual of the coach naming the team, mouthing platitudes about why one player is in, and another out, is deeply tedious for everyone concerned.

But on the Tuesday night after the thrashing in Brisbane the rugby writer for *The Press*, Bob Schumacher, got a very unexpected scoop.

On a miserable sort of night he found himself the only reporter at the park, waiting for the Crusaders to emerge from training. "They didn't come out of the changing room, and I was standing there on a lonely vigil that went on for ages."

Then Schumacher started to hear voices, raised in anger, with accusations and counter-accusations flying back and forth. "I overheard what was being said, and started to take notes. I guess some might say I was eavesdropping, but that wasn't why I was there, and really it was a case of happening to be in the right place at the right time.

"Eventually the manager, Chris Wilson, came out and told me that after a long, soul-searching session, with 'full and frank discussions' it had been decided to delay naming the team until later in the week."

The next day the story appeared in *The Press*, and Blackadder confirms that the details were accurate. "Vance gave us a real talking-to, and there was lots of finger pointing, it was a shitty session. Things were loose, we weren't performing, the coaches were under pressure, the players under pressure.

"I think in a situation like that you tend to go into your shell a lot more. You revert back to your comfort zone and you don't talk out.

"Vance was trying to find the spark in us. He went round the room — it was a moment of hell really.

"There was never any lack of effort by us in that first year. Our training was brutal but although we were in the professional era you can see now that we weren't professional."

In 1996 there was no video analysis, now a staple of pre-match preparation, and, most of all, the Crusaders were trying to stitch together a unified group who came from all over the country, without any lengthy pre-season camp to set standards, and establish any sort of group culture.

Playing Western Province at Lancaster Park was a chance for the Crusaders to redeem themselves with the home fans. They were ahead 16–9 until, with just 11 seconds left on the ground clock, the visitors scored a converted try to draw the game.

"We just didn't have that edge, and the bounce of the ball wasn't going our way. The guys were performing, but as individuals, not as a team."

Better times came against New South Wales, a night game featuring the return of Tabai Matson from injury, Mark Weedon and Con Barrell from suspension, and Greg Coffey, at 31 out of first-class football for two years, and only playing club rugby in '96 to help out his club side.

Matson had a blinder, Coffey was remarkably composed with his play and goal kicking, and suddenly things seemed to be firing again.

But it was back to the pits again the following week against Northern Transvaal. Led by the fierce Springbok flanker Reuben Kruger, they whipped the Crusaders, 34–18.

"I went off in the second half. I got kneed in the back and I thought I'd ripped my hamstring but I'd just crushed my sciatic nerve, which felt like a hamstring."

Blackadder was out for the next game, against the Brumbies at Lancaster Park, which would be the only Crusaders' Super 12 game he has ever missed, from the time the competition started in 1996.

The Brumbies weren't the force they became in later years, and the Crusaders might have taken the game. Instead they lost 29–7, and a pivotal moment involved captain Richard Loe.

At the start of the second half he had barged over for a try to keep the Crusaders in touch of the visitors, but seven minutes later it all turned bad.

Just as Pita Alatini was plunging over for a try near the posts for the Crusaders, a touch judge ran onto the field to tell referee Glen Wahlstrom that Loe had punched Brumbies flanker John Langford. The try was disallowed, the Brumbies kicked their penalty to touch, won the lineout, won another penalty, and kicked a goal. It was basically a 10-point punch.

Loe was stood down from the starting side, and Blackadder was named captain for the next game, against the Hurricanes in New Plymouth.

"I was pretty nervous," says Blackadder. "It was all blood and guts and Richard Loe took a count in my pre-game speech, and said I had a record of 36 "f's", so you can imagine what the tone was. Richard was okay about it. He would have liked to have played, you always do, but he didn't say anything to me, or make me uncomfortable. We were at that stage of the season where I probably didn't care anyway. The way things were going that season it's a wonder there weren't ropes hanging from the rafters in the changing room.

"While I was the captain I was bloody going to win that game. I can remember that even though we were down and out I was still proud of who the Crusaders were, and I knew how much effort they were putting in.

"We went out there at the Bullring, and had a bloody great game, and a bloody good win 36–13. It was easily our best performance in our Super 12 outings, and after we'd been written off it was great to get out there and win."

The euphoria didn't last long. The Crusaders flew to South Africa, and had a horror start in Johannesburg.

"I was rooming with Mark Weedon and he was the first to come down with a stomach bug, and it went through the whole team."

Transvaal, coached by former Canterbury legend Grizz Wyllie, were always going to be difficult to handle at Ellis Park. But the gastric epidemic gave the Crusaders no chance.

Emergency medical treatment from the team doctor could only do so much, and on the way to the game players were throwing up in the team bus. Stu Loe, on the sideline as a reserve, actually had to vomit while the game was being played. It was hardly any wonder the Crusaders lost, 55–23.

With the season nearly over the Crusaders rallied for a game in Durban against Natal that Blackadder rates as one of the bravest efforts of the season.

Natal were readying to play the final with the Blues, while the Crusaders were firmly at the foot of the table. "We were down and out," says Blackadder, "and we had Angus Gardiner out sick. So at King's Park we were thrown out to the lions a bit. But it was one of those games where, even though the score was 58–26 to Natal, we kept trying for the whole 80 minutes.

"We were back home for our last game, against the Highlanders, which was close, 29–27. Once again, we probably should have won. At this level it really is such a fine line between winning and losing.

"Lady Luck really wasn't on our shoulder that year. Nothing was going right for us and we were young. It was a very dark season, the first year of the Crusaders, and it certainly tested our supporters' loyalty. But out of all the pain came some bloody good years. We certainly built some resolve.

"I've never forgotten what it is like to lose. When I talk to people I say that it is, in fact, possible to come from being in last place, where we were in 1996, to win, as we did for three years."

A fortnight after Super 12 it was off to Napier for Blackadder, where he captained a Barbarians team, who played a trial against a shadow All Black test team, and were whipped 72–18. "We were almost set up for that game. It's not really a trial for selection when the players aren't scattered over the two teams."

The previous year Laurie Mains had his request to take 30 players on the tour to France, but it was a new regime in '96. Coach John Hart had powerful support on the NZRU council, and 36 players set off to South Africa, including Blackadder.

On the way the Tri-Nations game with Australia was played at the Brisbane Broncos headquarters, Suncorp Stadium, where a crowd of 40,000 people packed in. They saw a game that ranged from the sublime, a last gasp run by Andrew Mehrtens that saw Frank Bunce score and Mehrtens convert to give New Zealand a 32–25 win, to the crazy — an unprovoked attack on Bunce by Michael Brial.

The eight-match tour of South Africa was very different from the tour to France the previous year. "This time it was two different teams under one umbrella," says Blackadder. "If the test team were training we were holding tackle bags but not really rubbing shoulders with them. If we were preparing for our game they were coming off their game.

"We only ever roomed with our guys and they roomed with their guys. Sounds a bit strange but look at a normal week.

"The day of the test match the first thing we do is get on a bus and go away and train, have lunch at a totally different venue away from the team, and then meet up with the liaison guy and go and watch the test.

"We'd go to the changing room after the game, but the next day we would go to another venue, train with the test reserves in the afternoon, and then prepare for the Tuesday game.

"We usually stayed on a different floor in the hotel from the test team, so really we didn't have a lot to do with them."

John Hart didn't have a lot to do with the midweek team's training runs, which were usually controlled by assistant coach Ross Cooper.

"In all fairness," says Blackadder, "it's a lot to control two teams. That's a big job for one guy. Apart from one training we never had a full side to train with, to work on continuity. The midweek team was a supporting act.

"You certainly wanted to give all your support to the test team, but also to try and win our games as best we could.

"The mid-week team was captained by Taine Randell, who I already knew reasonably well. He was quite young then, but he did well."

The first game for the mid-week team was at Worcester against Boland. Like many country grounds in South Africa the surface was like rock.

Tane Norton tells the story of how, on the 1976 All Black tour, he was in the tunnel about to run on. He looked at the ground, which was a brown expanse of dust and what looked like gravel. Norton glanced across at his bullnecked opponent. "Not much grass out there," said Norton. "Yah, you're right", grunted the South African, "but we didn't come to graze."

Blackadder says the All Blacks put out a pretty good side against Boland. "But, by Jesus, they were tough. Some of the most bruising games I've ever played. I crushed my vertebrae in that game.

"Worcester is a rural town that seems to be in the middle of nowhere. There are a lot of metal roads, and when we went to the stadium and there was barbed wire everywhere, and a lot of police around with dogs. So you felt a little bit nervous there for a while, but the crowd just loved us and gave us a lot of support.

"The opposition sure didn't. Right from the very start of our campaign when Norm Hewitt went eye to eye during the haka I thought, 'This is going to be a big, tough game,' and it was.

"They were big, hard, hungry bastards who, come hell or high water, were going to beat you. It was a big hit out for the guys I think we were all pleased after the game, having won 32–21.

"With the All Blacks having won the Tri-Nations, I think the real fear for us in the midweek team was losing. We were in a really successful campaign, and wanted to play our part.

"One thing that I did envy the test team for was that they had the luxury of a neutral referee. We had the bloody local guy, who was always under pressure to see a South African team beat an All Black side."

The tests started at Newlands, in Capetown. In an odd decision the Capetown game was officially not part of the test series to come, but, strictly speaking, just the last game of the first Tri-Nations series. Whatever the technicalities, the All Blacks had to fight back from 18–6 down to eventually win, 29–18.

With the victory came the award of the massive Tri-Nations trophy, so big captain Sean Fitzpatrick struggled to lift it, and a remarkable scene in the players' tunnel.

Fitzpatrick was walking off, and was greeted by Sky television commentator Murray Mexted, who had played for the All Blacks against South Africa and lived in the Republic too. Better than anyone, he knew the enormity of the All Blacks' achievement. Mexted was crying, and he hugged Fitzpatrick, saying, "This is bigger than Texas."

Those were pretty much Blackadder's sentiments, although he wasn't actually in tears. "Zinzan and Robin Brooke, Sean, Justin Marshall, they were all awesome."

The next midweek game was in Port Elizabeth, a seaside town that turned on a dirty, windy, cold Tuesday night, and an Eastern Province team who wore Canterbury colours, and had recently been·coached by Grizz Wyllie.

"They were all over us for a long part of that game," says Blackadder. "We just had to grind our way back, more out of fear than anything."

Jonah Lomu sealed the game with a late try. It wasn't a great tour for Lomu, who the previous year had been the undoubted star of the World Cup. In 1996 he was plagued with niggling injuries, and didn't actually play a test in South Africa.

"If you've been in the test team, and come back and play mid-week it's bloody hard work," says Blackadder. "The opposition are fired up to get the better of you, because it's their chance for glory. It's not in the South African nature to ever go easy on you."

The next test was in Durban, another seaside town, which this time turned on summer holiday weather, with the water warm enough for hardier players to actually go swimming.

The test match was won 23–19, and Blackadder and the reserves were high in the towering stands of King's Park. "They never gave us tickets near to the All Black coaches and officials. We were up with the South African fans and every time they scored you'd get some big Afrikaner about ten feet away screaming at you in Afrikaans. They're pretty fired up and you can almost see the sweat dripping off their noses. You could see it in their faces, they were fanatical.

"The youngest players in the team always have to go and get the hot dogs at halftime, but over there you never send them off by themselves, we send a posse with them.

"But if it's a bit uncomfortable at times, you still feel very proud up there watching as a New Zealander. And to be fair to the South Africans who were around, once the game was over, and the All Blacks had won, they were happy to pat us on the back and shake our hands and congratulate us."

There were remarkable scenes at the next midweek game in Potchefstroom, against Western Transvaal.

"When we got to the ground it was a beautiful, crisp day, with the sun out, not a breath of wind, and the ground absolutely rock hard.

"We watched a game of schoolboy rugby, then it clouded over, and within minutes it started, absolutely torrential rain. In 15 minutes the ground was flooded, the whole changing shed got flooded, and people going into the stand had water halfway up their legs. It was unbelievable.

"It was a nice little country town, and we stayed in the local hotel. It seemed to be back in the 1950s. The ladies put on a feed for us and it was good old steak, sausages, eggs and bacon. We'd just started to have dieticians working with teams, so everyone was turning their nose up a bit, but we were right in the heart of the countryside.

"It brought me back to my Nelson Bays days, when we would be on a bus and stop for a good feed of that sort of stuff. I have to admit that I can remember thinking as I was running around, 'Jeez, I think I might have eaten too much steak.'

"We won there, 31–0, and despite the mud, it was the easiest game on that tour."

For the test team there was a chance to make history in Pretoria, where a win would make them the first All Blacks to ever win a series in South Africa.

"There was a real sense of patriotism towards New Zealand being in the stands that day," says Blackadder. "The guys were just playing like absolute legends.

"Simon Culhane had been in the midweek team, and when Mehrts was injured in the Durban test he went into the test side at first-five. I can remember Nibs picking up André Venter and driving him backwards, this little gutsy Southlander, about 5ft 4in, picking up a huge big Springbok flanker and driving him back. It just tells you what was on the line.

"When you saw things like that you couldn't help but feel proud of them. We were all aware of the fact the guys had created history. So many good All Black teams had gone to South Africa, and come away empty-handed. Teams in the past did have local referees, which in my experience over there is hard going."

In the crowd for the game was Fred Allen, whose 1949 team suffered four losses out of four. Nobody was more thrilled for the '96 team than Allen who beamed that he'd "waited a long time to see this."

In the stand at Loftus Versfeld the players, like Blackadder, Lomu, Taine Randell, Eric Rush, and Tabai Matson, who had not been on the reserves bench for the test, broke into a spontaneous haka.

Blackadder says that "after the Pretoria test the guys in the team were absolutely buggered. They'd been pressed all the way by the Springboks, which is what I think made it such a great series. It went right down to the wire."

On the field the All Black backs leapt in the air when Frenchman Didier Mene blew his whistle to signal the end of the game, and a 33–26 victory to New Zealand. Captain Sean Fitzpatrick says the last minute was, "without question, the longest 60 seconds of my life."

Thirty minutes after the test was over Zinzan Brooke was still shaking too much to sign an autograph. The All Black changing room, in a rare gesture opened to the New Zealand media, was a scene of absolute exhaustion, with players slumped against the wall, struggling to even lift their arms for handshakes.

But the players in Pretoria had one more game to go, the last test at

Ellis Park, and the midweek team had another challenge too, against Griqualand West, at Kimberley, up on the high veldt.

"All the riches of Africa were drawn out of Kimberley," says Blackadder. "It's the place where the diamonds are mined, so you think it might be a wealthy town, but the place is an absolute dive. Flying in, all you see is miles and miles of dry, burnt-looking grass. It's a hard old mining community, with a bit of farming thrown in.

"When you ask people in South Africa about a team like Griqualand West all they say is that they're a team of nutters. We seemed to be continually striking these raw-boned guys who were huge. They just took the game to us. Every tackle you made it felt like running into a brick wall.

"It might have been just me, but it seemed like every decision the referee, Tappe Henning, made went against us. We had to come back from being behind, and we had a chance in the last minutes for Jon Preston to win it for us, but the kicking tee mysteriously disappeared. It just went west.

"It would have been nice to win, and you certainly don't want to be in the team who lost a game on tour. We were disappointed to draw, but at least it wasn't a loss.

"They were a pretty good side, who have taken some big scalps. There's some real depth in the game over there. The South Africans run the Vodaphone Cup while Super 12 is on, and then run the Currie Cup at the end of the year, which tells you something about the depth of their rugby."

The last game of the intensive tour was in Johannesburg, and by now the All Blacks were very, very tired. Blackadder wonders whether a few younger players in the All Black team would have been a worthwhile change. "I know you don't give the jersey away easily, but when Glen Taylor went on for the last 30 minutes when Ian Jones was injured he played really well."

The Springboks won 32–22, which was something of an anti-climax. "From the time they played the old national anthem before the test, and you could see the locals standing up and roaring, you knew it was going to be a hard night.

"I wasn't there during the week, because the midweekers went to Sun

City while the test team prepared, so I don't really know what the attitude inside our team was. It had been quite a long year, and a really tough series, so you could understand how drained they were feeling."

When the team returned home the New Zealand Rugby Union flew wives and partners to Auckland, where the team had one last official function, a massive victory parade down Auckland's Queen St, which drew a crowd estimated at 250,000 people.

* * *

Back in Christchurch, Blackadder had two new roles to take on for Canterbury in the NPC. One was, for the first time in his rugby career, to be a fulltime captain.

Vance Stewart was coaching the NPC team, but with a new assistant, Blackadder's old captain from Canterbury B days, Steve Hansen. In Stewart's mind it was certainly time for a change of captain.

"We got ravaged in that first year of Super 12. We were under-strength, and, as hard as we tried, we got to the stage where we were playing international teams and we just didn't have players of that ability.

"In that pressure situation some people react in ways that you don't expect them to. Their demeanour can deteriorate. Toddy's sort of strengthened.

"At the end of it I think he thought, 'I can do a better job leading this team.' It finally sort of shook him into saying, instead of sort of sitting back and thinking about it, maybe he should say, 'Look, I'm keen to do it.'

"I think the captaincy side on the field and at training wasn't a really big issue to him. What terrified him more was the captain's role speaking in public and fronting the media.

"He was more concerned about that. He saw himself as a country boy, with a country background, and this was a thing for the townies to do. You had the people around him like Andrew Mehrtens, who are pretty slick speakers, good with off-the-cuff remarks, and Toddy struggled with that.

"But he was prepared at that stage to say, 'I'll do the best I can for the team, and I'll overcome the hurdle of speaking for the sake of the team.'

"In the team situation he was top-notch. It was a quiet way that Toddy did it. There wasn't a lot of yelling or screaming or swearing. He was all blood and guts on the field, so he could afford to talk quietly to the players, because they knew the standards he played to.

"He had a very good skill level, which was almost hidden, because he didn't always show what he could do. It wasn't Todd's way to flick the reverse pass behind his back, or the big overhead pass, or the wide miss pass. A lot of the time he was buried in the middle of the rucks with elbows and knees going.

"Toddy would never do the fancy things, because that wasn't his personality."

Blackadder recalls that after Super 12, he was happy to take on the Canterbury captain's role. "I felt that after what we'd been through, with no disrespect to anyone else, that I could do a good job. It was just a feeling I had. I know it's a slightly strange thing to say, but, although I'd never really captained any other side, I felt I was ready. When Vance asked me I was as keen as mustard."

The other change for Blackadder was in the position he would play. Canterbury suffered a run of injuries in the middle of the scrum, so Blackadder played the remaining seven games of the NPC locking with Steve Lancaster.

"Todd's best position at the time was certainly No. 6," says coach Stewart, "but Todd was always prepared to help out. I know when we lost the shield to Auckland at the end of 1995 they intimidated us to a certain degree, and we crumbled a bit. Our locks then were never really hard men.

"The likes of Robin Brooke could really get on top of them. So when it came to the NPC I thought that when we went against Auckland, who would be the person who would look across at Robin Brooke and not be bullied?

"Todd was the man. He had flint hardness, and a very good vertical jump too. When we did our tests we found that Todd had the best jump of our forwards. Mentally he could dominate people the way Colin Meads was able to dominate them in his day.

"It's disappointing to me to hear people say he shouldn't have been in the All Blacks because he wasn't a good enough jumper at the front of the lineout. Todd was by far the best jumper in the team at No. 2 in the All Blacks in 2000. When people say they should have had Troy Flavell there instead of him, why, when they played each other, did Troy Flavell jump at No. 4, and not against Todd?

"There's quite a difference between jumping at No. 2 and No. 4. At No. 2 you need a person with fast twitch muscle fibre, who would explode, and get up there. Todd was like that. I suppose the only downside for Todd was that as he got bigger he was probably harder for a lifter to keep in the air.

"I thought in the All Blacks that the team tactics, which probably required the ball towards the back of the lineout more, meant he never had the chance to dominate the front of the lineout, which I believe he could have.

"On international standards he was as good as anyone, and inevitably the people at the front of the lineout have had other areas of the game they offered. You want a ball player at the front of the lineout, which is what you got with a Colin Meads, or a Frank Oliver, and you certainly got with Toddy."

To Blackadder in 1996, "playing lock was a big change for me. Playing at loose forward, I don't think you even know what an engine room is."

With Blackadder locking, Scott Robertson went to blindside, Angus Gardiner was at openside, and a newcomer to Canterbury, Steve Surridge, was at No. 8.

At first glance, Surridge may seem an unlikely person to have ended up a Canterbury stalwart. Born and brought up in Auckland he's an academic with two degrees, one from Cambridge University, and is currently working on a third degree while he plays out his rugby career in Japan. He actually goes back a long way with Blackadder.

They first played together in the 1991 New Zealand Colts. "Overall," says Surridge, "I look back to then and Todd hasn't changed at all. The things he said now and then are exactly the same, which is amazing considering what he has been through.

"We had quite a good Colts team in 1991, coached by John Hart.

After we'd played Australia in Christchurch Todd invited me to stay at his place for four or five days as I had a judo tournament in Christchurch, and I needed a place to stay, rather than flying home to Auckland. Just out of the blue he invited me to stay, so I actually had four or five days at Rangiora with Todd and his mother.

"It was amazing. He took me down to Wrightsons and I'm pretty sure he convinced me to buy a Swanndri. I remember going back to Auckland with this Swanndri and it just didn't sit well at all."

Surridge, an outstanding sportsman in several fields, retired from rugby in 1993 because he was rowing. Then he went to Cambridge University, playing rugby there, and decided he'd like a shot at the new professional game in New Zealand.

"I rang up Harty and asked him where I should go. He suggested Canterbury or Taranaki. I rang up Canterbury and said to Vance Stewart, 'You don't know me, but I'd like to play rugby in Canterbury, and the only person who can vouch for me is Todd.' He called back and said, 'Yeah, come down and we'll sort something out.'

"So obviously they had asked Todd, because there is no way I would have got in otherwise. I didn't come from trials, no one had seen me playing.

"Todd had been in the All Black team in South Africa. I had been playing No. 8 in England, and he ended up playing lock that NPC. I was pretty grateful because at that time he could have made his mark, been forceful about it, said, 'I'm playing No. 8,' and cut me down."

To Blackadder, Surridge was, and remains, "a great guy, always enthusiastic and positive. Pipe's also famous for being a captain's nightmare. He's one of those guys that if we're going over a move, then after training is finished he'd want to practise it another 30 times. There were times when we'd have it all sussed, and he'd say, 'I think we need to come out and work on this.'

"He wants to get it right, and he'll go through every single scenario. He's an awesome player, who brought a real intellectuality to the side. He's a real thinker, and a lot of his ideas are really ground-breaking."

Surridge was also famous for treating his body the way a Formula One mechanic would treat a finely tuned Ferrari. One morning Canterbury trainer Mike Anthony was rung up by Surridge who said his pulse when he'd first woken was a bit high. "That means you're training a bit too much," said Anthony. So Surridge went back to bed and had a sleep.

The most famous Surridge incident involved Crusaders assistant coach Peter Sloane, a former builder. "Sloaney had gone round to help him build his bathroom, and Pipe got Sloaney all the tools he needed. But then he said he had to have a sleep because his pulse was up a bit. He left Sloaney to work in the bathroom on his own."

The first game Blackadder and Surridge played together for Canterbury was against King Country in the third round of the NPC. At that stage Canterbury had lost their first two games, both without their All Blacks, to Counties and Wellington.

At Lancaster Park against King Country things started to improve. The game was won, 38–27, and the Canterbury players who had been in South Africa were all presented with gifts in front of the main stand by Christchurch mayor Vicki Buck, to mark the success of the tour, with the team now dubbed "The Incomparables."

The following week a rout for Canterbury was on the cards at halftime in the game with Auckland. Thanks partly to an intercept try by Brian Lima, which saw the Manu Samoa winger not only stop a certain Canterbury try, but sprint 90 metres to touch down, the score after 40 minutes was 30–3 to Auckland.

Canterbury, in a sign of what was just around the corner in these traditional clashes, scored the only second-half points, a converted try. Auckland coach Graham Henry would suggest after the game that his team were very fortunate to be so far ahead at the break. "Auckland were a team who had flashes of absolute brilliance," says Blackadder, "and that meant they were always tough opponents."

Blackadder was locking behind Richard Loe on the loosehead side of the Canterbury scrum, an experience he enjoyed. "He's just naturally aggressive, and he sort of pulled me along with him. He was fired up at most times, and if you weren't pushing your bum off he let you know."

Richard Loe stories are legion, and just one example of the effect he could have on an opposing prop came in 1994, when he returned to the

Canterbury fold after being banned for six months for eye-gouging.

During the ban Trevor McKewen, later to be the chief executive of the Warriors league club, wrote a story in Australian *Penthouse* magazine in which Aussie prop Tony Daly suggested that as his career went on Loe had turned from a "tough customer into a dirtier and slimier player."

At the time, Loe was 33, and Daly no doubt thought he would stay in retirement. To his horror Daly found himself packing down for New South Wales against Loe in a pre-season game in Christchurch. Other Canterbury players recall Loe greeting Daly with the words, "Hello Fatty, I read what you said about me in the magazine." The best Daly could manage was a squeaked, "I was misquoted!"

Loe and Blackadder were key figures in the Canterbury team in the next NPC game, a thriller at Lancaster Park when Otago were beaten 43–22. Andrew Mehrtens returned to the Canterbury team for the first time since the All Black tour, where he'd been injured, and not only kicked 18 points, but gave the backline a confidence that had been lacking earlier in the competition.

By now Canterbury were heading towards a semi-final spot, and a win against Taranaki in New Plymouth, 38–21, and a powerful victory over North Harbour in Christchurch, 43–20, confirmed their ability.

The win over North Harbour came at some personal cost to Blackadder. "I finished with my nose hanging out to one side of my face. I ran into their halfback, Mark Robinson, and just about ripped my nose off. I went off to get some stitches, and when I came back on their prop Gavin Walsh spent all his time trying to biff it in the scrums. It was pretty tender at the time."

Two of Blackadder's close Canterbury friends, Stu Loe and Mark Mayerhofler, enjoyed milestones in the Harbour match. Loe played his 100th game for the province, Mayerhofler his 50th.

There was one more round left in the NPC in '96, and it was a battle, against Waikato at Rugby Park in Hamilton.

"It was a hard, grafting game, and I remember how, in the last few minutes, they were right down on our line, and Richard Loe really stood up against his old team.

"On the other hand, I didn't stand up so well at the team court session we had after the game. I think the top table at the time, Stu Loe and Matt Sexton, made me down a couple of glasses of rum. I've never been good at drinking rum. Steve Tew had been appointed our new chief executive at the Canterbury union, and as I was rushing out, it got the better of me, and the rum shot all over the back of Steve's beautifully white shirt. It wasn't one of my greatest experiences."

Canterbury finished third in the round robin, so travelled to Pukekohe to play Counties in the semi-final.

"We so much wanted to win for Vance in the semi," says Blackadder. "We knew that he was retiring after the season finished. He implemented so much for Canterbury that he doesn't get credit for, and we went through the wringer with him. I really respected him then, and I still do."

7. Honk if you're hurting

"Everyone was freezing, and tired, and hungry, and a bit grumpy"

Mark Mayerhofler is screaming with rage. The man they call Bubsy, who always has a smile at the ready, the guy Andrew Mehrtens says is "loved by everyone," has found his limits.

It's a beautiful, crisp, mid-winter day at Hanmer, a holiday town in North Canterbury, famous for hot pools, great scenery, and magnificent walks. Mayerhofler could not care less.

With the rest of the Canterbury NPC team he's near the end of a three-day, team-building visit before the provincial season starts. They've biked through snow, and carried bikes across freezing rivers. Now the most brutal of the activities, supervised by coach Robbie Deans, and his assistant Steve Hansen, is in full flight.

They're doing the stretcher carry, an exercise Todd Blackadder describes as "far from nice." Four teams have been named, with the heaviest man in each team directed to lie on the sack, which has two manuka poles threaded through it. The rest of the team have to carry the big man over a 4km course. Just to add to the occasion, it's actually a race.

"I think old Shag [Steve Hansen] had certainly been pushing Bubsy along, and he got told in no uncertain terms to go away," laughs Blackadder. "You can push someone so far, but every guy has his tolerance. For even Bubsy to snap, it meant you just knew a little bit more about the guy. We all learnt a little bit more about ourselves."

Mayerhofler agrees. "It was probably the hardest three days of my life. The boys still shake their heads over the stretcher carry. But it instilled in us all the real passion to do our best by the team."

To Blackadder, "The time we spent up there was one of the most beneficial things we've ever done. It taught us to be out of our comfort zones. We had quite hard outdoor activities, and also mental activities. The management did all the cooking. There was no television, and we set up all our season.

"We were up in the snow, and everyone was freezing and hungry, and tired, and a little bit grumpy. At the end it was all summed up in a debrief, and put into perspective, and we learnt a lot from each other.

"Also it brought us together as a team, in much the same way, I suppose, as the Army does. It gets you to understand how you react yourself, and how the guys around you react. Then it's how you react to them.

"When we did the stretcher carry, I was put in the stretcher. So the poor bastards in my team had a big fat guy like me to hoist up.

"Everyone doing the carrying was a different height, so the poles were at a different point on everybody's shoulder. When you've got a big load like me to carry it's harsh.

"You had to race down the road from Hanmer, go across this farm, and back down the road. It was a full circle, back to the hot pools.

"Poor old Fats [Afato So'oalo] was just out of Samoa, and here he was grabbing hold of every electric fence and getting a belt. There was mud up to your ankles, and after two or three days everyone was tired and shitty.

"They had Robbie and Steve and Don Hayes and all these other guys abusing the players and pushing them to see who was going to break under pressure.

"Our team actually won the stretcher race, but there's no worse feeling than lying up there and all these poor buggers are absolutely grunting their guts out carrying you. The test for the guys up the top was to see how you could encourage the guys carrying. I'd like to think that I played my part, but I felt bloody useless.

"I ran back and helped the next guys, and as we finished we went back and helped the next group.

"It was bloody hard work, but it refocused us on a lot of rugby things, our goals, and what we wanted to do as a team.

"We had a general theme too, and that was honking. Robbie and Steve had a video that showed a whole lot of geese flying in line, with wingmen, and a lead goose that breaks the air.

"We adopted that whole philosophy as our theme for the year. Whenever you were in trouble, or were hurting, or under real pressure, you'd call out 'honk' on the field, and all the boys would start honking. As ridiculous as that sounds, it brought some real resolve."

Robbie Deans says that when he started coaching in 1997 "our key thrust was attitude. There was a belief from the marketers that winning was the key in getting people along to the games, but I felt it was attitude.

"So we went about identifying the ideal attitudes, and then, as a team we went about aspiring to live by those attitudes. As a group we really put an emphasis on how we were going to include everyone and Toddy just grew with that.

"Toddy was the archetypal Canterbury man, so he was a superb guy to have leading the show. That whole emphasis just brought the best out of Toddy.

"A distinction between the amateur days and now is that, in the past, respect for the jersey and what it meant developed by osmosis. As you came into the team you were educated, by various means," Deans laughs. He began as a young fullback for Canterbury in 1980, when some of the hard men of the game, the Higginsons, the Ashworths, the Murray Davies made damn sure the new boys toed the team line, which decreed that if you weren't prepared to bleed for the jersey you could bugger off.

Fast forward to the new age of rugby. "In Canterbury in 1996 we had a lot of draft players," says Deans, "and we weren't successful in establishing a successful working environment.

"We identified the need to actually consider, rather that take for granted, that our culture, the one we wanted and needed, would happen.

"Toddy was the ideal man to lead us on values. He could have played in any generation and be welcome and at home. It comes from his background and upbringing. He came in with a lot of the values we sought. He identified with the tune we were playing."

Then there was the tactical appreciation. "As a leader he developed from one who was very much a 'follow me out of the trenches', to one who looked before he ran and became very tactically astute.

"He was always a good judge of people within the camp, and with the opposition. So he was always quick to decide who you'd prod a bit in the other team. That's a real asset on the field. It's such an important skill as a captain, when the heat comes on, and it's a tight game, and calls have to be made.

"We can give counsel and guidance from the stand, but ultimately it's the guys who are out there on the ground who can feel the chemistry. When you're on the field you can sense the state of the game, and of your opponents. Toddy was very good at not only having a good handle for his own people, but also for identifying opportunities.

"Once he became established and comfortable, that was a skill he developed, as he started to see how he could embellish his role as a leader.

"In the past, with things like lineout calls and scrum options, he probably hadn't given it much consideration. He raised his head and chased the leather. When he became captain he started to read the game, and he was good at it."

Change was in the air in Canterbury from the start of the 1997 season. As well as new NPC coaches in Deans and Hansen, Wayne Smith and Peter Sloane had control of the Crusaders in Super 12.

Smith's involvement with Canterbury rugby went back to his days as an outstanding first-five in the great Canterbury teams of the 1980s, coached by Grizz Wyllie.

As a player he was known for not only his attacking and tactical skills, but also his courage. His Canterbury captain, Don Hayes, says he was amazed at the way Smith would fling himself at the biggest opponent. "I'd say you could probably write the number of guys he really bowled on a fly's eyebrow, but he was always committed to it, and he always had a go. I admired him for it actually."

Smith's coaching path moved through being a staff coach at the Canterbury Rugby Union, coaching a club team in Italy, to running the New Zealand sevens team.

His partner at the Crusaders in 1997, Sloane, was a former Northland and All Black hooker, a man with an attitude forwards could relate to, especially when at training he would growl at the backs, in mock anger, "Get out of the way you little lizards, or you'll get crushed."

To Blackadder, appointed captain of the Crusaders for the first time, the arrival of Smith and Sloane "was so refreshing. I think it was the first time we had really worked on our skills, at a different level.

"We had a game amongst ourselves in Blenheim, and I remember specifically how Kevin Nepia picked up the ball and threw this amazing pass. He just showed skills we hadn't been used to.

"Smithy kept reiterating what he wanted from our forwards, vision and good handling. It was the start of a new era."

There were some other big changes from the way the Crusaders had gone into the first season of Super 12 the previous year. This time they headed for the regions.

It was probably just in the nick of time. For a start the players thrived on the reception they got in smaller centres. "We actually fed off going round the regions," says Blackadder. He laughs. "I guess the support they gave us made us feel loved for the first time. It was quite a change from '96, when nobody really wanted to know us apart from our own families.

"They were even talking about starting up a Hurricanes supporters' club in Nelson, and down at the bottom end of the West Coast where it gets near to Otago, they were starting to look a bit at linking up with the team next door, the Highlanders."

So first stop for the new-look Crusaders was Nelson, where, in a warm-up game against an invitation team that included Josh Kronfeld and Jeff Wilson, the Crusaders won 104–5. "They were a bit dark after that."

The Brumbies were beaten in Greymouth, and there was a good run against the Highlanders at Rugby Park in Christchurch, won 51–14. "Simon Culhane accidentally ran into my hip, the poor little bugger, and got concussed. Three or four of them got quite serious injuries. Josh hurt his shoulder quite badly."

The whole preparation was, Blackadder remembers, "bloody hard work. But there was nothing else for us to do. We'd been at the bottom, and the only thing we could do was fight our way up."

The first game of Super 12 was at Lancaster Park, against the Hurricanes, and the fans were rewarded with a 19–17 win.

The Hurricanes arrived with a pack that averaged 114kg a man, but the spirit that was rising in the Canterbury camp would be fully demonstrated. "We had the Hurricanes down in one corner, and we put down seven successive five metre scrums," says Blackadder. "I know that poor old Con Barrell's arse was hanging out, but I just wanted to eat up time.

"The win was vitally important. It was a sign that we were moving away from where we'd been, and the support the public gave us was being rewarded."

In the second round the Crusaders faced the Waratahs at the Sydney Football Stadium, and lost 25–8, the last 10 points for the Waratahs, two tries to Daniel Manu, coming in injury time. "It was an absolutely ferocious match," says Blackadder. "At halftime there was a penalty and I kicked the ball out. Both teams were almost crawling up the ramp into the stand.

"We went through all our loose forwards, and I think I made something like 26 tackles. It was one of the fastest and hardest games I've ever played in."

One of the more colourful imports for the Crusaders, John Akurangi, broke his arm in the Sydney clash. "He used to turn up for training in a convertible Jaguar with his dog in the back," says Blackadder. "I believe that he and Scott Robertson once drove through one of the pedestrian arcades in town in that Jag."

For the next game, against the Brumbies in Canberra, Blackadder found himself at No. 8, after an injury to Steve Surridge.

Future Wallabies coach Rod Macqueen was in charge of the Brumbies in '97, and they were developing the patterned play for which they, and Australia, would become famous.

For Blackadder it was a terrible night. For a start the Brumbies won 49–29, and from a personal point of view there was a moment that remains the playing low point in his rugby career.

It hadn't been a flash night for him in general. "I kept going for scrums to pressurise them, and every time I went to pick the ball up I'd knock it on or something. In the second half, we were down on points, and I was trying to do everything, and going nowhere.

"I took a tap, and I kicked the ball in the air from the tap, and it went out just past my fingertips. It hit the ground and bounced, and as I went to grab it, I knocked it on.

"Of course the crowd and the players all gave it heaps, and there was no shovel around at the time. At a stage in the game when things weren't going good it just felt terrible. It was a humiliating performance really.

"I remember the next day doing the debrief and we were watching the game on video, and then I did my tap penalty, and I heard laughs and I think I just snapped. Back then I just couldn't see any humour in the whole thing."

With time healing the scars, and the moment something he can now smile about, Blackadder reckons he was taught a good lesson by the horror moment.

"I found out that sometimes you can try too hard. Composure is a big thing in the game. Aaron Flynn said something quite comforting to me afterwards. He reckoned that he'd never seen me play an absolute shocker like that, but it was good to get the whole lot out of the system in one go."

The heat of public expectation, to improve on the record of two losses from three games, was certainly on when the Super 12 show moved into Timaru, for a night game against the Chiefs. They played in front of a capacity crowd of 8000 people at the Alpine Energy Stadium.

"Before the game I was sitting on the bench and we were under real pressure. It was a must win. Robbie Deans [the manager, for the first time, of the Crusaders] came and sat beside me and just put his hand on my shoulder. It was a welcome gesture I remember clearly.

"Our guys played bloody well, winning 24–15. It was a gutsy performance, especially as we were down to 14 men at the end. Just two minutes into the second half Mark Hammett was sent off by the referee, Glenn Wahlstrom, after he was supposed to have punched someone. It later turned out to be a slap, and he was only cautioned.

"We had to rearrange the forwards. Matt Sexton came on for Hammer, Mark Weedon got the chop, and I went to lock with Norm Maxwell. It was a long slog from there.

"But the game started off what's been a great time playing in Timaru. I love going to the regions. The people there don't get an opportunity to see the players much, so they really go out of their way to make you feel welcome.

"I'll give an example. That first year in Timaru in all our rooms there was a little basket of goodies from around the region, little pots of jam and honey. That sort of stuff makes an impression.

"We did signing sessions on the morning of the game. We regarded signing an autograph with a kid or an adult as a contract. You feel there's an obligation to give it your bloody best for them.

"When we're all in Christchurch we stay away from everyone, but when you go to Timaru, everyone knows you're there, and you do a lot of school visits, you meet a lot of people, and that contact all becomes part of what you're playing for."

There was a weird moment after the game. "I was talking to Brian Ashby [a radio reporter for Newstalk ZB in Christchurch] after the game on the field, and a full can of Speights whistled over my head by a few inches and took him in the face."

The interview was live on air, and the archive tape remains one of the classic moments in sports broadcasting.

You hear a clunk, as the can hits Ashby's headphones, and bounces off his cheek. Then there's a moment's silence, while he ducks in case there's more on the way. Then Blackadder says, "What the hell was that?" Ashby, sounding as surprised as Blackadder, replies, "It's a can of beer." There's a brief pause, and then it's back to the rugby.

"I guess it was a reminder," says Blackadder with a wry smile, "that it doesn't matter who you are or where you are, not everybody loves you. If it was aimed at me, when we'd just won, I'd hate to think what would have happened if we'd lost!"

Although the next game was lost, 28–29, the narrow defeat at the hands of the Auckland Blues was still one of the best games they'd played so far in Super 12.

The Blues at the time were defending champions, and they had a team loaded with some of the best players in New Zealand rugby. Their forward pack against the Crusaders contained eight All Blacks, from Zinzan Brooke captaining the team at No. 8 to Sean Fitzpatrick at hooker.

How astonishing that the Crusaders would come away feeling unlucky not to win, and to have, in the view of most critics, the better of the forward battle.

"That was the year when our self-belief started to develop," says Blackadder. "We started to feel, 'Hey, we can do this, we're a good side, we can beat these guys!' We went so close against the Blues, and none played better than our No. 8 Clark McLeod. He was absolutely superb."

McLeod, previously unknown outside Christchurch, was one of the young players Smith and Hansen had taken away on a development trip to Argentina at the end of 1996. The team, captained by Blackadder, was a mixture of NPC players and Canterbury Colts, and won three out of four games on tour. McLeod's play was so outstanding on tour that he had to be included in the Super 12 squad. "I was going to have to move back home," he remarked at the time, "but now I guess I can afford a flat."

A key moment in the game was when Leon MacDonald, then an outstanding 19-year-old who had recently moved to Christchurch from Marlborough, was taken out 10 minutes before halftime with a shoulder charge by Robin Brooke.

Down 13–6 at the time, the Blues struck back with two quick tries, the second, while the Crusaders were still trying to get their fullback back on the field, scored by Brooke in the same spot where he had flattened MacDonald. Brooke was suspended for two weeks after the

The Ranfurly Shield comes to Canterbury. Mike Brewer leads Graeme Bachop and Todd off the plane in 1994.

Stu Loe, a rugged prop, a man to rely on, a best mate, controls the ball for Canterbury.

Mark "Bubs" Mayerhofler, a man **Todd** loves like a brother, could score tries as well as save them.

Graham Jack, the sort of brave, gutsy player that sums up what made Canterbury and the Crusaders great in the 90s.

Two mischief-makers get together. Brilliant No. 8s Steve Surridge, with ball, and Ron Cribb.

Reuben Thorne: Nobody does more work, and he could be a great captain.

"Can you believe it?" Wayne Smith and Todd after 1998 Super 12 victory.

Todd and Priscilla after the 1999 Super 12 win in Dunedin.

"You beauty." Todd and Robbie Deans after the 2000 Super 12 win in Canberra.

Mates enjoy a record-setting moment. Justin Marshall and Todd, Canberra, 2000.

Another goal for Canterbury is about to be kicked by Andrew Mehrtens, a man Todd has seen so often at his best.

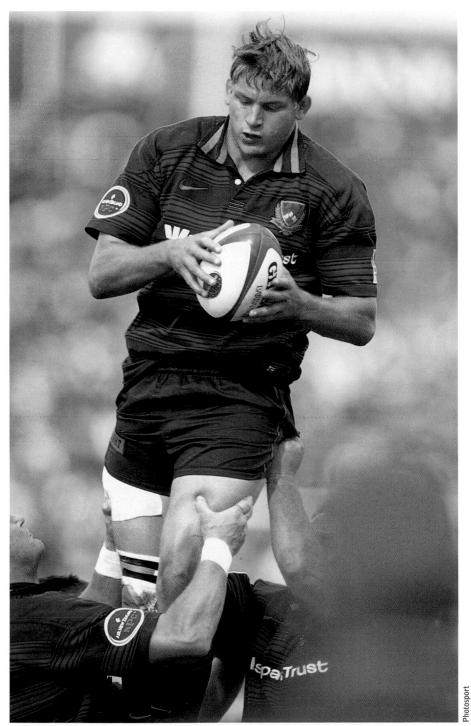

"The lineout abilities of Todd," says former coach Vance Stewart, "are greatly underestimated."

The team behind the team. Crusaders' wives and partners celebrate in the Eden Park changing room, 1998.

They love their footy in Canterbury. The fans gather to welcome home the 2000 Super 12 champions.

game, but was not even binned on the night.

"We were disappointed," says Blackadder, "but we had a real go. Looking back though, it's amazing some of the strange little things you remember games for. Norm Maxwell forgot his dress shoes that night, so he took the studs out of his boots, and was standing at the aftermatch in his boots."

After the excitement of the game with the Blues, the trip to Dunedin to play the Highlanders would end in deep disappointment.

"We were up by 17 points after eight minutes, playing magnificent rugby," says Blackadder. "The second try, to Daryl Lilley, saw 11 guys handle the ball. But then they started playing with superb ball maintenance, and we stopped going to them. We'd put in a good 80-minute performance against the Blues, but against the Highlanders we started like a rocket and ran out of steam.

"They beat us by out-grafting us that night. Once the rot set in, it was over. For a lot of us then the problem was our mental approach. We should have put the foot on the back of the neck against the Highlanders, and kept the pressure on. But what happened showed we still weren't mentally tough enough to grind out a win.

"We were doing debriefs after every game that year, and after we'd lost to the Highlanders, some guys said we needed things to keep refocusing during the game. In other words, that when we were 17 points up, we should have had a word or phrase to help us refocus again.

"I was standing up there at the whiteboard, letting it go, letting it go, and then I said, 'That's just bullshit. We didn't need to refocus when we were playing against the Chiefs, or the Blues. So why do we need to refocus now? We're making excuses for not being mentally tough.'

"Of course you do want to help motivate and refocus your players. It's not just the captain though. You should be doing it to the guy next to you, and each guy has to toughen up in his own head. When the pressure's on you've got to be doing things yourself.

"We took it on board. We don't waste time on nice words, or candy-coat it by saying, 'Yes, you played really well, but...' She's absolutely straight down the line. There's no bullshitting around.

"The whole team's in the same boat. It's a team game, and a team performance. If two cogs in the wheel aren't working the whole team goes down. So it's up to everyone to make sure that doesn't happen."

There were certainly signs of an improving attitude in the next game, in Christchurch against the Sharks, who had been finalists in '96, and had whipped the Crusaders in Durban that year.

This time the game was drawn, 26–all, and Blackadder's old mate Stu Loe, one of the cleanest props to ever pull on a footy boot, suffered the ignominy of being ordered off just 20 minutes into the game.

If the consequences hadn't been so serious the incident would have been like a surreal comedy. The big Crusaders lock Mark Weedon was stepping over a ruck when his boot landed on the back of Sharks' captain Gary Teichmann's head. Teichmann wasn't hurt, but in the heat of the moment referee Paddy O'Brien thought the boot that touched his head belonged to Stu Loe.

O'Brien called Loe out. It's true that many players feign innocence when a referee is lecturing them. On this occasion Loe certainly wasn't acting. The stunned look, and anguished question "What have I done?" were absolutely for real. Loe went to the sideline not knowing what on earth was going on.

Weedon would write to the judiciary saying that if anyone was guilty he was, not Loe. Despite that Loe was initially suspended for a week, a ban quickly lifted on appeal.

"I think that Paddy O'Brien apologised to Stu afterwards," says Blackadder. "Even Gary Teichman after the game knew it was all bullshit. He did feel something on his head, but it wasn't Stu."

With Loe gone, and injuries to the Crusaders' front rowers, No. 8 McLeod ended up at prop, and referee O'Brien ordered, for the first time in Super 12, golden oldies-style no-pushing scrums.

If the effort in the scrums had to be minimal, the heart shown by the Crusaders on defence was impressive, and so was the way Daryl Gibson sliced through the Sharks' backline when he ran from fullback.

"Today having Gibbo playing at second-five is to our style," says Blackadder. "I do worry that other coaches see him as just a second-five, and not the brilliant utility player that he is.

"In the modern game I don't think you want to get pinned down to one position, and guys often get selected for utility abilities. That's certainly the case with Gibbo. He can play fullback, and he's an outstanding wing or second-five. He's a good guy too, who's done really well with the Canterbury NPC captaincy."

There was dirty weather of the kind that plagued the Canterbury team in the grim year of 1992 when the Gauteng Lions came to Christchurch for an Anzac Day night game. For the first time the Crusaders held an opposing team scoreless, winning 23–0.

Then it was on to South Africa to play Northern Transvaal in Pretoria, narrowly lost 22–23. You could hardly blame Blackadder for having less than charitable thoughts about the referee in Pretoria, Jonathan Kaplan. He's the man who kept the 2000 Bledisloe Cup test in Wellington running for ever and ever, and in 1997 he called Justin Marshall late in the game for not putting the ball in straight, with the Crusaders hot on attack right in front of the Northern Transvaal posts.

"There were some dubious decisions in the Pretoria game," says Blackadder. "I don't have a great record with Kaplan. In fact, I don't know that I've ever won a game with him.

"But when we beat Free State in Bloemfontein it was our first win away from home, and you would have thought we'd won the championship that day.

"I'd never been to Bloemfontein before, and off the field I thought it was a great place. We went hunting, and they couldn't have been more hospitable.

"But they really take it seriously at the game. Out on the park there were oranges flying. Kevin Nepia was peppered by mandarins, and when the game started he went berserk. It was the sort of attitude we needed. That was a heroic win. It was brutal, but I enjoy those sort of games. I enjoy the forward contest. I really enjoyed the Otago game in the last round of 2001, because it was a blood and guts affair.

"Free State had some of the biggest buggers I've ever seen in the whole of my life. Their No. 8 was about 120kg. They had a massive team.

"The penalty count would have been horrendous. I can remember screaming at the guys to not give away a penalty, because it felt to me like the ref was just looking for a reason to give them the game.

"After we'd won, I've never seen a team more elated. In the changing room there were high fives, hugs and beers. It was an awesome occasion."

In the very last game of the competition the Crusaders gave a hint of what would come the following year. The Queensland Reds were demolished, 48–3, at Lancaster Park.

"Mark Mayerhofler had a blinder, and so did the team. It was the season that started us on the right track. We had good players. Guys like Steve Surridge, who was brilliant in our mix. We had Angus Gardiner, and Bubs. Guys who had been there in '94, and now, three years down the track, they were starting to emerge as senior players.

"We'd been through our darkest hour in '96, and we were starting to click as a side. Self-belief is one of the most crucial things you can have as a player, and we were starting to get that as a team."

Before the NPC season started, Blackadder would lead the first team designated as New Zealand A, in a game against the All Blacks, playing as the Barbarians, in Rotorua. His old Canterbury coach from 1991, John Phillips, was in charge of the forwards.

In a television interview before the game All Black coach John Hart said that blindside flanker (where Blackadder would play) "is a position we're really worried about. There will come a time when Michael Jones doesn't play for the All Blacks, and his replacement is going to be awfully important to grow.

"Charles Riechelmann has been given the opportunity in the New Zealand Barbarians team. While he's played most of his rugby at lock in the Blues, we think he's got a lot of the qualities we want. We hope we might be able to nuture that, and obviously with Michael in the squad that will help him grow that game.

"Charles Riechelmann has a huge defensive game, and that's important today in the blindside position, which Michael Jones has shown. He's also got speed, he's also got vision, and he's got hands, and he's a good lineout option. So he's got a lot that we want."

And Blackadder? "We always know that Todd Blackadder is there, and if we wanted someone to come in and pinch hit in a test, I know he would play very well."

Before the trial Blackadder met with Hart and his selectors. "The selectors were coaching the All Blacks under the Barbarians name, while we were staying up the other end of town. They told me they thought I was too slow, and had a lack of skills."

The game itself, although won by the shadow test team 29–22, was still a big day for Blackadder's side. "We really should have won that game. Our guys played bloody awesomely.

"We were leading most of the way. Paddy O'Brien came to me and he goes, 'Keep your guys on side.' I said, 'We are on side.' He said, 'I want them back another metre.' Then he whispered, 'It's coming from up there.' He was pointing to the grandstand.

"I didn't give a shit. But I guess not only were all the players under a bit of pressure, but the poor old ref was as well.

"We had a bunch of guys who thought, 'What the hell' and they went out there and had a go. You look at Glen Taylor at lock. He's an outstanding player, and outstanding bloke. He played that last test in Ellis Park in '96, and he's been bloody unlucky not to have an All Black career after that.

"I think I actually had one of my best games ever. When you feel that you've outplayed the other guy, and then you go into the same room, and the team's named, and you feel, 'Oh well, I obviously don't fit the job description.' They felt that Charles Riechelmann had a lot more promise than I did."

Blackadder took away his jersey, which was made of new space-age material, and a memory of a team performance he remains proud of.

Ahead was the camp at Hanmer, and captaincy of the Canterbury NPC team, now coached by Deans and Hansen.

"We were really struggling for locks. In 1996 I'd played lock in the NPC, then in '97 we had young Reuben Thorne, who was about 100kg dripping wet, and Graham Jack, who had really wanted to retire the year before. So those guys played so hard.

"The first game in the NPC was a ripsnorter against Wellington that we won 73–7. You couldn't have asked for more from the guys. Everything went our way that night."

Another win followed, Southland beaten 42–20 in Invercargill at Homestead Stadium. "That was actually a hard-fought game. It was a grind. We just tried to drive on a hot day, and it was another good graft. People might think these sort of games are easy, but they're bloody hard. I've never had an easy game down there."

Waikato then came to Lancaster Park, and gave the Canterbury side, now drawing 20,000 people to their home games, a real wake-up call, winning 24–18. "Waikato taught us a lesson. They played bloody well. We just got dealt to at the end of the day. Turnovers were our undoing. We just weren't tough enough and we had to get back to basics.

"Having had such an easy one against Wellington we'd started to loosen up a bit, and we struck a very committed Waikato side. We had a few lucky bounces, and the halftime score, 18–6 to Canterbury, didn't really reflect the game."

Two good wins on the road showed lessons learnt. Counties Manukau were beaten 30–18 in Pukekohe. "We showed a bit of backbone in that game," says Blackadder. "It was a blood and guts effort, a question of how much we wanted to win. We had to keep our belief and show some spine.

"In the last couple of minutes Mehrts threw me a really wide pass, and I passed to Fats [So'oalo], who scored a good try, which capped off a great game." Canterbury were now back at the top of the first division table.

The next weekend at the new Albany Stadium Canterbury showed they could graft their way to victory as well, with a 20–3 win over North Harbour. "It was 3–0 at the break. We felt the longer we could hang in, we could break them down," says Blackadder.

Now it was time for the biggest test of the season, a clash with Auckland at Lancaster Park. Canterbury playing Otago is always a hell of a game, but it feels more like brother against brother. You want real edge? You want signs in the crowd suggesting odd personal behaviour by the opposing players? You want people playing like their lives are on the game? Send an Auckland rugby team to Christchurch.

"Robbie Deans had taken us through the stages of the hard yards. Then it got to the Auckland game, and he said, 'This is the easy step.' I thought, 'Shouldn't this be harder than the hard yards?' He said, 'No, this is the easy step, because we'll be motivated, we've got a good side, we'll be fired up, and we've got these guys in our park for 90 minutes. They'll stay out there for 10 minutes at halftime. And they'll be ours.'"

The game would be the drought-breaker, the first win over Auckland for Canterbury for 14 years, Canterbury winning 20–9.

"The crowd was pumped, and the players were pumped," says Blackadder. "They put 13 All Blacks on the park, and we just went out and dug our feet in and gave it everything we had. This was the game when our forward pack picked up their front row and drove them right over.

"We put in hit after hit after hit. The tackle count for someone like Angus Gardiner was horrendous. He made 24 tackles, and forced five turnovers.

"When I look back on my career I can say I've seen Angus Gardiner in his prime, and it's something not many people have had the chance to see at close range.

"I believe when he was at his best, he and Josh were level-pegging. Josh has said that Angus is the only one in New Zealand rugby who has got the better of him the same number of times as he has got the better of Gus.

"I'm always going to have a biased view but I think Gus was one of the better No. 7s in the country. We called him Gutsa, which says it all really.

"He lived by the values that the team set, and was not shy about saying what was needed for the benefit of the team. He was the team sheriff off the field, where he was in charge of making sure the guys wore the right gear and so on. He had a way of doing it that was quite humorous although as the sheriff he wasn't afraid to pull his six-shooter out at times and gun a few guys down.

"Certainly as a player he was awesome. He played above his weight, and he had all the skilful attributes. He was a great linker, a great runner with the ball, and quite often you'd see him catch those high balls in the air. He was very athletic.

"I've never understood why he not only didn't make the All Blacks, but he was never in the New Zealand A team. Why not, I just don't know. When you played with the guy, and got to know him, you realised he was one of the best No. 7s Canterbury ever had."

After the win over Auckland, coach Deans was as pragmatic as he's ever been. To the gathered media he pointed out that, "We'll enjoy the moment tonight, but this win will mean nothing if we lose to Auckland in a semi-final, or a final."

Blackadder says that beating Auckland was "an unbelievable feeling. But then we went down to Otago and got our arses kicked."

One of the most rollicking characters in Otago rugby, Brendon Laney, was a late selection at first-five, after Tony Brown was forced out with injury. "Chainsaw" Laney, usually a fullback, or winger, plays with a freedom that can drive either his coach, or the opposing team, wild.

Inside the Canterbury camp there was some delight that Laney was Otago coach Glenn Ross's choice. They believed he would be a one-dimensional first-five, running at every opportunity, straight into the arms of the Canterbury defence. Wrong. Very wrong. "We perceived him as a weakness," says Blackadder, "and he had a blinder."

Laney ran all right, but the problem for Canterbury was that nobody could catch him. By the time he came off the field a powerful man with a chisel couldn't have scraped the grin off his face. "Jeez," he said to a reporter, "that was bloody amazing wasn't it?"

"We blew a lot of chances in the first half," says Blackadder, "and then they just kept on coming, wave after wave.

"At halftime it was 19–6 to Otago, and we were just hanging in there, and during the break everyone was saying, 'We've got to bloody score first.' Thirty or 40 seconds later Jeff Wilson was scoring in the corner. I guess the writing was well and truly on the wall.

"That year the tries Jeff Wilson was scoring were just god-like. They were struggling for most of the NPC, but they certainly didn't play poorly against us.

"The last of our round-robin games was against Taranaki, which we had to win to ensure a home semi-final. We won 40–21, and it was the good hard workout that we really needed.

"Before the semi we'd heard that Auckland were spending hours on the scrum machine. They had so many All Blacks in their side that I think they possibly thought we'd taken the round-robin game just on passion.

"But they were going to play merry hell with us in the semi. They were going to drill us. Zinzan had been joking with me and Justin Marshall in the All Blacks the year before, saying he'd never lost to Canterbury, and that Auckland would never lose to Canterbury while he was playing.

"What could I say at the time? I just kept it to myself and grinned. I know Marshy remembered it. It was nice for us to finally beat them.

"I think that was Fitzy's only loss for Auckland at Lancaster Park. In some way it was nice to see that players like he and Zinny hadn't gone their whole careers being on top of Canterbury. From my point of view it was good to give them a taste of what it was like for us for all those years.

"It was hard and brutal that night. The whole atmosphere was like a test match. They criticise the Canterbury crowds, but I'd take it as a mark of respect that when Auckland comes to town the stadium is always full.

"On the field it felt like two heavyweight boxers hammering each other. Every time Mehrts went into a ruck they were trying to ruck the shit out of him. There were no tries awarded. Stu Loe went over the line, but the try was disallowed. Knowing Stu as well as I do, if Stu said he scored it, he did.

"That was the game when Zinzan lost it. It was his last game in New Zealand. I don't think I could get a word in that night with Zinny and the referee Paddy O'Brien going hammer and tongs. They certainly weren't helping each other out.

"Mind you, I was too focused on the game to pay much attention. There was certainly a bit of honking going on that night I can tell you. It just proved that the earlier performance wasn't a fluke, that the boys could do it.

"At the aftermatch Steve Tew spoke and presented Zinny with a gift, which was a nice touch, because in his prime there was no better No. 8 in the whole of world rugby. The things he'd done with Auckland were just unbelievable, and he's a good guy too."

One of the more astonishing moments in the game came when

Fitzpatrick, famous as the most expert sledger in New Zealand rugby, was goaded into conceding a penalty to Canterbury by his 25-year-old opponent, Mark Hammett.

Eight minutes from the end, with the scores locked at 15–all, Hammett was penalised as Fitzpatrick tried to wrestle the ball away after a tackle near the Auckland 22.

Words were exchanged, and then, right under the nose of referee Paddy O'Brien, Fitzpatrick elbowed Hammett. The penalty was reversed, and Andrew Mehrtens kicked the goal for Canterbury.

What did Hammett say? Blackadder says he thinks "the two of them were probably exchanging cake recipes." If that's the case other Canterbury players reckon Hammett's recipe included phrases like "you're too old" and "past it."

It was certainly a turning-point in the match, says Blackadder, and "it takes a good man to get the better of Fitzy. Hammer certainly is a balls-out sort of a guy, a gutsy player. He'd be a terrible bugger to play against. You'd know you were going to get something you wouldn't want. I certainly wouldn't like to be marking him.

"He's also grown a lot in his approach. He is a very aggressive player and you can see that easily when he's on the field. But he also has some real leadership qualities.

"He doesn't mince his words if a young player is not pulling his weight, and every team has to have people like that. It can't always come from the top. You don't want the captain screaming at you all the time, the team has to be self-governing. He fits that role perfectly — if there's something to be sorted out he is right in there."

One of the more extraordinary examples from rugby of sheer determination working medical wonders came during the eight days between the semi-final with Auckland, and the final against Counties Manukau.

It involved Kevin Nepia, the 123kg prop who had moved to Canterbury from Auckland at the start of 1996, his way in his home town blocked by All Black props Olo Brown and Craig Dowd.

In the semi-final the medial ligament in his right knee was injured so badly it was just one grade from being snapped, and in need of immediate surgery. From the moment he came off just before halftime all that was on his mind was playing in the final. "All weekend my wife, Lisa, was icing my knee every three hours, right round the clock, until Monday morning. When we got to the specialist the prognosis was grim. It was a tear, and there was no rigidity in the knee at all. There was virtually no tendon holding it on."

The first specialist said it would be six weeks before he could play again. A second gave the opinion that it would be four weeks before he could even run, much less think about playing rugby.

"On the Monday I could hardly walk. I had my knee in a brace, and I was using crutches. On the Tuesday it was painful, but I was able to get on a bike in the gym. On Wednesday I was walking without a brace. At the gym I kept the brace on, and was able to use a rebounder.

"All through the week Lisa kept icing the knee, and I was taking anti-inflammatories to keep the swelling down. On the Friday I took the brace off and had the knee strapped. That night I got through a team training and they said, 'Yep, you can play.'"

While Nepia went through his medical regime, Blackadder was struggling to sleep easily. "There were a lot of nerves. I'd never been in that position before, not even that close to it.

"Suddenly we were in the final, and there were a lot of expectations, and a lot of things run through your mind too. I mean, could you imagine the opposition captain holding up the NPC trophy at our park? You've got all these things that you've got to think about.

"We weren't daunted by it, but there is a lot of pressure. I remember saying to Steve Hansen when we were getting ready, 'Aw mate, I need another shirt.' It was wringing wet. He went into the union office, and must have torn some drawers apart and found another one. That's what the nerves were like."

Stories published at the time said that while Blackadder was sweating, and other players were stretching, yawning and dealing with pre-game tension in their own ways, Nepia was being injected with pain-killers. Months later he would admit that all he really did was double-dose on the anti-inflammatory tablets.

At 2.35pm the knock came on the Canterbury changing room door, and Blackadder led his men down the slightly chipped, grey concrete tunnel onto the park. It's a moment he has always relished.

"There's no better feeling in the world than to lead your Canterbury team out in Christchurch.

"You've got your butterflies and your nerves, and then you get the ball and you just want to get out onto the ground. There's a 'whoosh' of noise when you come out of the tunnel, and the blood pumps through the veins."

The final was barely under way when Leon MacDonald was faced with George Leaupepe, the brutally strong Counties and Manu Samoa centre, on the rampage. MacDonald, at that stage still not out of his teens, is called Rangi, after the maniacal tackling Maori kid in the *Footrot Flats* cartoon.

Leaupepe had the goal-line in his sights when MacDonald hit him at chest height in a tackle so fierce it actually bowled the powerfully built centre off his feet. "Canterbury are renowned for their defence," yelled Murray Mexted in the television commentary box. "Have a look at this! What a way to stop your opponent when he has a clear run at the line."

In the heat of a game, says Blackadder, "You haven't got a lot of time to reflect on things, but when Leon makes a tackle like that it shows his level of intensity, and it rubs off on everyone.

"You saw Fats in that game, hanging on to Jonah Lomu. Mehrts tackling Jonah. Any other day they would have been swatted like flies. But because the team was so committed, and driven to winning that game, they hung on."

At halftime Canterbury held a 19–3 lead, and coach Robbie Deans was as fired up as any player. He walked into the changing room, and when the players hushed to listen to what he had to say, swept the health drinks off the top of the old fridge in the centre of the room. As the plastic bottles bounced on the floor he pointed at the bare top and snarled, "That bloody trophy stays here."

There's always a defining moment in a tough clash where the game turns, and in Blackadder's mind that moment in the final came just minutes after the second spell had begun.

Tony Marsh, the talented Counties second-five, had sliced open the Canterbury backline, and, on the 22 metres mark, fed his flanker Craig Glendinning.

"Somehow Angus Gardiner pulled out a try-saving tackle which could have let Counties back in that game. Not only that but he then got up and got the ball, and turned the game for us.

"In the next few years we had Scotty Robertson and Gus job-sharing, and while they complemented each other, I think that may have frustrated, not only Gus, but even Scotty at times.

"One week you're either in or out. Even in this modern era, you feel that you've been dropped if you're not actually starting the game."

There were men playing their hearts out right through the Canterbury line-up, and one of the more amazing tributes came when prop Kevin Nepia's knee finally gave way 15 minutes from time. As he was assisted to the sideline by Don Hayes the 1980s skipper remarked, in amazement, that Nepia was "the first bloody Aucklander to ever get a standing ovation at Lancaster Park."

Lock Graham Jack, older brother of 2001 All Black Chris, was a special hero to the people in the team who knew what he'd overcome to play the season out to the death.

"It was because of guys like him that we won that trophy," says Blackadder. "Jacko was ill with a blood disorder that they couldn't diagnose for ages, but he was such a gutsy bastard that he and Reuben Thorne performed, week after week. They certainly played their part in us winning that championship, putting in the effort they did. I will never look at that season without thinking of their effort.

"Graham's got a great nature, he's a great big spongy pud-grinner most of the time. He had to be an optimist to survive one of the worst streaks of luck I've ever seen on tour.

"It was in Super 12 in '98. He didn't play in the first game against the Golden Cats in Bloemfontein, and we went out for a few beers that night. We'd had a few, me and Robbie, and someone else, and Jacko. We were stumbling back from the pub and there was this big old concrete lamp-post, and we were just walking along and suddenly 'bang,' Jacko must have walked into it and the whole thing fell over.

"So we straightened it back up, and thought, 'Oh no' we could be in trouble here. Jacko was crook, so we put him to bed.

"The next day we were off to a team recovery first thing in the morning and we were all on the bus. Here's old Jacko lying in between the seats. We got to recovery and now Jacko is lying on the changing room floor because he is that crook he can't get up.

"Then he rights himself and we go down to play the Sharks in Durban, and he's named in the reserves. Then he catches the flu, and so he was out for that game. He just had a shocker, the worst tourist I'd ever seen on a South African trip."

In the NPC final the terrible luck was visited on Jim Coe, the Counties lock. "As fate would have it, Jim Coe broke his leg in that game. He was one of their hardest grafters, the guts in their forward pack."

But if the day was a nightmare for Coe, it was one of the more exciting for Canterbury. "It was one of the very first games where we had a really attacking mind-set. We had the attitude, 'No, we're not going for the points, we'll go for the lineout.' That was a bit of a change in philosophy. Most teams go for the points. We said, we'll keep attacking.

"Early on we had a couple of lineouts when we went for the drive. We nearly got a try but we got pushed out in the corner. We had the attitude, that we're wearing them [Counties] out. We're fitter than these guys, we're stronger than these guys, we want it more."

In the stands, coach Deans was delighted with the decisions his captain was making. If Blackadder, quite rightly, saw the Gardiner tackle on Glendinning as a crucial time, Deans believes a call Blackadder made to tap and run in the 60th minute was another major moment.

At the time Counties had come back to be nine points behind. An easy three points were on offer for Canterbury, when Counties were caught offside right in front of their posts by referee Colin Hawke. "Most captains," says Deans, "would have taken the shot at goal. But he recognised that it was time to put the foot on the throat, and that's what the game is all about.

"He started to back himself, and his own judgement. If you're hesitant, you're off your game. But if you back yourself, and you have the belief in yourself, then others will see that in you, and as you start to get success that belief snowballs."

From the tap, Marshall passed to Blackadder, who charged at the Counties line, turned to protect the ball, and, as the Canterbury forwards drove him forward, was able to slip the ball to Daryl Gibson for the try. Into his microphone Murray Mexted boomed, "To the players that would be ecstasy, to make a brave call like that and have it work."

Murray was in ecstasy himself six minutes from the end when Mark Mayerhofler dived in for a try. "That was superb, absolutely superb. In the replay have a look at the combination. They drew the defence on the short side, way over by the grandstand, and then Marshall swung it back, right over the top and Mehrtens was standing there waiting. It was on. It was called for. Then Mayerhofler running dead straight off Mehrtens gets the try. What a beautifully manufactured try that one was."

Well, actually, no. Not even remotely manufactured. "We tried a move which went horribly wrong," says Blackadder, who moved to the back of the scrum in the second half. "I ran blind, but 'oops no blind,' so I passed it back to Marshy, who threw it back to Mehrts, who was probably wondering what was going on. Then Mehrts and Bubs did a cut, and Bubs did a big dive under the posts. That was from something that had actually gone wrong."

In the dying moments there was a genuinely engineered try, which started with a pick-up from Blackadder at a scrum near the Counties line. "I managed to draw and pass, and put Justin over for a good try, which was a great memory.

"It was a great way to finish the season, although not a lot of us made the All Blacks to go to Britain. It capped off a great year for us, which had started back in the summer with Super 12, and to hold that trophy up was a reflection of all the hard work those guys had put in.

"When you look at the guys, Graham Jack battled the whole season with a virus, which they couldn't work out. Guys like Aaron Flynn, the hard-working guys, all came into it.

"We had our world-class players, like Justin and Mehrts, Fats So'oalo

143

that year was a pocket dynamo, and if you ask me Angus played so well in '97 he and Josh Kronfeld were by far the best No. 7s in New Zealand.

"But there were other guys not many people would even have known about. Right through the season we had five or six guys who were tackling bag holders, who would do a lot of physical work with us, so we weren't smashing ourselves up.

"They turned out to basically be a thermometer to see whether we were actually doing the work or not. They knew when we were at our best from how hard the hits were going in. They were club players, and guys on the fringe of the team, and in our win they were crucial too."

* * *

After the celebrations were over after the NPC victory Blackadder was selected for the end of year All Black tour to England and Ireland.

Steve Surridge would become an All Black for the first time, but there was no place for Mark Mayerhofler, the place many would have considered he had earned going to Waikato's Scott McLeod.

This was the tour where the first cracks in what had looked like an unbeatable All Black team in 1996 started to appear. It would also be a tour which would be remembered for one of the more bizarre actions by an All Black coach, when John Hart ripped into Norm Hewitt for what he saw as unacceptable behaviour when Hewitt was subbed off against England.

It was also a time when Josh Kronfeld, one of the superstars of the 1995 World Cup, was under real threat for his spot on the openside of the All Black scrum.

In his book *On The Loose*, Kronfeld says that, after being ripped to shreds by Hart for a perceived lack of intensity before the last home test of the '97 season, against Australia at Carisbrook, he was nervous about the end of year tour.

Sure enough, he says, when the tour started he was being compared unfavourably with Andrew Blowers, and being drilled for having poor skills and bad hands.

The person who Kronfeld talked about his situation with the most was

Blackadder, who says, "I remember talking to Josh on the bus, and saying, 'There's nothing wrong with your hands, you've got good skills.' The harder he tried, the worse he got. I know myself, when people mention that you've got a weakness, you can work too hard on one thing.

"You're trying to prove a point, instead of saying, 'I've got good skills.' If you can just relax it comes right."

There were some odd aspects in the selection of the 1997 team. Captain Sean Fitzpatrick was on tour with a knee that would never respond to treatment, so was a passenger for the first five games of a nine-match tour. Zinzan Brooke was selected despite announcing before the tour that after signing a deal with the London Harlequins club, he would not be playing in New Zealand again.

Blackadder wasn't involved enough with the test team to form any strong opinions about Brooke on tour, but Kronfeld says that "It sometimes appeared that he was just along for a swansong. Here was a great player with a chance to go out on a high, but instead he let himself down."

The first game was against Llanelli, at Stradey Park, where the All Blacks fielded a shadow test team.

In 1972 the All Blacks were beaten 9–3 by Llanelli, a cherished memory for the Welsh. "There's a great poem about Llanelli at Stradey Park that day," says Blackadder, "and as we were all going to the game on the bus Steve Surridge recited the poem. We were staying in Swansea, and when you drove into Llanelli you can't help but think about the valleys and the coalmines, the whole place was very cold. The valleys just run out of a few hills, and all the houses look the same. She's pretty dour stuff."

The All Blacks ran rampant, winning 81–3, and then it was the turn of the midweek team, led on this tour by Blackadder.

"I enjoyed captaining the midweek team. We had less pressure than the test team, and we had a good mix of guys. We had Bull Allen, who loves a laugh, good old Anton Oliver and Gordon Slater. You know what you're going to get out of a guy like Gordie. He'll give it his guts on every occasion."

Walter Little, in the twilight of a great career, remained one of the hard cases of the team. One incident on tour sticks in Blackadder's memory. "We were waiting to join the test team to go to Old Trafford, and Harty and the team officials were waiting in the foyer. And waiting, and waiting, for Walter.

"The message must have got to Walter not to come down to the foyer, because he'd obviously been out having a big night. He had to run all the way down the stairs, take the back exit, run all the way around the hotel, and then jump into the bus.

"They knew that Walter was somewhere, they just didn't know what condition he was in. He came screaming up into the bus with his bloodshot eyes. Then they came on board asking, 'What's happened to Walter?' We called, 'It's okay, he's here.' Then away we went.

"Jonah Lomu was in the midweek side at the start of the tour. He was good as gold. Jonah is only ever treated differently at times by the coaches, he doesn't ever ask for special treatment. I think he enjoyed being with the midweek guys. I'm not saying he desired it more than playing the tests, but in our games he gave it death.

"Jonah's matured a lot. Last year in the All Blacks one of the senior players was late for a meeting, and Jonah gave the team a dressing-down about standards of being an All Black. He just showed such leadership skills. If the captain's not at the helm, you need guys who will jump up and take charge, and he did it that day. You need guys to do that within the side."

Another man Blackadder remembers fondly from the '97 tour was Aaron Hopa, the towering Waikato No. 8, who would tragically die in a freak diving accident the following summer.

"I roomed with Aaron a couple of times on that tour. He was a top man, who I got on really well with. I met his Mum and Dad and his girlfriend Tracey after he passed away, and they were lovely people. Since then I've talked to Tracey quite a bit.

"He was such a talented player, a hard worker, who loved his rugby. There was no silver spoon in Aaron's mouth. He was actually working delivering rubbish before he went on that tour. He was from a straight-up background, an awesome guy.

"Regardless of which team you play for at provincial level, no matter what the rivalry, once you get away together in a New Zealand team, you all get on like a house on fire.

"Midweek has a different feeling than a test side. It's a case of let's get out and have a go. In 1997 John Hart would be at our final team run, but the rest of the time it was Ross Cooper, and the trainer."

Blackadder's first game as an All Black captain doesn't ring any great bells for him. "It wasn't that exciting. It was a night game, against Pontypridd. They played well, although the score, 51–8, doesn't reflect that."

Like so many All Blacks, Blackadder fell in love with Ireland on the quick visit that followed the Pontypridd game. "The midweek team do a lot more promotional stuff than the test side. That's not always a bad thing. One day in Dublin, after we'd trained, we went into a big Canterbury International shop, then had to go and drink Guinness, and were taken home in a horse and cart. So you can see that it's a tough life.

"Dublin was beautiful. Ireland is certainly a place I'd go back to again. I remember we went out to play golf, on a links course. We all retired to the clubhouse very early, even though we had two buckets of balls each.

"When you tee off on a links course there's a bit of a fairway in front of you, and in the distance there's the green. What's growing in between you could bale hay with. It makes playing the course a very tight affair."

It was at the venerable Landsdowne Rd ground in Dublin, where fans pile off trains right at the ground, that Blackadder made his debut as a radio commentator, calling the game with Graeme Moody.

"I was a bit nervous about it," says Blackadder, "worrying about things like whether the wind was blowing from left to right. We'd hardly started talking and a train rumbled under the stand.

"We went on air and Ireland played pretty well in the first half. The All Blacks looked just a little bit shaky before they got on top, but by halftime it was 27–15 to the All Blacks.

"At halftime Graeme goes, 'Aw well, just hold the fort mate, I've got to go away,' and here I was, talking to the whole of New Zealand for 10 minutes. I started making up stories and telling people what we'd been up to during the week. In the end I quite enjoyed the whole experience."

The entire squad then moved back to England, where the midweek team started what amounted to a three-game series against England's second-string side, variously named Emerging England, England Rugby Partnership XV, and England A.

"We were basically playing what was our test series against the same team. We won the first, against Emerging England, 59–22, in Huddersfield.

"We played on artificial turf, and it was one of those nights when every decision I made went our way. There were times when I could have taken points, but I went for the scrum, and did the sort of things I'd been doing with the Crusaders.

"I thought I'd try my hand with the All Blacks. I felt that we had nothing to lose, why not have a go? Let's have a really attacking mind-set."

Before the game Kronfeld told Blackadder he was "going to rip this one," and he did. Kronfeld had been on the reserves bench behind Andrew Blowers for the test in Dublin, and he played so well at Huddersfield that he had to be selected for the test against England at Old Trafford, in Manchester.

That's right, at Old Trafford. To give a game to the fans in the north of England the home of Manchester United was made available to the English rugby union.

Nothing unusual about the score, 25–8 to the All Blacks. But as well as the venue there was something weird about how the English players did a lap of honour after they'd lost by 17 points. Perhaps they were celebrating the fact that in the first half Martin Johnson had got away with king-hitting new All Black captain Justin Marshall in the face. He was caught on video though, and suspended for a week, missing a test with South Africa.

The only sign of any dissension in the mid-week group came after the game in Bristol, won 18–11 against familiar rivals, now called the England Rugby Partnership XV.

"At the debrief we had one of the guys saying that perhaps we should have taken the points in the game, rather than going for lineouts or tap kicks," says Blackadder.

"I was really pissed off about that because unless you've got everyone thinking the same as you it's never going to work. I'm not saying that's the reason some things didn't work at Bristol — some might not have come off with the best will in the world — but it showed me that perhaps we hadn't all bought into the idea of attacking as much as possible."

The test in the weekend was against Wales at Wembley, used because the traditional Welsh home ground, Cardiff Arms Park, was being rebuilt for the 1999 World Cup. Welsh people in the crowd sang beautifully, and the All Blacks won 42–7.

But the aftermath of the game inside the All Black camp was ugly. That night Blackadder had the distressing sight of Norm Hewitt in tears, after a violent verbal attack by coach Hart.

"Norm came into my room crying that night," says Blackadder. "It should have been one of the greatest days of his life. I don't think Norm did anything wrong. It sickened me."

It all began 25 minutes from the end of the test, when Hewitt, about to throw the ball into a lineout, found Sean Fitzpatrick, who had been on the All Blacks reserve bench, at his elbow, asking for the ball.

"Normally when you're going to be subbed off," says Blackadder, "you get a series of different coloured cards. The trainer would run on and tell you, 'Red card mate, you're coming off.'

"There was a mix-up, and Norm didn't get red carded. All of a sudden Sean just turned up. Norm was surprised, and walked back to the bench."

In Fitzpatrick's book *Turning Point*, Hart says: "Norm wasn't impressed, which really disappointed me. People can say that if he knew he was going to come off maybe he would have handled it better. I would argue that with the substitution rules as they are now, that's just part of the game."

Hart says he had never "addressed a player like I did him that night for what I thought he'd done to Sean and the team. I know how hard it was on him because he'd been fighting for that position for so long. But there was a wider picture and I think he forgot it for that split-second."

Blackadder sees it very differently. "John Hart told Norm he was a disgrace. He told him that the people in Wembley had not come to see Norm Hewitt play, they'd come to see Sean Fitzpatrick play. I've got nothing against Sean, but people had actually come to see the All Blacks, not one man.

"Norm had just been replaced, and I've never seen one guy walk off the field looking happy. I saw Justin just a few months before against Australia looking pretty grumpy at Carisbrook. You never see me jumping for joy when I'm pulled, and of course Norm was thoroughly enjoying the test. They were having a good win, playing at Wembley, the sort of things you can tell your grand-children one day.

"Now he's being reprimanded for the way he handled it. People had come to watch Sean, not you, which is so degrading.

"Norm was told off again in front of the team the next day, and he had to apologise in front of the team. I don't think you'd ever realise how much that hurt him. It was wrong.

"No one should be subjected to that. It was such a nothing thing, which could have easily been defused if Sean had stepped in. But nothing was said, which was a shame."

Hard on the heels of the Hewitt upset came another strange dispute. Fifteen minutes before kick-off against the England A team in Leicester, Irish referee Alan Lewis came into the All Blacks changing room.

"He said we all had to change our sprigs," says Blackadder. "He was not allowing 21mm sprigs. We were ready to go. There were threats that we'd have to put the game back.

"When you're preparing for the game and the referee walks in and says change your sprigs, it puts you off the stride. There's nowhere in the world that you can't wear 21mm sprigs. Certainly you never go into a changing room and say, 'Boys, you have to change your sprigs.'"

Unhappy as they were with the referee, the All Blacks, on a cold, muddy, miserable night, had quite enough composure to beat England A, captained by No. 8 Ben Clarke, 30–19.

Now Blackadder and his midweek men, happy that they'd stayed unbeaten, could watch with fascination the last test of the tour, against England at Twickenham.

The horrors that lay ahead for the All Blacks in 1998 were hinted at in that game, although most of the New Zealand rugby media were still worshipping the All Blacks and their charismatic coach.

Blackadder wasn't quite so impressed. "The signs that would crop up the next year were showing. Justin didn't lose it in that game, but he was getting frustrated, and I'd suggest it was because of the amount of ball he was getting that was crap.

"The English really ripped into us. There's a real rivalry between England and New Zealand, and it's pretty brutal at times.

"We drew the game 26–all, but to me it felt like a loss that day. England are a team who are very big and imposing. People wonder why it is that nobody plays very well against them. I think it's because they're very good defenders, and their tackle lines are a lot higher.

"What happens is that when you're getting hit high in a tackle, up around your chest, it means you can't place the ball so it'll be good ball.

"England are huge, so every time they tackle you it slows down getting the ball back. They'd been coached by John Mitchell, and I thought at Twickenham they really took us on up-front. They were away to 17–3 after 15 minutes, and we were probably lucky to come away with a draw."

8. A bit like a dream

"Draw your swords boys,
we've got a battle"

Wayne Smith knew there was something special in the air. He could see it in the eyes, in Todd Blackadder's in particular. "When he got that look you knew the others were going to follow him, and it'd take a hell of a lot to beat you."

Smith saw the signs on the day the Crusaders' campaign of 1998 would finish in triumph on the manicured grass of Eden Park, but along the way there would be losses, soul-searching, ugly rumours, and a courage and commitment that has rarely been matched by any team.

This was the year the "potential" tag used for the Crusaders was discarded, replaced by the word "champions." It was the start of an amazing three-year winning streak.

The '98 story began with a complete review of what had happened in the 1997 NPC competition. Smith, his assistant coach Peter Sloane, Robbie Deans, who would manage the Crusaders after coaching the Canterbury NPC team, and all the other officials from both teams, plus every single player, got together in November and exhaustively talked things through.

Explained Smith, "We first trained together, in November, doing weights and aerobic work, and then, when we got together in January we worked on the vision, the game plan, and to build the environment.

"While the Crusaders are a regional team, we're still the Canterbury Crusaders, and we're still red and black."

To hammer home the point, in February the squad gathers in a white-walled roomed under the stand at QE2 Stadium, home to the 1974 Commonwealth Games, where Dick Tayler set the crowd and the country alight with a brilliant win in the 10,000 metres. But on the screen of the television set in the team room the players watch rugby images, and rugby heroes.

With the help of Gilbert Enoka, a key man in the forming of team attitudes, Smith and Sloane have put together a video with scenes of great Canterbury rugby moments, and interviews with rock-solid red and black men, former All Black captain Tane Norton, and the 1980s leader, Don Hayes.

Norton and Hayes have something more in common than being exceptionally good rugby players. They are also deeply honest, humble, decent men. As role models they don't come any better.

"The video was very special to us," says Smith. "It was the way we wanted to establish our culture."

As it usually is with the Crusaders, there weren't too many signs of the riches to come from the early season warm-up matches.

After a promotional tour around the regions, to Ashburton, Timaru, Blenheim and Nelson, the first game was in Invercargill, against the Highlanders. The men from Otago won 83–23, the Highlanders running in 14 tries. "We won't be taking anything out of this game," muttered coach Smith at the time.

Blackadder, who was a spectator that day, wasn't so downcast. "When we are working hard with our fitness the game is secondary, apart from being a hit out. I'm not taking anything away from the Highlanders' win, but the Crusaders do have a pretty poor pre-season record.

"Going to Coolum, on the other hand, was a bit of a disaster. It was so hot. We played the Blues and the Waratahs at Coolum, and played Queensland at Ballymore."

Although the Crusaders beat the Blues 33–0, Blackadder doesn't have happy personal memories of the game. "I broke a bone on Lee Lidgard's head. I may as well have been punching a brick wall. He kept on grabbing my jersey, and I remember warning him. I think I would have needed a club to get the message through to that guy though — he's a fairly traditional prop."

The Crusaders lost 19–36 to the Waratahs, and 24–41 to the Queensland Reds, but the real blow was having Afato So'oalo rupture an anterior cruciate ligament in the Waratahs game. "He'd had an exceptional year for us in '97," says Blackadder. "Fats had been one of those match winners that every team loves to have."

In the opening game of Super 12 there was a very strange experience for the Crusaders. Leon MacDonald, big-hearted Rangi, was lining out against them at Albany for the Chiefs.

There had been a long and hard-fought battle behind the scenes over MacDonald between the New Zealand and Canterbury unions. The All Black selectors wanted to see him playing first-five, a position firmly held down at the Crusaders by Andrew Mehrtens.

The Crusaders wanted him as a fullback, and included him in every squad they nominated to the New Zealand union, down to submitting him as one of their 15 core players. It was all to no avail. In 1998 the national selectors were all-powerful, and MacDonald, happily settled in Christchurch, had to pack up and shift north.

"He had a blinder against us," says Blackadder. "He played outstandingly, and kicked five penalty goals, so once again we got narrowly beaten, 25–23, by the Chiefs. Then early in the competition the poor guy got injured, so he came back home anyway."

The oddest moment in the game came seven minutes from the end, when Kevin Nepia was sinbinned by referee Steve Walsh Snr. Ian Jones had crashed down from a lineout and Walsh blamed Nepia for tipping him over. Video replays showed that Nepia was actually nowhere near

Jones, whose own support players lost their grip at the top of his jump.

If Nepia being binned was a strange mistake, what happened next bordered on the surreal. Chiefs' captain Errol Brain, apparently believing another innocent man, Angus Gardiner, was responsible for what had happened to Jones, punched Gardiner in the face. The touch judge reported the incident, but Brain was just cautioned.

Let's just run through that again. Nepia does nothing and is binned. Gardiner does nothing and is punched so hard he's forced out of the game. Brain punches Gardiner and has a finger wagged at him. The Chiefs get the penalty.

"Look at the referee," says Blackadder wryly. "Is it any real surprise? It got really weird at times.

"We actually got Steve Walsh in pre-season one year to talk to us, and he gave us a few interesting tips. But I think he got a bit rattled for a while. I don't think I was harping at him, I'm usually quite controlled. In the last two years I've got frustrated at times, but I put that down to the standard of refereeing.

"When you've got someone like Mehrts in there chipping away, I think he shakes the refs a bit of the time. He never says anything derogatory, he's just talking about the laws of the game, on which he is quite astute.

"I think most referees find that a little unnerving. Most players don't know the rules that well, and don't snap at the refs. So the ref can easily say 'You're penalised because of whatever.' But Mehrts says, 'No ref, under such and such a section that shouldn't be the case,' and he rattles them."

A very good win, 33–12, over the Waratahs at Lancaster Park was tempered by the loss of Justin Marshall in a freak accident. In the last minute of the game Marshall hauled in a slightly high pass from Daryl Gibson. In the process he tore his Achilles tendon, and had to literally hop over the line.

It was the first of a series of injuries, in which Gibson was always the innocent bystander, that led to team jokers Marshall and Mehrtens dubbing Gibson the Black Widow. Marshall would not play again in 1998's Super 12.

"Apart from Marshy's injury, it was a great night," says Blackadder.

"The boys were on fire, none more so than Kevin Nepia. He was a big man, who gave it his all. He'd really fired down here, after being a fringe player in Auckland."

Nepia did get an early introduction to the more earthy culture down south. "It was quite interesting," says Blackadder. "We had a meeting in '97, when we thought we were getting a bit burnt out from over-training. Neeps suggested we have our training jerseys washed for us. He had this new theory and he basically was told to 'shut up, we do our own washing down here.'

"He'd showed in the '97 final how much guts he had, when he selected himself to play in the final. When it counted, it put everything in on the field."

A Blackadder mental snapshot from the next game, against the Queensland Reds at Ballymore, was of lock Graham Jack lying in the showers, the cold taps turned on full, trying to cool down. "When we walked into the changing room, it was so hot I didn't want to lie down. So I went past the hand-basins into the shower room, and there was Jacko, lying in the drain with cold water pouring all over him.

"In the first half we were just holding on. It was exhausting. That was another of those games in Queensland where the sweat was just popping out of our skins. We got to halftime down 9–6, and they went away to win 35–9.

"It was so hot that after the game Steve Surridge was taken away to have fluids pumped into his body. Our players were absolutely stuffed in the last minutes.

"I remember vividly when Dan Crowley punched Angus, and Gus, who had taken a few whacks, was so tired they carted his poor body off the field. In a way it showed how much commitment Gus puts into every game he plays. Crowley was suspended for two matches.

"We were breaking our necks the whole game just to hold them off. It was very trying."

Back in Christchurch the Crusaders had the bye, and then the build-up to the game with the Auckland Blues at Lancaster Park had its own controversial tweak. Mocking Auckland is certainly part of the social fabric in Canterbury. There have been billboards saying how lucky

Canterbury beer drinkers were that they didn't live in Auckland, and one pub in the central city promoted live telecasts of Super 12 games in which Auckland was always advertised as Dorkland.

But nobody in the team was thrilled when major billboards by a Crusaders' sponsor appeared that asked the question: "What do you call three Aucklanders without power? The front row."

Aucklanders, fresh from a summer of electrical blackouts weren't in the mood for teasing, and Blackadder says he didn't laugh much either.

"I've never liked that sort of campaign. It's not sensible by sponsors. The game is hard enough without firing people up. When you're with your team and you are looking for any sort of motivation, something like the front row campaign, that's ideal.

"I think it goes against the sort of people we are down here in Canterbury. I don't think we are like that naturally, poking the borax at their front row when they're best in the world, the All Black front row."

How much the Blues were fired up by the sniping from the sidelines is debatable, but they certainly started well, racing to a 24–9 halftime lead, and holding off a big comeback by the Crusaders, to win 31–24.

Blackadder's wee personal horror moment came just before the break. "I remember we were right on their line and it was a lineout. I missed a tackle on Jason Spice and he ran through and linked up with Caleb Ralph. When Caleb runs he glides, and he just ghosted away for the try. I went through a little nightmare patch, where every tackle I missed teams were scoring from."

On the Monday after the game, Andrew Mehrtens held nothing back in an interview in *The Press*. He described the refereeing display by the old Canterbury favourite, Steve Walsh, as atrocious. His main complaint was the charge that Walsh had allowed the Blues players to hold the ball on the ground after a tackle.

While that little rocket was ricocheting around the media traps, Blackadder was stunned by a mean-spirited rumour he heard on a local talkback radio sports show.

To say things weren't going too well for the Crusaders on the results sheet at that stage could be compared to suggesting the Ice Age was a bit of a tough time for the dinosaurs. The Crusaders had won one out of five, and were firmly planted at the bottom of the table.

Coach Smith suggested straight after the Auckland game that "being at the bottom is irrelevant. We've just got to keep an eye on the next game, and win it. Positions on the table change overnight." They may be sensible words, but this is rugby, in a rugby hotbed, and for some fans common sense doesn't get in the way of outrage.

"I remember driving down to pool recoveries at QE2 on the day after the Auckland game," says Blackadder. "I was listening to a guy being interviewed on air who supposedly had talked to my mother. He rang the station and said Mum had given him the inside information that Robbie was coaching the team, and Wayne Smith was no good.

"Mum had known the Smiths for years and we'd been family friends. When I heard it, I rang up Wayne's wife, Trish, because hearing that live over the radio at a time when things aren't going that well, when everyone is out for blood, there's just no need for it.

"Basically we were getting bagged left, right, and centre. Todd Blackadder shouldn't be the captain and we needed a whole new team. I remember listening to it on the way to QE2 and just thinking, 'Aw, hell.' We were trying really hard, and apart from Queensland, when we were never in it, the scores were actually pretty close."

The only truth in the "Deans is coaching the team" claim on radio was that Todd's mother, Carolyn, knew the man who called by sight, but no more than that. She had certainly never spoken to him once about rugby, or suggested that Deans was running the show.

Carolyn's not a woman who takes a slur on her family, and old friends like coach Smith, lying down. She tracked the caller down by phone, and, once he'd admitted that he'd made the story up to get his 10 seconds of fame, told him what she thought of his actions to the point where he was in tears. He said he would write her a letter of apology, and he wrote to the radio station admitting he had never spoken to her about the Crusaders.

"It shows you just how much people get carried away," says Blackadder. "He makes up a story to bolster his opinion, and a radio announcer lets him go on when there is really nothing factual to support his story."

The reality was that the Crusaders were a very good side, and a hungry side. "You can't get away from the fact you are on the bottom, and it's bloody hard work being down there. But we had a really good attitude, a week-to-week attitude and we didn't dwell too much on where we were on the table."

There was also a rock-solid commitment to taking the game to opposing teams. "We had a real attacking sort of mindset, the whole team did. Everything we did was attacking, we tried everything. In the Auckland game we were a bit behind on points, and we had a lineout and they went on to score. Your decisions out there are the things you live and die on. In the Crusaders there was never any criticism. Everybody was of one mindset."

Smith recalls that as a captain "Todd didn't want to coach the team, but he spent time talking with us, so we could run things by him, and he understood what we were doing.

"We trusted him totally to run the side on the field. In those early years, sometimes we wouldn't kick for goal, and often I'd have the media into me afterwards, and my stock answer was that 'Toddy makes the decisions on the field, and we trust him.'"

Next up were the Northern Bulls, at Lancaster Park, won 31–20 by the Crusaders. "Matt Sexton and Elton Moncrieff, who was at halfback for us in that game, both got sin-binned for professional fouls," says Blackadder. "Then Rat [Sexton] snapped his Achilles tendon when he got back on the field.

"I think I missed Joost van der Westerhuizen and he went through and scored another bloody try, so for two games in a row they scored from a missed tackle by me."

On the bright side the Crusaders had their bonus point for four tries by halftime, and Mark Mayerhofler showed why he was the epitome of the players' player. "Bubs saved a certain try just before halftime by catching Franco Smith and turning him on his back, dragging him with one hand back from the line. I never saw anyone more committed than him. When he played it was almost like having an extra player, another loose forward who was out in the backline."

Where the season really got on track for the Crusaders was in Timaru, in an Easter game against the Brumbies.

"The whole town was behind us," says Blackadder. "It's amazing when you look at it with the Crusaders, that over the years the turning point has come when we have gone around our regions, and basically got out of our home comforts a little bit. Or in South Africa when we're right out of our comfort zone.

"In Timaru we'd gone into the streets, meeting the public and signing things. We'd gone round and done little coaching schools with the kids. The people repaid us with great hospitality, and huge support at the game.

"It was an awesome match to play in. It was brutal and fast and we just took the game to them, winning 38–26. The Brumbies had been in the final the previous year and they were a great side.

"It's a game I remember specifically because with all that had been happening, we just got back to basics, and decided to do some hard running. I was playing No. 6 then and we started with moves where, if Bubsie took it up I'd run off him. It was a smash, crash sort of display.

"You remember funny little things about great games. Steve Larkin was playing fullback for them, and we put a chip through in the corner. There were three of us surrounding him and he just side-stepped the whole lot of us, 'bang, bang, bang,' and was gone.

"We thought we had him covered easily, and thought 'We'll get this bloke and put him over the sideline.' But I might as well have been twiddling my thumbs. It was a great effort by him."

The man playing first-five for the Brumbies, David Knox, made his mark on the night in a less impressive way. To the astonishment of everyone, Knox, known in the sport as a man whose physical presence would not threaten the proverbial sick kid on a pot, had a bit of a slap at Andrew Mehrtens. Mehrtens had apparently teased him about his advancing years.

"Knox is a very mouthy sort of guy," says Blackadder. "To be honest he's one of those guys everyone would like to smack, he's one of them. He was never short of a word, and the year before when we played the Brumbies, when we were losing he was giving us a lot of shit behind the posts.

"Well, the one thing I don't think you should do is to be mouthing off. When we played them in Timaru we just focused on shutting him up, and giving him a hard time. I think we based a lot of our play at running at him and trying to smash him.

"He wasn't famous for his robust defence, and then Mehrts delivered a little bit of payback verbally, so we certainly had no sympathy for David Knox as he was cowering behind the line."

At his home Blackadder has kept a plaque that was presented at the end of the 1998 Super 12. "It shows us at the bottom of the table after round five. It lists all the teams and the points, then it's got the Crusaders in the final and the win.

"It just shows you when you think you are down and out, you should never give up. Every game we had a team of guys where no one held one thing back.

"Beating the Brumbies was a huge win because suddenly you were back in contention again, and we went from bottom of the table up to the top four in four games. Once we got a roll on it was unstoppable. Every game we played was just open throttle.

"We were playing 'nothing to lose' football. We had a nice little team culture that year. As an example Reuben Thorne and Norm Maxwell were injured for most of the competition, but they got through every game.

"The reason they got through every game was that we had Graham Jack and Steve Lancaster at training, who basically did all the work for Reuben and Norm. You could train with a full pack with the other guys slotting in, doing all the grunt work.

"Then, when it came to the game, Reuben was getting an injection to play and Norm was injured as well, but they went out there and rewarded the guys who had worked for them with bloody good performances. That's what sort of a unit we were."

The Western Stormers were disposed of 27–25, and then, on a mild autumn Canterbury night the old foes the Highlanders came to town.

There was drama in the Crusaders just a couple of hours before the game started. Kevin Nepia bent down to tie a shoelace, and found he couldn't stand up straight. With Nepia's back out, Greg Feek, a young prop who had arrived from Taranaki, got his first start in Super 12.

He might have wondered what he'd struck in the first 40 minutes. The pace of the game was sensational. Mehrtens, always a leader in training time trials, confessed that he was "stuffed" at halftime, and the rest of the team didn't feel any better, with the Highlanders holding on to a 21–16 lead at the break.

Enter the inspirational Norm Berryman. Big Norm was a star for Northland in his teenage days, and, until he was injured, might have been an All Black at the 1995 World Cup. In a shadow All Black test team playing in Harlequin jerseys he ran in four tries against Waikato, a performance overshadowed in memory by the Achilles tendon injury suffered by Zinzan Brooke in the same game, which threatened the great No. 8's World Cup.

By the time Berryman came to Christchurch he was at a crossroads in his career. Everyone knew he was gifted, but was he too much of a daggy boy to ever hit the big time?

When he first arrived the Crusaders wondered about him too. "We were a bit worried there for a while," says Blackadder. "He wasn't off the rails or anything, but he certainly seemed very easy-going, more than we were used to. I know old Sloaney had a word to him. I don't know what he said but it sure worked, because suddenly he was a different guy."

Straight after halftime in the Highlanders game Berryman made a break from his goalline. With the capacity crowd in a state of near hysteria he bumped one, two, three, four, five, six opposing players off, until he was finally dragged down 30 metres from the Highlanders line. From the ruck Mayerhofler sprinted the rest of the way for a try under the bar.

"Norm was a star that year, he was a game breaker," says Blackadder. "Just to see him mucking around with a ball at training, it was almost magical, he was so skilled. He was instrumental in our success, and yet he was another draft player that wasn't wanted up north.

"We seemed to have a thing of picking up guys who would come down to Canterbury and play so well. I like to think that Canterbury gave those guys, like Norm, and Kevin Nepia, and Ron Cribb, a lot, but shit, they gave the team a lot back with their enthusiasm and their performances.

"One thing I did pick up was that things have changed since I first joined the team. You have to make everyone absolutely welcome. It doesn't matter if you play one, or 100 games, it doesn't matter how many games you play, what matters is what you do on every occasion that you play.

"You have to have that attitude, and all the guys going through that whole era would do anything to help anyone else. There were no put-on smiles, we meant a lot to each other, we were all good mates. I'd say we bloody loved each other.

"It pisses me off when people say, 'Oh these guys get paid, of course they should be playing hard.' Money never comes into the equation of how much you give in a game of rugby.

"You do it from in here." He punches his chest. "You do it for your mates, you do it for your province. You do it for your own personal pride, and for your family. I've never gone out there and thought, 'Oh well I'd better make this tackle because I get paid well.' That's not the reason you play."

The all-for-one attitude brought a last-minute fourth try, a 40–24 win, and a bonus point against the Highlanders. Tabai Matson dotted down, with 13 players flying into the drive from a lineout.

"We tried a few new things that year. We had a few moves on the scrum where the backs came in and we were trying a lot of different things.

"That year our lineout drive was absolutely superb, and instead of going for a lot of kicks at goal, we were probably the first team to start kicking for a lineout, and then trying to drive over."

In Napier the Crusaders faced the Hurricanes, a good team with a sensational fullback in Christian Cullen. By now the Crusaders were operating in a fully professional way, not just on the field, but off it too.

"The way we were doing our debrief, and our analysis," says Blackadder, "was something really new to us. But every game we went into we knew who to target, who they were going to throw the lineout ball to, what moves they were likely to use. All we had to do was get out there and play.

"Christian Cullen had a good game in Napier, but Bubs Mayerhofler caught him from behind after a 60 metre run, which just shows you the calibre of Bubs. Reuben Thorne ran someone down too, and this is our

100kg lock, who is running on an injured ankle."

The Crusaders got their bonus point in the dying minutes, won the game 39–17, and had the pleasure, for the first time, of a crowd of fans at Christchurch airport a few days later to farewell them as they headed to South Africa.

Blomfontein sticks in Blackadder's mind for more than the rugby. One was musical. "We had our own bus and the guy was playing *Eric Clapton Unplugged* everywhere we went on that tour." Another was rustic. "A few of our boys went out with local farmers, being flung around on the back of utes, out on the countryside where the Boer War was fought. We were shooting, and were allowed to bag a Springbok."

The Golden Cats were having a nightmare season in '98, with internal divisions, and disputes over coaching directions, but they were still loaded with Springboks. They had flashes of brilliance, but couldn't match a team as unified as the Crusaders, who won 34–25.

By now Aaron Flynn was looking totally at home in the halfback jersey he had inherited when Marshall was injured. "When he got his chance he was one of the players of the year really," says Blackadder. "He got better and better with every game, he just kept stepping up. He was outstanding, a guy who everyone had belief in.

"He'd been doing all the work in pre-season, so he just slotted straight in, and being the great man he is he just went for it."

If the game with the Brumbies was the sign the Crusaders were out of their early season doldrums, the last game of the round robin, against the Sharks in Durban, was the performance that suggested they could go all the way.

"That was one of the gutsiest games that I'm proud to say I was involved in, a sensational game," says Blackadder.

It was also a game that Wayne Smith regards as one of Blackadder's greatest hours as a leader. "To be champions as a team you have to buy into something bigger than yourself. That year we worked really hard at identifying what we were part of, and giving it real significance.

"Toddy bought into the whole thing. He loved the whole values thing, the attitude of winners, and being part of something special.

"He was the ideal captain for that perspective, because from what we set up in the campaign, he could draw very powerful imagery. It needed a captain who was absolutely sincere to make it work. We had these little swords made up, and we used to wear them on the lapels of our blazers.

"Against the Sharks in Durban, we desperately wanted to win and get home to play the semi in Christchurch. For his captain's talk all he said was 'Draw your swords boys, we've got a battle tomorrow.'"

The Sharks game came at what amounted to a crisis time for Stu Loe, probably Blackadder's best mate among the Canterbury players. "Stu is a top man, the salt of the earth, and a bloody good mate. When he was playing I always felt the team went better with him in it. You get attached to some guys and know they are reliable. No slur on the other guys, but when someone is a good mate and a honest grafter you lean towards them a little bit more I suppose. Stu's just a good honest bugger really, and every team needs one.

"He's good fun, he likes a beer and I suppose we like the same things. When the team's away we always go for a walk, and we keep out of the shopping malls.

"He's a straight-shooter. This is an example. Sometimes there's a meeting where coaches will prompt you to say something. They look at you, and you have to say, 'Yep, that's right.'

"There was all this stuff on the board and we are about to play Orange Free State in '97. Because I was the captain I knew Sloaney and Smithy were going to be prompting Stu to say something. It came time and Stu was obviously prompted. Peter Sloane sort of looked at him. Stu just said, 'Aw, it's all on the bloody board.'

"Stu was pretty much an elder statesman at the time when we played the Sharks in '98 and his career was basically on the line in that game. That's a lot of pressure on one man's shoulders. But he went out there and led from the front.

"The whole team played just unbelievable rugby before a capacity crowd who thought the Sharks were just going to tear us apart, they were super-confident. They really thought, 'It's all over for you guys.'

"But we had our support too. The one thing we really noticed, that we had never had before, was the unbelievable amount of faxes and support from home. The whole team room just had stacks and stacks of faxes, and there's no better feeling.

"It was a ferocious game, but our forward pack was so committed, all of them. God knows how Steve Surridge did it, but in that game they were attacking, and attacking and he managed to turn over the ball. When you remember big games you remember little pieces of commitment you see.

"Mehrts had a dream game, and Norm Berryman got two brilliant tries. From turnover ball we were dangerous, with real attacking ability. There was so much to play for, because if we had lost that game we would have had to stay another week and play them again.

"Mark Hammett was on fire, and smashed his way over for a try. I remember in the last ten minutes just trying to keep everyone from being sent off. It was hammer and tongs and with replacements coming on, they were pretty fired up. Things could have got out of hand very quickly."

The game was won 32–20, and the Crusaders were on their way to Christchurch for the semi-final.

Blackadder and Angus Gardiner were more than ready to go. They'd roomed together in Durban, and Gardiner remembers how Todd's son Ethan was having a birthday the following week.

"Todd said, 'I have to get home. How can I miss his birthday? Bugger it, I'm packing my bags.' So he went over in his room and packed his bag. This is the afternoon of the game. I thought, 'What the hell, if it's good enough for him, it'll do me. So I backed my bag too and said, 'I'm with you Toddy.' In the team talk he said, 'Bugger this, we are not staying here another week.' And we didn't."

The Crusaders began the semi-final at Lancaster Park looking like a team who would win by 50 points, ahead 20–0 after 15 minutes. Norm Berryman had scored twice, waving to his adoring fans on the bank as he jogged back from scoring, and then Daryl Gibson, racing into the line from fullback, added a third try.

But the Sharks, a team captained by Gary Teichmann, loaded with test players like fullback André Joubert, first-five Henry Honiball, lock Mark Andrews, and prop Ollie le Roux, were never going to lie down.

"Looking back on that game," says Blackadder, "we didn't have a lot of legs left. We'd been going so hard for so long, and when the Sharks came back and scored, Jesus we were nearly down and out. We were almost gone.

"I was that shagged I remember the ball being kicked back and I had to run back to get it and I was gone. I picked the ball up and I could hear a voice somewhere. I just passed the ball, I can't remember who I passed to.

"The Sharks had a six-point lead 12 minutes into the second half, but it was a charged atmosphere, and we were relentless in that game. We didn't have a lot of petrol in the tank but managed to hold on when it got really tough, and win 36–32. I think that showed the character of the team."

The final would be played at Eden Park, against a Blues team captained by Michael Jones, with Jonah Lomu and Joeli Vidiri on the wings, Carlos Spencer at first-five, Robin Brooke and Royce Willis locking, and Olo Brown and Craig Dowd propping.

"The Blues were definitely the favourites, and they were going for their three peat," says Blackadder. "They had a lot more All Blacks, and we were the sort of team where everyone thought we were playing above ourselves, and when is the run going to be over? Compared to the Blues we were a team of nobodies.

"I think they targeted our forwards that day. I mean, who wouldn't? We had a few elder statesmen up front, and some skinny locks, held together by some skinny loose forwards. You know, why wouldn't you target us?"

Coach Wayne Smith says reaching the final "was a bit like a dream for us. While we'd established that was what we wanted to achieve, I think deep down inside we didn't expect it to happen so quickly.

"I remember getting off the bus at the Centra hotel in Auckland, and walking in, and it was all decked out in red and black. They'd really gone to a lot of effort to make us feel at home.

"Then I said to Toddy, 'What are we going to do in the morning? We've got a long day, the boys are going to be hyped up, what'll we do?' He looked out the window, and said, 'Well, why don't we have our lineout drills out in that car park there?'

"I guess in Rangiora the car parks don't fill up too fast on a Saturday. We wander over there in the morning, and there's cars coming in and out all the time.

"Mehrts is hyper-active, running round and round in circles. Every time we did a move he'd run through 10 cars and round again and pass the ball back, and, it was like taking out a team of kids who were so bloody excited to be there, and nervous at the same time."

Blackadder says that from the 2.35 pm kickoff "the game went so fast, and the intensity was absolutely electric. They were all over us in that first half and Norman Berryman was off injured. In those games you haven't really got time to think, 'Oh hell, are we going to lose with him gone?' It's just a case of, 'Get the next guy on.' It's like that.

"It was 3–0 to us at halftime. We staggered our way into the shed, bloody lucky to be up three points. They were all over us, and we were tackling our hearts out, that good old Crusader defence. But we were just holding on by the skin of our teeth.

"I think people expected us to come out and dominate the game at the start, but Auckland actually came out with a hiss and a roar and surprised everyone.

"I remember saying at halftime, 'We're playing like shit, and we still won the first half.' It was just to try and have a little relief, although probably no one listened. The best thing was that we were in the game.

"The tide was against us, but we were still up 3–0. Then they scored the first points in the second half. Lee Stensness, a very elusive runner, scored a try, and then Adrian Cashmore drop-kicked a goal.

"If the Auckland boys look back they might agree that the pivotal moment in the game was when they had just scored their try. Auckland were attacking in the top left-hand corner and they put scrum after scrum in and we were absolutely just holding on with our lives.

"There was a time when it twisted and it was almost touch and go whether [referee] Paddy O'Brien would give a penalty try. But he didn't, he put it down for another scrum, and we ended up getting out of there and back down the field.

"That was a moment in the game where we needed to hold on against a far bigger forward pack, but it showed the sort of character and determination that had developed. It felt like, 'If we could hold them out here boys, we could do this.' They could have sealed the game there and then.

"As that game went on we got better and better. We were in the hunt and we could smell the kill. It was the first time for us in a final like that, and we had gone through such a hard run to it.

"Then the boys dug their toes in when it came to scrum time and we started to get the belief, the hits kept coming, we started getting in their faces, waves of attack started happening.

"Norm Maxwell got his try when the ball came loose from a tackle. He scooped it up, dummied a couple of times, scored, and 'bang' we were right in the game."

Adrian Cashmore and Andrew Mehrtens traded penalty goals, and, with only a minute of regulation time to go, Mehrtens is passed the ball some 20 metres from the Blues line.

He has no preconceived idea of what he will do, but through the white noise that is the roar of the local crowd he can just hear winger James Kerr yelling, "Chip it, chip it." He drops the ball to his right boot, and lobs it just short of the goal-line.

Mehrtens says he watched the ball "bobble around, and take a horrible bounce" for the two Auckland defenders, Cashmore and Junior Tonu'u. Coach Smith says it was "a very good option, very well executed by a player who had nailed every kick, and taken every right option for the previous eight games."

Kerr flies to the ball, dives, and scores the try. Back where he made his kick Mehrtens is stunned. "I couldn't really believe we'd scored from it." He regains his composure in time to kick a difficult conversion, and although the Blues try one last surge the game is over with the score 20–13 to the Crusaders, and the Super 12 title is won.

Blackadder now has to make a victory speech. He quickly has a word with Gardiner, a school teacher with a double degree. "Let me run this by you," says Blackadder. Gardiner listens. "Sounds bloody good to me, go for it."

Drenched in sweat Blackadder steps up on the temporary stand in the middle of Eden Park. He thanks the red and black supporters for a "tremendous year." He then has the presence of mind to thank, province by province, the six smaller unions that join with Canterbury in the Crusaders.

It's a remarkable example of grace under pressure, although many details of the game itself are largely a blur to him. "For me, playing in that final, it was just tackle after tackle, ruck after ruck, it was played with such ferocious intensity.

"Often the biggest games, you think, 'I should remember every minute of that game because it was so special' but they are just a blur because you are so flat tack."

The celebrations after the game were made extra special by the fact that manager Robbie Deans had arranged for all players, even squad members who weren't on the field or the bench for the game, to be joined by their partners in Auckland.

After the game Prime Minister Jenny Shipley came into the changing room. "She was wearing red and black," says Blackadder with a smile, "so you knew the country was in good hands. Over the years, when I missed out on the All Blacks she would always write me a nice letter, and she's come into our changing rooms a lot.

"It's actually meant a lot to our guys. She's a Crusaders' supporter, and she sent a fax in Canberra in 2000 to ring back after the final, and we rang back at about 4 am. I think one of her minders took the message.

"It's nice that she makes the effort. It's nice that she comes back to the shed, and puts up with everyone wanting to have a photo taken with her."

The Crusaders and their partners flew home on a chartered Mt Cook plane. "We had the plane all to ourselves," says Blackadder. "The celebrations were flowing, and the Canterbury union's chief executive, Steve Tew, was pretending he was a flight assistant, going up and down the aisles with a drink trolley.

"The captain on the flight asked me up the front, and we were talking through to Christchurch, and they told us there were a few people at the airport, but we had no idea what it would really be like.

"When we hit that airport, from where you come down the escalator, right out to the front, there was no room to go through. It was absolutely packed by red and black people, condensation was dripping off the ceiling.

"It wasn't out of control, but people were diving over other people to pat you. I'll never forget it as long as I live, going through that crowd.

"For some reason I can't remember Angus's partner, Maria, was hanging onto the back of my blazer, and we snaked our way out there like a conga line, shaking people's hands on the way. It was chaotic.

"It was a bit scary to see the kids there. Robbie Deans actually picked one up out of harm's way. I'd be surprised if some people didn't faint, but since that day it's never been quite like that again because they've got better at controlling the crowds.

"There were two buses for us, and the buses were rocking. Some people missed them. We couldn't work out who was on which bus, so we went into town to the casino. We had a meal for the team, and after all that had happened, the build-up, the game, the tension, a few beers, we all went home after the casino. We were exhausted.

"We'd all worked so hard for it, but never in our wildest dreams did we ever think we'd be picking up the Super 12 trophy at the end of it. We thought we had a good chance, and we had a bit of belief, but to beat the guys who'd won it twice, at Eden Park, after being in the team in 1996, when the wheels were off the truck and bouncing along beside you down the road, it was amazing.

"Our whole focus was to win the Holy Grail, which was our aim that year. Blood, sweat and glory was our motto, and I've never felt prouder in my life, because it was a really gutsy effort."

The ultimate salute for the Crusaders came the following Wednesday, when a parade through the centre of the city drew well over 100,000 people, a crowd estimated by council traffic officials to be larger than the number of people drawn in for the annual Christmas parade. In 1998 in Canterbury the Crusaders were officially bigger than Santa Claus.

What does Blackadder believe were the key elements behind the Crusaders' triumph in '98?

"You'd have to put a lot down to the great coaching we had. Smithy and Sloaney were inspirational.

"As a player, what you're looking for from your coach is consistency.

You're looking for what he thinks of you, what you need to improve on, how he's going to make you a better player. Some coaches seem to select players that suit their style, rather than getting players and refining what they do.

"With Smithy and Sloaney we'd had them the year before, and we'd been working on our skills levels. If you know Sloaney you'll know he wants the basics done properly, and, as far as the basics go, he really got the best out of us. He was a hard taskmaster, but a fair one. He just wanted you to do the best. He was a bloody good guy who kept empowering you as forwards.

"Smithy at times likes the technical side, and puts a lot of time into debrief and analysis, whereas Sloaney was a bit more of the old school, Alex Wyllie-type guy who likes to see the grunt work being done.

"When they took over in '97 they were looking to see what we had. We were pretty happy that we improved, and then in '98 it was the first time that we really had a video of who we were as Crusaders, and we had a set of values, a set of beliefs, and one focus, and that was our whole theme, the Holy Grail.

"We had a video that only the team saw. We saw it at the start of the campaign, and once again at the end. We had images, and we had all these things about who we wanted to be, and how we wanted to be seen.

"Our song was 'The Search for the Holy Grail'. We had a belief, and after we went through the wringer at the start we just grew extra arms and legs.

"We were a well-balanced side. I'd have to say that our team culture was what got us through that year. We were a team in every sense of the word. Not so much a team of stars, but a champion team, which shows what good coaches we had.

"There was a lot more emphasis on skills than we'd had before. A lot more analysis, a lot more work on the top six inches. Incorporated with that was hard work.

"They weren't into flogging you, but they wanted it done with skill, and they worked on things that we'd never really worked on before.

"We worked on spread defences, very tight defences, and after having us in '97 Smithy certainly took us to another level. We were thinking and doing things we'd never done before, and it was really, really refreshing.

"Smithy gave us a defensive pattern that we all bought into, and it worked. Unless you absolutely believe in the defensive pattern it will never work. He gave us a system of staying inside the man, going forward, marking from the outside in, so he can only go round you. If he cuts back inside you you've got the body angle right.

"But if you don't believe, or don't want to help your mate out, it won't work. You have to make your tackle, or I have to compromise my body position if your man cuts in. That year there was just wave after wave of red and black jerseys.

"A lot of people talk about team spirit and team culture, and I attribute that to what you see on the field. What is team spirit and culture, unless you're actually doing it on the field? You can have the best fun off the field, and everything is a box of roses, but where you really need it, and where it's all glued together, is on the field, every time.

"You can tell from body language how tight you are as a unit. If someone drops his head because someone else has made a mistake, that just tells me that things aren't as tight as they should be. Instead of dropping your head, you should be thinking of what can I do for the team to make it right for the next guy?

"We worked on all these things, how we tackle, how we contest the ball, every little technical detail, and put so much emphasis on it. That's when it comes down to team spirit, to whether the guys are lining up with you.

"I know the All Blacks [in 2000] tried to take it on, but it takes more than just a couple of weeks to get it ingrained.

"When the 2000 All Blacks were named, there weren't a lot of guys from Canterbury in there, and we were trying to talk about Canterbury defence. Well, what is it to the other guys? It might have worked for the Crusaders, but do they really believe in it enough to work for them? At the start it's always hard."

After the euphoria of the Super 12 win, defending the NPC title, with Mayerhofler, Mehrtens and Marshall away with the All Blacks for the first three games, was always going to be tough. So it proved.

"Our first game against Otago was bloody hard," says Blackadder.

"Tony Brown was outstanding for them, and losing 41–23 certainly wasn't the start we were after.

"Apart from that effort, which was pretty poor, we started to go pretty well. We had a big win against Southland [52–12], and played very well at Athletic Park, where Canterbury hadn't won for some years, winning 40–28.

"We had all our All Blacks back for the game with Auckland, and it was great to back it up from the previous year, beating them at home 50–17. Mehrts and Justin and Reuben Thorne just had blinders that day. They played superb rugby. Auckland were at full strength, as we were."

Northland, who came to Christchurch as such underdogs the TAB was paying $1.01 for a Canterbury win, were beaten 40–17, and then came a 34–6 defeat of Taranaki, in New Plymouth, described by Blackadder at the time as "our most complete 80 minutes of the season so far."

That wasn't the case when North Harbour came to Christchurch for the next round. "We were up by 28–0," says Blackadder, "and Harbour started coming back into the game. We just seemed to be running out of steam. In the end we scraped through 31–29."

Coach Deans hoped that the near thing would be a warning for the team as they headed north for a Ranfurly Shield challenge against Waikato, which, if Canterbury won, would also give them a home NPC semi-final.

"We had a better side in Hamilton in '98 than we had in '94 when you look back at it," says Blackadder. "But I think in the whole context of the year, we were just starting to show the signs of being absolutely knackered.

"We fell into the trap a little bit of getting away from our basics. In the first scrum against Waikato I was trying to do some move, and their halfback, Rhys Duggan, whacked it down, and shot away and scored in the corner. It was like, 'Welcome to Hamilton boys. Did you guys want to take the shield away from us?' It was hard from the start.

"I've never really seen a crowd like the people that day in Hamilton, they were so volatile. Mind you, they had plenty to cheer about. Aaron Hopa was playing No. 8 for them, and he had an outstanding game.

"There was a real crucial time when we had about eight scrums right on their line. We had scrum after scrum and I swear that I got over the line, but [referee] Paddy O'Brien didn't see it.

"It didn't really matter though, because Waikato played out of their skins, and they were a far better side on the day, winning 29–23. They treasured the Ranfurly Shield. I thought our preparation was good, and you play to win, but they were just unstoppable. They were playing with their lives really, and they deserved to keep the shield."

The last round-robin game, against Counties Manukau, was most notable for a sensational performance by Joeli Vidiri.

"He virtually beat us on his own, scoring four tries," says Blackadder. "We were 21 points up in the first quarter, and they clawed their way back to beat us. We had a good side, full of All Blacks, with a lot of experience. But it was like flogging a horse. You just can't keep on galloping, and basically we just ran out of legs.

"Then we had to get back to Hamilton to play the semi-final, and although we were right in it at halftime the wheels then fell off, and we lost 32–13.

"One of the most disappointing things was that it wasn't nice to leave a guy like Stu Loe, who had given so much to Canterbury, and equalled the record set by Murray Davie of playing 123 games at prop for Canterbury. We would have liked to give him a good send-off. But we were just buggered, with no more legs.

"It's a really fine line today between how coaches and trainers train you, and how you feel physically. There has to be a really fine line and balance there.

"A horse doesn't bolt every time you want it to, and it's the same with players. We'd all been through the wringer that year, and a coach is never going to say, 'Gee, you guys are tired, we'll have to balance it a bit.'

"You want more out of yourself, the guys around you want to win, and you play to win, but in '98 the NPC was a classic example for us of a team being right in it, but then not being able to keep the foot down. So we were put away by some determined, committed teams.

"It was an enjoyable year though, it really was."

9. I knew I was gone

"You can say what you like,
but you give someone a fair go."

Why was this man smiling? Todd Blackadder was walking off Eden Park after a humiliating subbing. He'd been replaced just nine minutes into the second half of the first test he'd ever started in.

He was smiling to hide his rage. He was furious, "but I was never going to give them the satisfaction of seeing how upset I was. At halftime I knew I was gone. I was just totally pissed off, but I remember walking off and smiling at Bubsy Mayerhofler on the sideline."

That's not, of course, how it's supposed to be. Your first test start is described by most All Blacks in almost mythical terms. Players say they sneaked their jersey on in their hotel room to see how it looked. Others were almost too nervous to warm up in case they injured themselves before the game. In a famous quote Justin Marshall said he stared at his jersey to see if he was "man enough to put it on."

Blackadder's situation was very different in 1998. His brother Scott, who travelled with their mother, their grandmother, and Todd's wife,

Priscilla, to Auckland for the game had wished Todd good luck the day before the game. Todd replied, "It's a bloody waste of time."

To understand his attitude let's look at the background to that game against England.

Blackadder had just finished Super 12 as a triumphant captain of the Crusaders, and a dynamic presence on the side of the scrum. His winning captain's speech at Eden Park marked him out as a man who could handle not only the physical side but the media attention too. As Keith Quinn would comment at the time, "Blackadder doesn't need any public relations training because he always says the right thing."

On top of his Super 12 form he played well for a shadow All Blacks team, playing as the Barbarians when they thumped a New Zealand A side 55–4 at Albany. He could hardly be left out of the squad, although Blackadder remembers that after the game coach John Hart mentioned almost every player but left him out. It would certainly prove to be an omen.

At the time, the All Blacks were in a state of flux. In 1996 new coach Hart had inherited a captain in Sean Fitzpatrick, who then led the team to the first-ever series win in South Africa by the All Blacks.

But by 1997 Fitzpatrick as a player was living on borrowed time. A chronic knee injury meant he was largely a spectator on the end-of-year tour of Britain, and Justin Marshall took over the role for tests with Ireland, Wales, and England.

With Fitzpatrick gone by the start of 1998 the selection of a permanent captain was crucial. Marshall was still in the team, but happy, he would state publicly, to no longer be captain.

Although Blackadder had captained the All Blacks midweek team in Britain in '97 he had never played a test, and Hart turned to test flanker Taine Randell, who he moved to No. 8 to captain the side.

The path for Blackadder in the All Blacks looked entirely stalled. Josh Kronfeld was in the No. 7 jersey, considered the best in the position, not just in New Zealand, but in the world. At No. 8 was the new captain, and in the No. 6 jersey was Michael Jones.

"We went down to Queenstown to prepare for the England tour," says Blackadder. "I was playing in the No. 6 jersey for the Crusaders, and

Michael Jones had gone to number 6 in the All Blacks, so it was going to be a hard task to get past him.

"Michael Jones is Michael Jones isn't he, one of the greatest flankers ever in the game to this very day. When you've got Josh on the other side and Taine as number 8, it was a pretty hard trio to break into."

The team for the first test, as he expected, saw Blackadder in the reserves for the All Blacks.

While there were players in the England team like Jonny Wilkinson, Danny Grewcock and Matt Perry, who would later be big names in England and Lions sides, at the time there was universal derision about the squad the English had brought to New Zealand. More than a dozen of their top-line players were unavailable for the tour, most under orders from the clubs they had contracts with to stay home and freshen up for the next northern season.

The most excitement in the lead-up to the Dunedin test was the suggestion that England had sent a spy with a video camera to check out the All Blacks training in Queenstown.

Being on the bench after playing every game in Super 12 was a new experience for Blackadder.

"No matter what you say you don't always feel that close to the game as a starting player. Even to this very day as a reserve, while they all say it's the same as starting, you never really feel the same.

"Maybe if you have always been coming into the game off the bench, and you're more used to it, then it may be easier, but certainly in Dunedin, when Michael Jones went down, the old heart was pumping the adrenalin through the body.

"It was just great to run on in my first test. It went pretty fast and I think I made a few mistakes. But generally it was just good to get the first one under the belt."

Something very special was that midfielder Mark Mayerhofler was playing his first test in the All Blacks. "It was great to share that moment with Bubs. We'd been through the wringers and everything together and he felt like a brother to me, old Bubs."

The test was won, 64–22. "The team for the next test in Auckland was named in Dunedin before we departed and the impression I got from the coaches, and through the media, was they weren't very happy with the first test even though we won by so much."

There was a weird aftermath to the Carisbrook test. It was alleged that at a Dunedin pub late that night All Black reserve hooker Norm Hewitt and England hooker Richard Cockerill had a full-blown fist fight.

To this day Blackadder is bemused by the whole thing. He was there and swears that "Norm and the guy Cockerill were just laughing and joking. There was no pushing or shoving and all that sort of stuff. I don't know where all that came from. They seemed to get on all right to me.

"There was a big to-do over that. It was in the papers and on television. For some reason it was as if the All Black management were accusing Norm Hewitt of something he didn't do, and then the media blew it all out of proportion. Everyone was poking their nose in.

"There was no altercation whatsoever." Eventually the story would be revealed as a very tall tale that grew as it was repeated.

Blackadder had happier things to think about, as he looked to Auckland. "I was certainly delighted to be named in my first test and I was really looking forward to it. As a reserve when you're called into the test team, you look forward to running through everything as a team, to get to know the moves."

But right from when the team assembled in Auckland it was obvious the Eden Park test wasn't going to be an occasion to remember for Blackadder.

"Basically I knew on the Tuesday I was going to get arseholed. Straight into the first team run and after the first ten minutes I was pulled out. Isitola Maka came on, and there was a reshuffle in the loose forwards.

"In the first week of being named in the test team, you need to know all the moves, and you have to get to know the guys around you. So when you're pulled straight away, you get the feeling things aren't too bright.

"I wasn't too sure who was doing it or what they had in mind, but I got the impression straight away that it wasn't a good sign for me."

If the treatment was upsetting, it was not, says Blackadder, because there was any truth in the rumours of a major personality clash between himself and coach Hart.

They're certainly from very different backgrounds. Hart, born and bred in Auckland, is a product of the corporate world, climbing through the ranks at Fletchers head office in Auckland. Blackadder is almost the epitome of the Kiwi good keen man, for whom the outdoors is a natural environment.

But while they may have had different ideas about rugby, there has never been a major personal disagreement, much less a nose-to-nose shouting match.

"I first had John Hart in the New Zealand Colts in 1991, and I thought he was absolutely inspirational for the Colts. We had an unbeaten tour, and I thought he was absolutely great.

"Since then we've always got on quite well really," says Blackadder. "I know people always look for negative things. When I was in his touring All Black teams it was always the mid-week side of it and I never really had a chance at a test team, but that was his call, because he was the coach.

"Look, as far as a one-on-one relationship goes, it was fine, there was no bitterness. Well, there didn't seem to be anyway.

"I'm not very sure how he looked on me as a player. I do know that he must have looked at me through those years as not being up to test standard because otherwise he might have given me a chance. But during those years he never really did give me a chance."

As well as being more of an observer than he wanted to be at training, there was, in Blackadder's mind, another contentious issue in the test build-up.

"This was the lead-up to the Sean Fitzpatrick game where we had a small No. 2 on the sleeves of our jerseys, that was basically a farewell to Sean.

"Even in the whole build-up to the game it was all about Sean Fitzpatrick. I have no animosity against him, he's been a fine All Black but, as I was sitting there listening to John Hart, as he talked about the game, and the reasons why we were honouring Sean, and the whole motivation towards the game, I couldn't help thinking: 'What's wrong with us, the current team?'

"I wouldn't like to have a game dedicated to me, because I've had my chance to play, and it's not about one person, it's never about one person.

"It's not Sean's fault they dedicated a game to him, but I think in rugby you have your chance, and then it's time to move on.

"I couldn't help thinking in the All Blacks when Harty was delivering his speech before the game, 'Hell, what's wrong with us? Why don't we want to go out there and win for us as a team, and for New Zealand?' It doesn't matter whether you are a provincial player or an All Black, you still do it for your mates and your team."

Wayne Smith had been brought into the All Blacks as the back specialist coach, and says he can remember saying to Blackadder in Auckland, "You're in the All Blacks now, and it should be more special than red and black. If that means taking a leadership role, which this team needs, you've got to take it.

"I felt that he didn't want to be seen to be taking the leadership role, although he might have felt that he was pushing in as a new boy.

"I felt that he had a lot more to offer because of his leadership qualities, the way people all round the country reacted to him, they all liked playing with Toddy.

"He didn't get a fair go, but I also felt he never really pushed hard enough to become an integral part of it. He should have been there, and he should have been there in 1999. But he didn't do enough in terms of leadership of being there. He was reticent in coming forward.

"What I was saying, make yourself feel included, although that is a hard thing to do. Players get a feeling for, they seem to know their place in the scheme of things, whether they feel comfortable, or part of it.

"Whether they can buy in to the vision or the goals which you have to do if you are really going to contribute. He might have felt that wasn't there."

Josh Kronfeld might help explain why Blackadder wasn't in a position to impose himself on the All Blacks. In his book *On the Loose*, Kronfeld notes that he went through a phase with Hart in 1997 when "my self-esteem was plummeting, and so was my faith in myself as a rugby player."

What happened to Blackadder in Auckland, wrote Kronfeld, was that "Toddy was getting some of the same treatment I'd got from Harty. I felt sorry for Toddy, and saw him as being made to carry the can. No one gives more for the cause of a team."

During the week in Auckland there was plenty of reason for Blackadder to feel he wasn't long for the All Blacks. "I was only spoken to once or twice all week about the game and I just picked up those little vibes and, as it proved, I got the first half, and that was it really.

"When I look back at that game, while things didn't go my way I didn't think I did too badly.

"The game itself was very loose. Having been a captain I look for qualities in our teams, of hard work, and it certainly wasn't done that day. And if there is a job to be done I'll get in there and do it, that's what I am.

"But I don't blame any of the players for being dropped. It wasn't their fault I wasn't selected."

If there was any doubt over what his future held under Hart it was soon dispelled. "I knew in the changing room after the game that I was gone. Harty walked into the changing room and shook some people's hands, and not others. He didn't shake my hand. So I knew that was it for me."

What disappoints Blackadder still is that he was subbed so early in the game. "It was hard work to be in my very first test and to do that to someone, I thought was pretty shitty. I still do. To have all my family up there too, Priscilla, my Mum, Nana, and brother up there I felt like I'd been short-changed a bit in what should have been a proud moment.

"You can say what you like, but you give someone a fair go, and to walk off there just after halftime wasn't nice. I felt bloody let down."

His mother recalls that "I was sick, and Scott was devastated. I think that was the worst Todd's ever been hurt in his entire life."

After the game Todd asked Scott, "What were the seats like?" Scott replied, "Priscilla and I had these big poles right in front of us, right in the corner of the stand." Todd said, "Yeah, that bloody figures."

After the test, won 40–10 by the All Blacks, Blackadder was dropped for the rest of the season.

There were attempts to suggest he'd been dropped because of shin splints. That wasn't really the case.

"I did have shin splints that were really bad. I had them right through Super 12, and there were times during Super 12 when I couldn't run properly.

"If you've ever had chronic shin splints, it's not pretty. I've got scans at home where it shows small fractures up and down my shins. I was getting cortisone needles right up and down my shins so I could run.

"I was rung up on the Sunday night and told I wasn't in the team any more, because of a lack of form, which was pretty disappointing, but you've got to accept those decisions.

"Then they wanted me to captain New Zealand A to Samoa. I needed a chance to get my legs right, instead of pounding them away on the hard grounds in Samoa. So I pulled out of that.

"The next day it was announced that I was out because of injury, which was technically right, but I was dropped first. It was only afterwards that the shin splints were mentioned."

As for Blackadder in the Hart era, the two England tests in 1998 were really the end of the trail.

"I didn't have any real contact with the selectors from that time forward. I was called on in 1999 to captain New Zealand A, who were going to play the All Blacks. We'd gathered in Christchurch, and I was just sitting down with the New Zealand A coach, Ross Cooper, going over a bit of stuff for the week, working out when we'd get out of the hotel, to go out for a feed.

"I think it was the day before the All Blacks came to Christchurch that I found I had to leave the New Zealand A camp.

"Right through to the end of the Crusaders' Super 12 campaign, including the final against Otago, Norm Maxwell was crook, he was basically run down. So with him being out of the All Blacks I came in to cover him, for that one game.

"I thought we'd had a pretty good side in New Zealand A, and as it turned out they played well against the All Blacks. When I was warming up on the sideline the crowd was going mad. It was almost embarrassing.

"But I felt sort of proud too, in a wee way, without being egotistical. Here I was at home, and the crowd were getting in behind me.

"By the time I got on, there was about 15 minutes to go. I would have liked to have had a bit more of a chance. That was me really. They thanked me for being in the team, and I went back to New Zealand A.

"In all fairness to him, in 1996 Harty had a champion team, and in

1997 things were much the same. In 1998 things started going wrong, and it was the first time he'd been under pressure.

"It came as no surprise that he didn't pick me. I don't think he'd ever been very fond of me. The things he used to say through the media, in a roundabout way, there was never any real praise for me, not that I expected him to praise me.

"I don't think I ever figured too much in the equation and when you look back through those years they were some of my best years in rugby."

When Blackadder returned to the All Blacks in 2000 as the captain he got a letter from John Hart, wondering if Blackadder wanted to meet him to sort out some issues in the media. "It was nice of him to write, and I did reply to thank him, but other than that I just let sleeping dogs lie."

10. Locked in

"I've got this idea Toddy"

Steve Hansen and Todd Blackadder are driving from Christchurch to Ashburton on an October Saturday afternoon in 1998. Hansen's at the wheel, and they're on their way to wave the flag for sponsors Air New Zealand at the NPC third division final. It's an easy drive across the plains, and there's a relaxed mood in the car too. They've known each other for years, since the days when "Shag" Hansen was captaining Canterbury B, and Blackadder, then a tall, skinny kid from the Belfast club arrived at team training.

Hansen, who has taken over Peter Sloane's job as Crusaders forward coach, broaches the topic he's really in the car for. "I've got this idea Toddy."

Blackadder's ears prick up. "What would that be Shag?"

Hansen plunges straight in.

"Look, I think we can get your All Black jersey back, and actually get someone else an All Black jersey. If you swap positions and go to lock, and we put Reuben to No. 6, we can get you an All Black jersey and get Reuben one too."

Hansen will never forget the response.

"Well, if you think Reuben can be an All Black at No. 6, then I'll change."

To this day Hansen finds it amazing. "Todd was showing the qualities that make him special. He was thinking about someone else, and not himself. We talked a bit more, and obviously he was disappointed with the way he had been treated in the All Blacks, although he never complained too much.

"The key thing that we talked about was that he could play like an All Black, even though he wasn't picked. He took that on board, and hopped into lock, and he's been a huge success."

Blackadder says he was "a little apprehensive about the change. I'd been involved so much with that No. 6 jersey, and it meant such a lot to me. I'd been an All Black and played NPC as No. 6 and, of course, won with the Crusaders as No. 6. I felt it was my natural position, and still do in a lot of ways.

"It certainly wasn't easy, to give your jersey up that means so much to you to someone else. What made it easier for me was Reuben at that time was playing lock, and so I knew the guy I'd be swapping with.

"It would have been a lot harder if I hadn't respected him so much. It's not an easy thing to do. Then I found that dealing with the captaincy was a little bit different. It's far easier to call the shots from the side of the scrum than it is from lock. The last picture you see as a flanker is there in front of you, and that can have a lot to do with how you make your calls.

"I had to put a lot more faith in the guys around me." Blackadder laughs. "That wasn't easy either, but it certainly worked for us anyway."

If handing over his prized jersey was a wrench Blackadder could see logic in the move. "I was a lot bigger than Reuben and perhaps they saw him as an upcoming player naturally suited to No. 6. When you look back on it now it was probably a wise move. He's now a No. 6 All Black."

Hansen says, "I have no doubt that the work Toddy's put in at lock has shortened his rugby career. He's not a big tall man, and he gives 100 per cent, in every scrum he gives 100 per cent. The boys will tell you he's a good scrummager, and round the paddock he's always one of the top tacklers. To ask him to give so much it's probably knocked his body round a lot."

There were other changes in the tight five. To the surprise of many, Canterbury had introduced two new props for the last game of the 1998 NPC season, Greg Somerville and Dave Hewett.

"When they said Greg was coming into the side to play Waikato, I'd never heard of him. We kept everything under wraps, we didn't want a lot of extra external pressure going on them.

"Now I've got to know him, and he's a top man. A great thing about him is that he has a very distinctive laugh, and you hear it a lot, because he's always joking.

"Yoda's one of those modern day props. He's athletic, and a good runner with the ball, but he does the hard work too, and he's a great scrummager. Being so young he has a long way to go in the game.

"Tiger Hewett is a very interesting guy. He had a great job as a financial adviser, and really rugby was just a pastime. He got better and better in the game, and I know it was a toss-up whether to take what might have been the easy option of sticking with his career.

"Instead he chose the cut-throat life of rugby and he's a great prop with enormous potential. He started his provincial career at 27, but he's made the New Zealand A side, and has the talent to be an All Black. I don't think age is a barrier to performance, especially in a prop."

The 1999 Crusaders, with their captain now a lock, went to an Australian Institute of Sport training camp at Thredbo, in the Blue Mountains, outside Sydney.

"It was a great camp. We were in mini groups getting to top of mountains, doings thing out of our comfort zone, like abseiling, climbing up rocks, that sort of stuff.

"It was a ski lodge, not over the top, but nice. While we were there the Australian swimmers were too. The camp had a field, a gym and a pool and it was a little bit at altitude, so in general it was excellent. We had the time to set values and foundations, and work out our expectations for behaviour."

As had almost become a tradition for the Crusaders there was a pre-season loss to the Waratahs in Sydney, which, to be fair, was followed by a victory over Queensland.

Then it was the real thing. Blackadder says he "had never been so fit at the start of a season because all the boys who weren't All Blacks at the end of '98 had a good month to six weeks off. By the time we got to Super 12 we were flying."

The rest of the country, especially the odds-makers at the TAB, had obviously thought winning the title in '98 had been a stroke of luck for the Crusaders, who started the season at $9 for a win, rated third among the New Zealand teams.

The odds shortened quickly after a 48–3 hiding dished out to the Chiefs at the newly named Jade Stadium in Christchurch. Playing lock seemed to agree with Blackadder, who, as coach Smith was quick to point out after the game, had "a stormer."

Blackadder says that "everyone put their hand up and performed. I remember getting [Chiefs fullback] Todd Miller in the headlights of my truck at one stage. I gave him a bit of a good stomp-over. It was my first big game at lock too, so the team going so well was a good way to start."

There was a big crowd, and big expectations, for a repeat of the previous year's final, when the Crusaders and the Blues played a historic match, the first ever under lights at Eden Park.

Sadly the game was a fizzer. Referee Paul Honiss blew for 30 penalties, and although the Crusaders emerged with a 22–16 win, the match was most notable for collapsed scrums, and a referee who didn't care to play the advantage law.

The next week's game, playing the Hurricanes in Christchurch, was a bitter-sweet experience for Blackadder. His good mate Stu Loe was now in the Hurricanes.

"It felt funny playing against Stu, we'd played over a hundred games together. I missed the big bugger, and then I found myself playing him at Jade Stadium.

"I was pleased that they didn't beat us and, in a way, I was pleased for him that it was a draw, 18–all, because there was no shame for anybody. I think we were pretty lucky to get away with a draw as they certainly were coming back."

Evidence that playing lock didn't limit how much Blackadder was able to fling himself around the field came when he made two late try-saving tackles on Tana Umaga.

The quirkiest story from the game involved dread-locked first-five Mal Arnold, a West Coaster who was drafted out of Canterbury to the Hurricanes. When he lined up a conversion of a try by Christian Cullen that would tie up the game, Arnold said he "just had to kick it. Cully had bet me a Big Mac combo that I couldn't get it. I couldn't pass up an opportunity like that."

It wasn't so much fun when the Queensland Reds came to town a week later.

"They cleaned us up," says Blackadder. "We'd been getting away with things we shouldn't have been. They put their big forwards out in the backline and smashed us with quick switches of play. We learnt some valuable lessons." The Reds won 36–23.

Things perked up against the Brumbies in Canberra. "It was the first game we won in Australia," says Blackadder. "It was no easy feat to win there, but we'd become a good touring team."

As well as the 28–21 win, there was the sort of incident happy teams love, for the material it gave for internal mickey-taking. Prop Greg Feek raked the head of a trapped player in the ruck, and the man needed stitches. Where the humour, for everyone else in the team, came from was that the gashed victim was Feek's flatmate, Daryl Lilley.

By now there was some pressure in New Zealand for Blackadder to become All Black captain. Taine Randell had lived through the terrible losing streak of five test matches in 1998, and team-mates, and former All Black captains like Wayne Shelford and Colin Meads, were speaking up for Blackadder.

Dissenters suggested that Blackadder might be too unsophisticated to deal with the new breed of urbanites in the test team. Steve Surridge had three years of post-graduate work at Cambridge University behind him, a lot of that time spent studying management skills.

"The biggest thing that emerged about a leader," said Surridge in '99, "is that he must be honest and upfront with you. You won't find anyone more honest than Todd. He understands people.

"It's a myth that he couldn't work with Aucklanders. He thinks deeply about things, and can read people. Someone like Mehrts is pretty urbanised, and Todd gets on really well with him. Todd thinks about things a lot more than people give him credit for. He has a great depth of knowledge, but he keeps his words to a minimum, and he doesn't use them until it's necessary. They have more impact because there aren't too many of them."

If pre-season losses were almost a tradition for the Crusaders, so too, it seemed, was a mid-competition slump.

First it was a 23–6 loss to the Highlanders at Carisbrook. "We played quite well everywhere but on the scoreboard that night," says Blackadder. "Tony Brown kicked a lot of goals and they found holes in our backline defence."

From that loss the team flew to Cape Town, to play the Stormers, for another loss, 28–19. "It felt like we had lead weights in our legs. The Stormers really gave it to us during that game," says Blackadder. "I know I felt like I was a Thunderbird puppet. I was running around but my legs had gone, everything had gone.

"We had started the competition so well, but every year you go through a bit of a low before you peak. We do so much conditioning, and work on our fitness in summer that when we start a campaign we begin really well, then peter off, and, because we have done the hard work, we then hope we can come back. Against the Stormers we were going through a bit of a lull."

Blackadder enjoys touring in South Africa, where "we have a lot of laughs," and when they moved to Pretoria to play the Northern Bulls, one incident sticks in his memory.

"We have this thing called Crusader of the Day. We have a terrible suit, like a white robe with a big red collar, and whenever someone was a bit silly or said something silly they had to wear it.

"We went out to this restaurant that had live animals on show. A cheetah was standing on a table with two chains on it so that it couldn't gouge us. It was a truly magnificent animal, and we were up patting it. The lady in the restaurant was telling us about it, that it was a bit like a cat. If you ran it would chase you.

"Fats So'oalo was wearing the Crusader suit and they got the cheetah down and were walking it back to its cage. The Crusader suit started flapping in the wind, and the cheetah pounced on Fats' back and started clawing at him.

"The whole place got cleaned out, everyone there was just running for their lives, before they got it under control.

"In the game the Bulls fullback, Marius Goosen was going for a try and Fats streaked over and cut him down right in the corner. I had him on after the game that the cheetah was chasing him across the field and he was running for his life. After that, before every game I'd just walk past, scratch his back, and say 'cheetah.'"

By the time of the Bulls game the Crusaders had dropped to eighth on the table. Another loss and there wouldn't have been time to get back into the top four.

"In that game against the Bulls, I wouldn't say we were playing badly, but it was hard work up there at altitude. It feels like you can't sprint, you can only go three-quarters everywhere you go, you just feel flat."

With seconds, rather than minutes, to go, Andrew Mehrtens kicked a famous winning 35m dropped goal, which he celebrated by giving a vigorous middle-finger salute to the crowd with both hands.

The lead-up to the dropped goal was probably as noteworthy as the aftermath. Justin Marshall remembers holding the ball to feed a scrum being set straight in front of the Bulls' posts.

"We were all tired, because it was incredibly hot," recalls Marshall. "I sort of looked to Toddy for a bit of advice. I can picture it now. I turned to our leader of men, the sweat fair hosing off him. His jersey's hanging out, he's sucking in air, and he says to me, 'Just bloody do something!' Then he buries his head in the scrum. Classic."

Blackadder laughs at the memory. "It was certainly a great piece of captaincy. Marshy was going to Mehrts '50.' That's our code for a dropped goal and Mehrts was going, 'No, no, throw it to Leon.'

"I was nicely composed as captain, and instead of saying, 'Why don't we set up here chaps, and then we'll go for the dropkick,' it was just 'bloody do something, I don't care what it is.' As it turned out he threw it back, and Mehrts slotted the goal."

Mehrtens says that he almost blew the kick anyway. "I thought they would all expect the drop kick, so I wanted Ron Cribb to run from No. 8. They'd follow him, and then we'd sweep blind, and catch them on the hop. In the end Justin didn't hear me, and I started moving to where I shouldn't have been. I had to go back to grab the ball. It turned out to be the best thing we could have done."

In what he later called something "completely out of character", Mehrtens then flipped the bird at the vocal Pretoria crowd. Straight after the game he grabbed coach Smith and said, "Can I come to the press conference?" At that stage Smith, who had seen the goal but missed the gestures, didn't know what he was talking about.

Mehrtens apologised at the conference, and Bulls captain Reuben Kruger generously said he might have done the same thing in the circumstances, but it took a meeting for Mehrtens with the New Zealand union in Wellington, and more public apologies, to set it all to rest.

Of more pressing interest to the Crusaders was to get on a roll to the semi-finals. Their next game, on a superb Nelson day, didn't hold much promise at the start.

"Before the Nelson game things had been going a bit scratchy," says Blackadder. "It was a straight-up team talk, I can tell you. I think going to Nelson, in the times that we've gone to our regions, after a tough tour, has always been so timely.

"To walk through the main street, and to see the red and black jerseys along the walls, and the people wearing their red and black, you feel like you owe them something.

"Smithy always said that every time you sign an autograph, you're signing a contract with that person, and in a small town, it does feel like that."

The Crusaders needed crowd support in the first 30 minutes of the game, as the Cats raced to a 31–6 lead. "I don't believe any team in the world could have kept that Cats team out in the first half.

"It was amazing. I was standing under the posts after one of their tries,

Jenny Shipley, then Prime Minister, considers Todd's offer to take the role of Minister of Sport in her new Cabinet.

Choice. Slade McFarland and Norm Berryman flank Todd on the 2000 Super 12 victory parade.

Photosport

A gentle suggestion to the referee that his decision might need more consideration —
Jade Stadium, against South Africa, 2000.

Photosport

"I bet the bugger kicks this." Todd considers John Eales — Wellington, 2000.

The ball is secured, and so was the win against South Africa at Jade Stadium, 2000.

"It's always good to be home." Todd and Priscilla with daughter Shinae and son Ethan.

and the crowd was so deathly quiet. It was surely a time for someone to yell out, 'Come on you useless bastards,' but there wasn't a word, just stunned silence."

Seven minutes from halftime the comeback finally started. "We'd been working on this lineout move, where we ran down the back, and it went to Justin, and he put a guy in the hole. We thought we'd try it, and Greg Feek scored a try which started to turn the game.'

The Crusaders then caught fire. By halftime it was 31–23 to the Cats. And by the end of a stunning match the score was 58–38, and the Crusaders were in fourth place on the table.

"That turned the season," says Blackadder. "It was an absolutely gutsy performance. There was some great football. You saw [reserve halfback] Oggie Flynn come on and play on the wing, and he was one off the ruck for a try to Leon MacDonald. I felt really proud after that game."

It took tremendous composure to keep the winning streak going. The Sharks, always a big Super 12 threat, fired to a 22–6 halftime lead at Jade Stadium.

The Crusaders rallied, and came back to win, 34–29. Straight after the game Smith said, "The guys have got belief in themselves. At the break everyone knew they could still do it."

Looking back now, Blackadder agrees. "We've always done very well at focusing at halftime. We get into the shed, and there's not a lot of talking or finger pointing. We just focus on how we're going to do it.

"The coaches and I get together, and we talk about the things that we think can win us the next half. Then we talk about those things with the team.

"The whole team sits down, and we all change our jerseys at halftime. Then we reinforce what needs to be done to each other. It's pretty casual, there's no getting up, saying your piece, and then sitting down. Anyone can say anything. We've always had an environment, right through the team, whether you've had one game or one hundred, your contribution is just as important.

"It's important that everyone speaks up, at times. You don't have to agree with everything that's said, but at least you know what people are thinking.

"It's the same before a game, everyone can say whatever they like. We've had old Marshy so psyched up at one stage he was going to run out with Mehrts' jersey. He was laying the law down, grabbed the jersey off the hook, and was getting ready to run out with No. 10 on. That's what it's all about.

"With the Crusaders we've never really gone in with a game plan set in concrete. We've always looked at what we wanted to do ourselves, and had several plans that we could go to. We knew that some teams had certain moves, but they might change during a game.

"We had such a lot of experience, and had been together for so long, that we could change a game plan on the field with just a couple of words."

Facing the Waratahs in Sydney, in the last of the round-robin games, the Crusaders needed one bonus point to make the last four. They did better than that, winning 38–22, and scoring four tries for a bonus point.

In the process there was a Blackadder moment many of his players still remember. South African referee André Watson had called Blackadder in to tell him that he wanted his team to stop holding the Waratah players down on tackles.

"Speak to your players," barked Watson, "or someone will be binned."

Blackadder walked to his team. He hauled out his mouthguard, and smashed his fist into his open hand to emphasise his point. With his back to Watson he said not a word about professional fouls.

"They don't bloody score," he growled. "Keep the defence up."

Blackadder says now that "I couldn't imagine a captain coming back and telling his players to stop professional fouls. I have said at times, 'Just cut all the penalties out.'

"The first year at Bloemfontein I was running around telling our guys to not even think about giving a penalty away, because I felt the referee was looking for ways to win it for them. There are occasions like that.

"But in Sydney it called for a bit of reinforcement on the defence. After the win [38–22] it meant we were in fourth place, and depending on the results we could have had to play the Stormers in South Africa."

Against the odds the Highlanders lost to the Hurricanes, and the Stormers lost to the Cats, so the Crusaders would face the Reds in Brisbane in one semi-final, rather than, as expected, the Stormers in Cape Town.

Several of the Crusaders, including Blackadder, were out celebrating the win over the Waratahs at a few Sydney bars. "God knows how, but Robbie [Deans] and the Aussie liaison officer, Stu, found us," says Blackadder. "We got back together with Smithy, and we had to decide whether we'd stay in Australia, or did we go home? When we put it to the team, we decided that we'd go to Manly.

"It was one of the best things we'd ever done and I believe it set up the winning run. If we'd gone home we would have gone to our own environment, come back, trained, and had a lot more travelling at the end of the week.

"Instead we stayed at Manly by the beach. We spent a lot more time together as a team. We trained, we played beach volleyball, just had a lot of fun together. We do enjoy each other's company as a side.

"After playing the Reds in an early round, we'd picked up on a few of their calls, and we made our best guesses over what they'd do in the semi. We thought they'd do a lot of kicking to us, and put on a good chase."

Andrew Mehrtens regards the 28–22 win over the Reds as one of the most satisfying of his career. "Everything the Reds did, we anticipated. It was the best example of a team controlling a game tactically that I've ever been involved in."

To Blackadder, "It was an awesome performance, right from the start. We were back on defence in the corner, and Feeky flicked it up, it went out to Caleb Ralph, and he almost scored at the other end. We had a real belief, and after the week in Manly we were always going to give it death."

That night, where the Crusaders would play the final depended on what happened in South Africa between the Otago Highlanders and the Stormers. The Highlanders scored an excellent 33–18 win in Cape Town, which meant that on the Sunday the Crusaders cruised home to Christchurch, while the Highlanders slogged back to Dunedin from South Africa.

Blackadder watched with a tinge of pleasure the big welcome at Dunedin airport when the Highlanders got back. "In the lead-up to a final there are always a lot of nerves, and a lot of pressure, and I was pleased to see the airport crowded for them.

"They were probably knackered and tired, and just wanted to hop into bed, but that wasn't going to be possible straight away. That thought flicked through the old brain."

The final in Dunedin had Otago fans in a frenzy of excitement. It must have seemed a good idea at the time to theme the final with the phrase "Party at Tony Brown's Place," a play on an insurance company's television campaign about a fictitious Kelly Browne.

Everywhere you went in Dunedin there were people in blue T-shirts carrying the message, and not just scarfies. One blue-rinsed lady walking through the Octagon the day before the Sunday final matched the shirt with pearls, a grey skirt and high heels.

"I don't know how much the 'Party at Tony Brown's Place' was a distraction for them," says Blackadder, "but I'm sure that poor old Tony Brown just wanted to get out there and play footy. I bet he didn't want to dedicate a party to himself before the job was really done.

"I saw a billboard when we were going to the ground. It had something like 'Todd plus 14 versus Taine plus 32,000.' Those little things get your hackles up a bit."

There were actually 41,000 people at the final, but the billboard writer was probably spot on. Around a quarter of the spectators were Crusaders fans.

"When we ran out," says Blackadder, "it felt to me like the crowd was red and black everywhere. Even up at the Auckland final in '98 there was red and black everywhere."

Justin Marshall was a key figure in the victory. Byron Kelleher had been playing brilliantly behind the Highlanders' pack, but in the '99 match he was overwhelmed by the combative Marshall.

"Justin is a gutsy bastard," says Blackadder. "I love the guy. He likes to win everything, and he's a top man off the field too. He loves a party.

"He's not the new age mould really. He's one of life's tough battlers. He's one of those guys who has had to work hard on his game all the way through, and that's the sort of guy he is. He's worked hard for everything, and I admire those qualities.

"He's bloody good for me. He pushes me along. If it's a crunch game, and I may have been off my game a bit he'll say, 'I want you to lead today Toddy. We need you to lead.'

"A lot of people tend to think it just comes naturally, but a captain's no different to any other player, sometimes you need people to push you along.

"Justin's an emotional guy, and for some reason some people around the country don't like him. In 2001 in Dunedin Justin got some stick for standing on Byron Kelleher's hand. The way I saw it, it looked like Byron was trying to have a go at him. I honestly believe that if I hadn't grabbed Byron when I did both our New Zealand halfbacks would have been out for a couple of weeks.

"When Justin came to Canterbury from Southland he had his mud flap on, the long hair in behind. We were training down at Rugby Park and Richard Loe was telling him how to put the ball in. Justin said, 'Just shut up and push. I'll put the bloody ball in.' Loey just zipped it straight away.

"He gets in the odd stoush, but it's only because he wants us to win so much. That's the sort of guy he is, and those qualities are what make him a great All Black, the most-capped All Black halfback.

"He's a runner, and he's like another loose forward he's so physical. He's also a good leader. When I went from blindside into lock he took over a lot of the decision-making within the side.

"I didn't think that Marshy did anything wrong when he was the captain of the All Blacks in 1997, although when he's not captain he doesn't have to worry about the peripheral things, and he leads from the front anyway.

"A halfback today has to know the lineout calls, and the scrum calls, and he's got to know when and where to call them, so he's a link between the forwards and the backs.

"He also has the basics to do well, and everyone scrutinises his passing and kicking, so that's enough to take on for anyone."

As was the case in Auckland the previous year, Blackadder found that in the final "things seem to go so fast that the only specific memories I have of the game in Dunedin is Fats So'oalo whacking the ground with both hands after he scored his try, and Gibbo putting the ball down with his hand in the air after he'd scored his try. And, of course, the look on everyone's face when we'd finally won it.

"I don't think that in the first year anyone really expected us to win, and I don't think they did even in this game. But we certainly had a real belief.

"The crowd at the airport back in Christchurch was just as big, and so was the parade. We picked up Fats halfway through the parade. We asked him where he was and he said, 'Ah, too many rums last night.' There are magic memories in winning it twice.

"I thought I had one of my better years as far as Super 12 goes. We'd won the championship, and I thought if I was ever going to have a shot at the All Blacks it would have been then. But I never kidded myself, right from the very start, that I'd make the World Cup."

One who did was the player of the day in the final, Reuben Thorne. The switch from lock didn't pay off for Thorne during the Tri-Nations, won by the All Blacks. But after a humiliating 28–7 defeat in Sydney in front of 107,000 people, probably a worse display by the All Blacks than the later loss to France at the World Cup, there was suddenly a demand at national level for a tireless worker like Thorne.

"Reuben one day could possibly be a great captain," says Blackadder. "I believe he has those leadership qualities. He's straight up, and people warm to him. You know that whatever he is going to ask of his players, he's prepared to do himself.

"I suppose if you don't know him he seems a quiet sort of guy, but within the team, he's one of the characters. The boys get into him a little bit about his big deep voice.

"He's very tough, and his work ethic is well and truly his strength. To me he has all the traits of a perfect Canterbury player, a hard-working, unassuming sort of guy who gives it his guts every time. You can't ask for more than that.

"I think that some people believe, because he is not so prominent in the open, he is not doing the work. But when I look at the whole loose-forward combinations today I think a No. 6 is being asked to do a No. 8's job at breakdowns. You used to see the No. 8 right up the No. 7's butt, so that the No. 6 had the opportunity to read the situation, and maybe run off the breakdown. But now Reuben is playing the No. 8 role, and no one is more hard working than him."

When the World Cup squad was announced eight Canterbury players were included, and coach John Hart decided against his Cup squad players being involved in the NPC. As a result it was a radically different Canterbury team in '99.

"It was actually quite exciting to have so many new guys," says Blackadder. "A lot of the players who started in '99 are becoming regulars now."

Blackadder ran alone to a standing ovation from the Jade Stadium crowd for the first game of the NPC, against Taranaki. It was his 100th game for the province, and it was a win, 34–16, followed in Invercargill with a 34–5 defeat of Southland.

"Then the Waikato boys came down and certainly gave us a towelling, 20–6. They're a good team Waikato, and they're respected in Canterbury. So the games are always battles."

Then came the visit to Pukekohe Stadium, remembered by some Canterbury players for the time Norm Maxwell forgot his dress shoes, and wore boots without sprigs with his blazer and uniform trousers.

This time it was Blackadder's turn for a footwear emergency. Angus Gardiner remembers it well.

"Toddy, Steve Surridge and I had got into a bit of a routine before games. We'd drop our bags and go to each other's rooms and solve all the problems in the rugby world in a space of 30 minutes before the game. We'd have it all worked out just before we got on the bus.

"So before the Counties game here we are chatting away in the midst of our cups of tea at the Waipuna Lodge in Auckland and there's a knock on the door and the manager pops his head in and says, 'Guys, we're waiting for you.'

"We were late, the captain and two of the most senior members, were late for the team meeting and we went in all very sheepish. It was the first time Toddy had been late and me too.

"Anyway, the bus trip was a long one to Counties. When we got there and rushed in, Todd realised he'd left his boots behind in the hotel. It was hilarious, because who the hell has got feet as big as that?

"He couldn't get boots to fit, and we're saying, 'Oh my God, he'll have to play in sandshoes.' A car got sent off to the hotel, and he squeezed into Chris Jack's boots.

"At the time Chris Jack, in his first season, was obviously coming through and the standing joke was that wearing a young fellow's boots makes you play better. We used to make Chris Jack say to Toddy, 'You're wearing my jersey now. If you don't mind can I have it back please?'"

Jack spent most of the game sitting on the sideline in sandshoes. Blackadder played the whole game in boots that he remembers with a wince "were just a tad too tight. It was a nice wee reminder that you pack all your gear, and double-check it."

Boots aside, Canterbury played very well against Counties, clocking up an 82–22 win, and then edged past Auckland in Christchurch, 12–10, with a last-minute dropped goal by Daryl Lilley. The plan was for new first-five Aaron Mauger to take the kick, but the ball was taken up again by mistake, Mauger ran to the blind, and Lilley had a shot he said he "would probably never strike as well again in my life."

With four wins from five games, notes Blackadder, Canterbury "for a young side had been doing extremely well. But then we went up to Northland and got cleaned out. Nothing went our way. We got screwed in the scrums and lineouts, and Northland just kept coming and coming.

"They played bloody well with a lot of guts, and we didn't do the basics. I remember we were trying long passes out wide, and we were dropping them."

Northland's captain, Glenn Taylor, had a superb game for the victors. "Glenn Taylor is a guy that I would have had in the All Blacks," says Blackadder. "He's a guy who's been overlooked in the prime. He's a very hard worker. There was no question about his scrummaging, his lineout work, his work at kick-offs, so what was the problem that kept him out?

"If you compared him to someone like Ian Jones, he was far more physical than Ian. He was an inspirational guy too. It would have been very easy for him to go to another union, but he stuck with Northland, and that night he inspired them to a 27–20 victory."

The Canterbury season rounded out with a 35–16 away win over

Otago, a 27–6 home win over Wellington, and a 19–11 loss on the road to North Harbour.

"We were up and down and not learning our lessons," says Blackadder. "It's a thing that comes with a lack of experience, although in '99 it wasn't just the younger players, it was the older players too. We were playing on emotion rather than playing clinical rugby. When we lost the game at North Harbour it meant we ended up in fifth place, and out of the playoffs."

There were some hotly disputed decisions that led to Frano Botica kicking four penalties to give Harbour the victory, but Blackadder would shortly have even bigger decisions to make about his own future.

Former All Black great John Kirwan had been playing rugby in Japan for the NEC works team, and he came to Christchurch with a Japanese manager to offer Blackadder a big money deal.

NEC's offer was for five years, at $NZ500,000 a year. There would be free accommodation for the Blackadder family in Tsukuba, about one hour by train from Tokyo, and generous airfare allowances to bring family and friends to Japan, or to fly back to New Zealand for visits.

"At that stage," says Blackadder, "I knew I probably wasn't going to be in the All Blacks ever again. When it was touch and go whether I'd go to Japan, that was in my mind.

"I'd gone away with my family on a little holiday. We hired a little mini-van, and toured round Central Otago, and when it came down to the crunch to whether I stayed, or whether I went, we were in Wanaka.

"We were staying in a little camp, having a fish, catching some trout. That was the setting. The money was just ridiculous if you just wanted to do it on a dollar basis.

"But it's more than dollars or cents. You take the kids into consideration, and what the move would mean for them. But they're pretty versatile. Priscilla was great. She said she'd support me whatever I wanted to do.

"So the things that you then weigh up are your family, your lifestyle and, really, what I wanted to do as a rugby player. Whether I still had things to contribute.

"The thing that made me want to stay really was that as a kid my dream was to play for Canterbury. Then, to play for Canterbury, was fulfilling my dreams.

"The major thing that made me stay was that I still felt I had something to offer to Canterbury rugby. I basically felt I wasn't ready to let go of my dream.

"Things had changed a little bit at the New Zealand union. David Rutherford had taken over as chief executive. He wanted me to stay, but that didn't sway my decision. I signed up purely as a Super 12 and NPC player. I'd resigned myself to that being my lot. I still felt I had something to offer."

11. Visions of victory

"Every time I dreamed of holding
that trophy up for the boys"

When Andrew Mehrtens was a kid in the 1980s his favourite song was "Give It A Boot Robbie," a song dedicated to Canterbury fullback Robbie Deans, that was hammered to death on what was then the leading radio station in the province, 3ZB. Deans was a classical fullback, strong on the tackle, fearless under the high ball, and dead-eye accurate with his kicking. He was from one of the great Canterbury settler families, the Deans from Scotland, who arrived even before the first four ships in 1850.

Robbie's great-uncle was Bob Deans, immortalised as the All Black who scored the try against Wales that wasn't allowed on the 1905–06 tour of Great Britain.

As a player Robbie had reached the heights, and as a coach he already had the 1997 NPC title to his credit when he took over from Wayne Smith to coach the Crusaders in 2000 with Steve Hansen.

Todd Blackadder believes there's more common ground than differences between Smith and Deans. "Smithy is a extremely innovative guy. None of Smithy's training runs were ever the same. He got us thinking and worked on making us more skilful.

"Robbie's very similar but a bit more aggressive, a lot more competitive within himself. Smithy gets just as fired up but in another way. I've never seen either one talk down to a guy, and with both of them you know there are no hidden agendas. With those two guys, all the hard questions that are ever asked at training to the players are only for the benefit of the players and the team.

"If someone is not doing something, Smithy will question you. So does Robbie to a certain extent but they just go about it a little differently. Smithy is a little bit smoother I suppose, in the way he delivers the message.

"Robbie is a little bit more direct and straight to the point in the way he delivers his. In a nutshell, Smithy might ask you and Robbie might tell you. Robbie is almost a forward in a back's body. I suppose it's that North Canterbury, Glenmark attitude.

"But one is as easy as the other to deal with, and I'm friends with both of the guys. In the end, you get to the same point anyway. Whether you agree with them or not you are quite free to fight for your argument.

"Smithy might ask you, even though he already has his own mind made up. He just wants to know where you are, and that's his way of doing it."

Deans has his own carefully formed opinions about Blackadder. "There's an awareness more and more that there are two kinds of intelligence. There's the traditional IQ and there's the EQ, the emotional quotient. Todd's got that in abundance. In the pragmatism of life, Todd's outstanding. Your academics may have an ability to acquire, and then regurgitate, a mass of information, but they don't necessarily identify what's important at a particular moment in time.

"His emotional intelligence makes him very perceptive with people, and you have to be as a leader. You have to be able to understand where people are coming from to be able to move them to where you want them to go when you come together as a group.

"One of his great skills as a captain was to be able to observe. He wasn't a guy who was verbose, he was very dry humoured, witty in his own way. He'd use humour to prompt people into action.

"From a coaching perspective he was a great link, because he could relate to us, and he always had a handle on what we were looking for, and he was a great conduit between us and the players.

"You combine that with his ability on the ground to recognise the moment, and the result was superb."

There were significant changes in the Crusaders squad for 2000. Angus Gardiner was gone, off to play for Bath in England. "I can remember walking off with Angus after our last NPC game in '99 against North Harbour," says Blackadder. "We'd played together as loose forwards for years and he was probably one of the unluckiest flankers in New Zealand rugby.

"Being with him all along, going through the grades with him, I put my arm around him as we walked off, his last game in a Canterbury rugby jersey. It was sad to see him off, he deserved to have gone further in the game at a national level than he did. He didn't even play for New Zealand A, or get a trial, and he would have graced an All Black jersey."

Gone too was another man whose friendship stretched back to teenage days, Steve Surridge, who had accepted an offer to play in Japan.

In his place at No. 8 was a North Harbour player unwanted by the Auckland Blues, Ron Cribb. The first few times Cribb turned up at Crusaders' training there was a general sense of amazement. Sparkly shirts and trendy [that week] flared trousers stood out from the crowd. "Cribby's quite a fashionable sort of a dude," says Blackadder. "He had these clothes that weren't exactly moleskins."

There was another cultural shock, after what's renowned as the comparatively relaxed approach of Harbour. "He was late to the first training session, and well and truly got a blast from our trainer, Mike Anthony. If anyone knows Motsy, he detests lateness. And so it should be.

"So right from the very start, I wouldn't say they were hard on Cribby, but they certainly set him guidelines. I think he, and his partner, did enjoy the environment.

"Off the field we are pretty much like a big family. I'd like to think that the atmosphere, and the mixture of guys we have here, helped

Cribby play his game. In his time here he went from being not wanted, to being an All Black.

"His Dad, Jim, is a hard case. He came down every weekend, so we got to know him. Cribby's a really humorous guy, a bit of a prankster, like moving your bag so you can't find it. He'd almost be in the same category as Steve Surridge. For some reason we had two really annoying No. 8s in a row.

"We had Cribby and Slade McFarland from North Harbour in 2000 and I think we've been very fortunate with the guys we've got, they have been superb. None of them have been a distraction to the team in any way. They've all given the team something."

The campaign started in Westport. "We went through three or four intensive days going through the protocols, which is time consuming and mentally draining," says Blackadder.

"It's the hardest time of the year in many ways. We're training physically pretty hard out, working on our moves, and also doing a lot of mental work on what we want to achieve.

"In saying that, there are a lot of DB promotions where you go out and have a beer, and get to let your hair down, but it's back to a hard training regime the next day. There is no better way of getting a side together than having a few beers and get to know someone away from the footy field.

"There are less dramas on the Coast and I think it's a very good environment for team building. You're back to the earthy people.

"When we went to Invergargill, and beat the Highlanders, 19–18, it was the first pre-season game where I thought things were ahead of schedule for that time of the year.

"We were still working hard up to that game, on our speed sessions, our weights, and our conditioning sessions. We hadn't slackened off any of those, yet we still played well in that game. It wasn't the result I was looking at, it was the performance.

"Then we went across to Sydney and played the Waratahs in the hosing-down rain and lost 16–3, then went to Timaru and lost to the Reds.

"Pre-season you're looking for specific things in your game. The Highlanders game showed me that the attitude was already there because we worked so hard all the way through.

"In the game with Queensland, the way they took us on, putting more guys on and cleaning out through the ruck, it was obvious we were going to have to be a lot better at that. You are only looking for certain things in pre-season, such as combinations.

"With the gap between the seasons, and the gaps between the teams, getting shorter you get punished if you don't prepare properly. In 2001 we were punished for it, because we had just three weeks to prepare a side for Super 12. The better campaigns have involved months of hard preparation and work, and then the final product has been excellent."

In 2000 Blackadder literally limped away from the first game, a 27–24 win over the Chiefs.

"When we first saw Rugby Park in Hamilton we went 'phew,' and when we went back to the hotel I shot down to the Waikato River to see if there was any water in it. I'd seen some dirty droughts in Canterbury but nothing like that. I've never seen such a dusty, hard ground.

"I don't know I'll ever forgive Stu Loe for it, but he had a saying that 'every day is a 21mm day.' In other words, for a forward you wear your long [21mm] sprigs every single day. Good old Stu. I remember hobbling my way to the team court session that night. I could only walk on one-third of my feet. I was being held up by blisters, big huge blisters.

"Ross Cooper, the Chiefs coach, at the after-match came up and said he wanted us to complain about the state of Rugby Park. It was atrocious, it was rock hard. I got a try and I should have just placed the ball... just getting over I took a big patch of skin off my calf muscles."

It had all started pretty happily for Blackadder. "There had been something in the paper calling the Waikato rugby people 'bogans' because they were playing AC/DC's music before the game. Being a little bit fond of it myself I knew we were in for a good day. It's amazing what you listen to as the ball is about to be kicked off.

"We were actually pretty lucky to win, because they had a kick at goal miss in the last minute. But as far as Super 12 campaigns had gone in the past it was a good start."

The Crusaders had a week off with the bye, then faced the Blues at

Jade Stadium, emerging with a 32–20 win. "Ron Cribb gave us that X-factor in 2000, and he gave us a really well-balanced loose forward unit with Reuben and Razor Robertson," says Blackadder.

"You could not help but love Scott Robertson. His whole enthusiasm, he's just a pumped-up sort of guy, always smiling, with a boyish keenness. There's a Razor Robertson fan club at Jade Stadium, and every time he runs out he never forgets to wave to them.

"In the changing room it'll go round and everyone will say their bit. Razor will talk about 'keeping things tight, you know what I mean?' He'll thump his chest and say, 'Keep it real.'

"He helps put a great balance in our side, because the Canterbury way is that we get pretty down to earth and don't mince our words, the grafting sort of language. Then he'll come out with that 'keep it real' stuff, which we all enjoy. He's such a sincere guy that it works for all of us.

"It is a laugh a minute with all these guys. We joke about everything. But you couldn't be accepted into a team like ours if you didn't earn respect by getting out there and playing. There's no point in being the joker of the side if you can't front with it on the field."

There was a personal milestone for Blackadder in the next round, against the Queensland Reds in Brisbane. When he ran on the field he became the first New Zealander to play 50 games in Super 12.

At halftime the occasion didn't seem much fun. The Crusaders were down 16–3, and struggling. Then, 10 minutes into the second half, Justin Marshall read an inside pass from Reds first-five Shane Drahm. He grabbed the intercept, and ahead lay 80 metres of open space.

"For somebody like me," says Marshall, "who hasn't got the fastest set of legs in the team, knowing that you haven't got a lot of support is not a nice feeling."

There was support, recalls Blackadder, but it was strictly verbal. "I was on halfway thinking, 'Ahhh, thank God. Go mate go. Go Marshy go.' When you can hardly walk yourself, the best you can offer is to yell.

"It was just so close — it was one of those games that could have gone either way until Justin's try. That was the real game-breaker. Queensland at home are always tough."

Inspired by the Marshall try the Crusaders went away in the second half to win, 27–19.

The game against the Stormers in Nelson was preceded by minor controversy, when television commentator Keith Quinn suggested that Super 12 games should only be played in major cities.

It's a view Blackadder vehemently disagrees with. "I remember thinking at the time that you can't put a dollar value on a game like the one in Nelson. It's more than just people through the gates, or more than television people saying they can't get their camera crews to Nelson.

"It's about playing the game within your region and fostering the game of rugby in the top half of the South Island. People come from the West Coast and Marlborough and Canterbury to watch those games.

"If you stop taking your team around the regions what are you doing for rugby to foster it there? Today you have hardly any time to go round your regions pre-season, and you're asking those people to support you as a regional team. You never get anything for nothing. You have to give something back to the people who support you.

"Think of the kids in those regions who want to play rugby, and be a Crusader. You'd like to think there are one or two, or 10 or 20 in the crowd who want to play footy. When they see the Crusaders they can have a day where they feel part of it."

The game itself saw the Crusaders make it three from three, with a 47–31 victory, scoring six tries, one of them by Blackadder. He still smiles at the memory. "It's a story to dine on for years. I threw a dummy and ran through. With the years the distance will probably get longer and longer.

"Lots of friends from Collingwood days came to the game. They have a marquee with a band playing, all the partners go up too, so it means a bloody good weekend."

Ron Cribb was in such outstanding form he was already being tipped to become an All Black. One tackle on Percy Montgomery, the Stormers fullback, was so fierce it was suggested a headstone should be erected where Montgomery was buried.

Marika Vunibaka, the Fijian winger, was firing too. Vunibaka had been in outstanding form at the 1999 World Cup for Fiji, although he ran into some judicial trouble after some push and shove in pool play.

Off the field, says Blackadder, "he's a little shy with strangers, but in the team he's fine. The big bugger just grins and his big pearly white teeth stick out and everyone has him on. He's certainly got wheels — when we did the pre-season sprint tests he was like a rocket. For sheer pace, he's awesome."

The first 50 minutes against the Highlanders at Jade Stadium were immaculate, the home team ahead 39–12. From then on, it was almost all Highlanders, but the Crusaders hung on to win 42–36.

At four for four, the winning roll came to a halt against the Hurricanes in Wellington, at the city's new waterfront stadium. "I felt that we were playing well," says Blackadder, "and then Jonah Lomu got the ball." Lomu's dynamic form exposed the problems Norm Berryman was having with injuries. Sadly there would be no more match-winning displays from Berryman in a red and black jersey. The game was lost 28–22.

The annual visit to South Africa started in Durban to face the Sharks. "I remember reading in the programme before the game how Olly le Roux was saying, 'It's time we put these Crusaders in their place' and that sort of stuff.

"We knew we'd be playing a very committed, fired-up team, and sure enough they were." The Crusaders gritted it out, winning 32–24, with all the bench on the field at the end. "It shows the calibre of our reserves," says Blackadder. "When they come out we don't seem to lose anything. In fact it gives the rest of us a boost."

Heading to altitude at Ellis Park was never going to be easy, with the Cats coached by Laurie Mains, and that was certainly the case. Down 17–6 after 21 minutes, Blackadder had vivid memories of the brilliant way the Cats had started in Nelson the previous year. But this time there wouldn't be an equally brilliant Crusaders' comeback. "Basically they blew us off the park," says Blackadder. The Cats won 54–31.

Back on home ground, says Blackadder, the Crusaders "tightened everything up and against the Bulls we went out there to play for each other. It was magical to watch. It was a high-speed game, with very few mistakes." The Crusaders romped to a 75–27 win, and the pace was on again the following week against a tougher team, the Waratahs, won 22–13.

"It was a ferocious game, and I can clearly remember being on the sideline trying to talk, and when you can't catch your breath, all that comes out is sort of 'aaah hmmm.' It was bruising."

The Crusaders displayed lateral thinking for their last round-robin game, against the Brumbies. Both teams were already guaranteed a home semi-final, but a win in the round-robin game would decide who might have a home final.

Amazingly, Blackadder says the Crusaders "never really focused on trying to beat them for a home final. Robbie said, 'Lets go out there and smash them.' They'd been cutting defences to pieces until then. So our whole focus was to go out and hurt them as much as we could in case we never got to play them again.

"We were very defence orientated in that game, but when you look at it in the context of the whole season, that set us up to win the final. We went out there that night and although they scored two tries, they were a bit lucky to get either. I really think we softened them up that night."

There was certainly plenty of passion among the Crusaders' players. Four minutes from the end Justin Marshall started to storm off the field when he thought he was going to be yellow-carded by referee André Watson.

Marshall was furious that Watson blew up a maul that Marshall was convinced was still moving: "I saw him reach in his pocket for the card, so I said, 'I'll save you the bloody trouble,' and started walking off."

Amazingly Watson, in the confusion, changed his mind so Marshall saw out the game, although he was cited, appeared before the judiciary, and ordered to make a public apology.

"Marshy's a very competitive person," says Blackadder, "and I don't blame him for showing his frustration. We were just getting a roll on, and we were a couple of metres from the try line, and the ref said we were static. Marshy lost it there for a couple of seconds, the old eyes rolled back."

A worry about whether Marshall would be suspended for the semi-final, against the Highlanders, was the only major concern for the Crusaders, despite the 17–12 loss.

"I think we walked off the field feeling a lot rosier than the score showed," says Blackadder. "The spectators probably said, 'Gee, these

Brumbies are good, they're probably going to win the final.' But there were a lot of grins in our changing shed, because our boys were in great nick, we'd just gone out there and put big hits in for the whole game and we were feeling pretty good. There was a lot of petrol left in the tank."

If Marshall escaped a ban, he was struck at training with a calf-muscle injury, that would keep him out of the semi-final, and final. His first-five partner, Andrew Mehrtens, on the other hand, having missed the Brumbies game with an injury, was back for the semi.

While the Crusaders were more composed than might have been expected after the Brumbies loss, there was still high tension before the semi-final.

"We put our gear on the bus at the hotel before the game, then we had our meeting, so you get to the ground about an hour before kickoff. We went to go to the game and the bus had broken down, no power, lights or anything.

"Poor old Shandy [Crusaders manager Darren Shand] was on the phone trying to organise another bus, and we only turned up half an hour before the game. But as it turned out, the bus driver had it in drive instead of neutral or park and that's why it wouldn't start — it was just a bit of high tension. It actually helped take our mind off the game and relax a bit more."

The game against the Highlanders was the last time Josh Kronfeld would play in New Zealand, and was the last time Jeff Wilson played in the 2000 season.

But the fireworks all came from the Crusaders, with Mehrtens in commanding form, and a 21-year-old who until then was a club player only, Ben Hurst, stepping into Marshall's boots with amazing aplomb. Usual reserve halfback Aaron Flynn was also injured. "It was such a shock, and felt so unreal," Hurst would say later, "that I was actually more nervous before the Christchurch club final than the Super 12 games."

Mehrtens kicked eight from eight shots at goal, and his tactical kicking meant the Highlanders played most of the game in their own half, the Crusaders winning, 37–15.

"Mehrts would be one of the greatest first-fives Canterbury have ever had," says Blackadder, "and he's certainly one of the characters within the side. He's a different guy, and a great guy.

"On his day he's absolutely brilliant, and I've been lucky enough to see him plenty of times on his day. You don't see many footballers like Mehrts.

"He's always joking, and he's very quick-witted, but he is one of those guys who is very passionate about things, and speaks his mind. Mehrts is good at everything he does, whether it's golf, or tennis, or rugby, and he's intelligent, but in most ways he's just a normal joker. He likes a beer. He's passionate about the red and blacks.

"There's a little clip when Bruce Deans scores in the corner in the 1985 Shield game with Auckland, and Mehrts is right in the corner, jumping up and down, right on the sideline in his little red and black shirt. We have a laugh about it in the team.

"People have to remember that he came onto the scene and straight away was into the All Blacks, and he's played bloody well for them. He was put up on a pedestal and was expected to perform all the time. But really, he's still young.

"Mehrts is a guy who tries to please everyone, and he finds it very hard to say no. He can run himself ragged. In some ways it worries me about guys like him. He never gets a chance to get outside the goldfish bowl, and it's hard on people like him at times.

"In 2001 all that happened was he had an injury. He had one in 2000, and because he's so good he gets by, and he gets selected because he's a match winner. He's been playing under that sort of pressure for so long."

Come the final, in Canberra, and Blackadder's frame of mind could not have been more positive. Before all three Super 12 finals he's played in he had an experience that he's never revealed before. An extremely practical man, he still finds it difficult to explain what more fanciful people might call almost mystical moments.

"I don't know if it was a dream, or whether I just willed myself, but on every occasion I could picture myself winning."

Does he think it was something he literally dreamed while asleep, or was it more like a day dream?

"Well, it's very hard to remember your dreams, isn't it? So I don't know whether it was just a feeling, or whether I dreamed about it. It was something that happened on the Monday or Tuesday before every final. I just dreamt that I was up there holding up the cup.

"Whether I just wanted to picture it in my mind, I don't know. But all the ones I've dreamt about, it's happened.

"The only one I've ever told is Justin Marshall. I said to him, 'Don't worry about this one, I've dreamt about it.' He may have thought I was just joking, but I wasn't.

"I don't know if it was the power of positive thinking, but I visualised every one. Never for a second did I ever think we were going to lose. I'm not saying I have visions or anything but I always believed we were going to win it. Every time we've been in the final I've always dreamt of holding that trophy up for the boys."

Canberra, a city that in winter often offers weather that hints more of Antarctica than Australia, was freezing when the final started.

"It was quite low-key for us before the game," says Blackadder, "because it was over there, and to the locals we were just going to be the team that the Brumbies were going to beat to win the Super 12. So the pressure was on them, which was great for us.

"In the team room all the faxes from home were around the wall, you could feel the support. I remember Robbie talking to us before the game. He said, 'There is a storm coming and it ain't the weather, it's going to be us.' It was something a little different and got everyone's hackles up.

"It snowed the night of the final. It was that cold that when you ran out there sucking the air in almost took your breath away. We just went for it, with nothing to lose. Those are the games you love, when there are no expectations, and nothing to lose.

"Man, it was tough though, a bruising game. You didn't realise it at the time, you didn't have time to feel the tackles or anything like that. It was interesting afterwards looking at the stats, where there were guys like Scott Robertson putting in 32 tackles. We had been averaging about 12. At one stage the Brumbies put nine phases on, without making the advantage line, which just shows you how punishing the tackling was.

"Every guy was just absolutely throwing his life into it. Just shows you how much it meant. We were the sort of team if we were in a game we had a good shot at winning it.

"That was a beautiful try of Ron Cribb's, when he put that little kick through and regathered. We never realised he was going to do that, I don't even think he realised he was before he did it, but it certainly turned the game.

"We knew that we had to keep attacking, and, although we spent long periods without the ball, when we did get into the Brumbies half, we were close enough for Mehrts to keep piling points on. We kept chipping away, until it came down to Mehrts' kick."

Down 19–17, it was four minutes from the end when Mehrtens was asked to kick for goal from 42 metres out, into the freezing wind. He recalls that he was battling with cramp at the time.

"I tend to get it in both legs. It's not so bad running around, it's when you tense up and extend your leg, so making a tackle seems to bring it on. Towards the end I can remember making a tackle, and then just sort of sitting beside the ruck, sticking out my legs in front of me, like a little kid at school.

"It's when you're kicking that it really grips. You can kick, but then on your follow through it really rips hold of you. I was worried that knowing I'd be in some sort of pain after the last kick might make me hold back. So I really tried hard to give it everything, just whack it, and then it's over, and whatever happens won't matter if you've kicked the ball properly. It did come off nicely, and in the end I don't think I even cramped up."

Ahead 20–19, that would be one more penalty awarded to the Crusaders. Blackadder remembers that "there was no one around to kick it out. I was going to have a go myself, but I said to the ref, André Watson, 'How long have we got?' and he said, 'There's still time on the clock.' I thought, 'Shit, I'll get someone else.'

"It was a huge effort, but because we'd done the work all through the year, we knew we had it in us.

"There's just no better feeling in the shed, with the beers, and the hugs, and the sighs of relief after all the work that goes into it, but we never got to see the Brumbies after that game.

"They said they had a feed for us, and we went up to a room and had a meal, just by ourselves. In rugby someone has to win, someone has to lose, and it's good to have a beer with the opposition. So it felt a little bit cold. You should get together. To me it's the whole essence of footy, going hard out, then having a beer after the game.

"We went back to the hotel, and had a night to die for. We had a bit of a court session, and the whole foyer to the bar was open to all the Canterbury supporters.

"Once we got back to the hotel it was one non-stop party. Nobody went to bed, we just went straight through."

12. Private lives

"It was pretty cool when Dad came to school"

Priscilla McKay and Todd Blackadder first met when they were both teenagers. Todd was doing a welding and fitting course in Nelson with Priscilla's brother, Scott, and the boys would come back to the McKay's dairy farm in Collingwood for the weekends.

There were no romantic sparks at first. Priscilla, working as a hairdresser in Nelson, says that she and Todd were good friends, like mates. "In a way he was like a brother, one of the family. Todd was always the one in the group who made sure that everyone was okay. Even when he was young he had a caring attitude."

Priscilla had gone to the local Collingwood area school until the fifth form, when she went to Christchurch for a six-month hairdressing course. When she came back home she soon found that she didn't really enjoy life in a salon in Nelson, and worked at several jobs while Todd farmed in the area.

Then he moved back in Christchurch. "I hadn't seen him for more than 12 months, when he came back for a friend's 21st. I saw him across the room. He was always just a good mate, but then I saw him from a different perspective. So we'd known each other for about four years before we started going out together.

"After the 21st he went back to Christchurch, and we wrote letters, and kept in touch on the phone. At Christmas I came down to Christchurch, and we had a couple of weeks together. Then I decided, okay, I'll move down. He was living down there, and wasn't going to come back to Golden Bay.

"It's pretty relaxed where I lived, and guess I was a bit of a hippie girl from the sticks."

So was Todd in those days some smooth city slicker? Priscilla laughs. "I wouldn't have called him a city slicker. He fitted in [at Collingwood] like he'd always been there, which is why so many people there got on with him."

Priscilla was no rugby fanatic, but rugby in Collingwood is more than just a game. As it is in so many rural towns in New Zealand, the sport is part of the area's social fabric.

"I was mildly interested in rugby," she says. "I can remember watching All Black games with my Dad. I liked Sid Going, I thought he was pretty cool. I'd get up at 3 o'clock in the morning to watch games with my Dad. But I don't know if I did that because I liked the footy so much.

"Most weekends I would go and watch Collingwood play. It was such good fun, and it's a real community thing. That's probably why you get swept into rugby. In little places it's a way that you all get together.

"Even now I'd probably only know about three rules, although I pick up a lot sitting with Todd's Mum, Carolyn. I once said to Todd, 'Don't you think you should sit down and tell me what it's about?' He said, 'To be quite honest with you, if you knew all the rules, can you imagine our conversations after the game? Why did you do that? Why did that happen?'

"A friend he knew had a partner who actually coached rugby, and after the game the poor guy got absolutely drilled."

When Priscilla first came to Christchurch, she and Todd lived with his mother. "We lived with Carolyn for about 12 months, and it was good, because I really got to know her."

Priscilla and Todd went back to Collingwood to get married, in the rose garden of her old English teacher's home. "We got married in February, and the next weekend there was rugby, so there was no honeymoon."

Very quickly, as Todd became a regular in the Canterbury team, rugby would be a major element in their lives.

"Once he was in the Canterbury team I was very nervous. I had to get a whole new wardrobe, that was the biggest dilemma. I'd never been involved in anything like that. It was nothing like Collingwood. Here you worry about whether you're wearing the right clothes, you're careful about how much you drink.

"I worried about what I was going to talk to people about. That was when I first met Karen, whose husband is [Canterbury team masseur] Errol Collins. She felt in the same boat so we cobbered up, and have been friends every since.

"It doesn't worry me now, not at all. As the years have gone on Karen and I have conversations about what it used to be like. I was absolutely petrified of one Canterbury player's wife. I don't know why, but to me she was so confident, and so intimidating, and so immaculately presented.

"It was a couple of years before I realised that she was fine. There was no need to worry about her."

Rugby has given Priscilla moments she will always treasure. "The first Super 12 win in Auckland was amazing. I was sitting next to Graham Jack, because he wasn't on the bench. We all had terrible seats, right up the back of the old stand. Every try that was scored he'd jump up and give his partner, Adele, a cuddle, and then turn round and give me a cuddle. It was so emotional. I'll always remember that."

All Black announcements are an exciting memory, and "the Australian test in Sydney in 2000 was huge. That was an amazing game. I got a bigger buzz from that one than the game with Tonga, when Todd captained the test side for the first time."

The All Blacks' partners were all shouted to the Sydney game by the New Zealand Rugby Union. In the professional age it's not something that happens a lot. "I'll always go to the games in Dunedin, and Nelson," says Priscilla, "but not too many apart from that. When we do go to a Canterbury or Crusaders game there's always someone that'll organise. Penny Deans is a great organiser. She'll say, 'Who wants to go to Nelson?' Then she'll organise and book the flights, and accommodation."

As well as the fun there's a downside to life with a modern rugby player. "The thing that probably I get sick of is when Todd's away for more than three weeks. I can do three weeks quite adequately, but longer than that I get a bit sick of playing Mum and Dad.

"You need some back-up. I do miss him, but because we've done it for so long, it's quite normal for us," Priscilla laughs. "When he hasn't been away for a while, and you might get a bit niggly, as all married couples do, I think, 'When are you going away again?'

"When he first started going away, I wasn't happy about it, but it's just what he has to do. You can't say, 'You're not going, you're not allowed to.' You just learn to live with it.

"Two or three weeks isn't so bad. The longest he's been away is six weeks, and that's a long haul. But I try to think, 'You're not the only one missing him.' The kids miss him, and so does his Mum. He's very close to his Mum."

The Blackadders have two children, Shinae, a pretty 10-year-old, and Ethan, a strapping six-year-old. The idea of being quoted in a book sees them react in ways that mirror their ages.

Shinae is a little bashful, but says that while she finds rugby "a bit boring" it's pretty cool watching Dad play.

Her classmates are well aware of who Dad is, and she often comes home with scraps of paper for him to sign. There's been no jealousy from school friends. When Todd returns from a tour there's always a home-made card from Shinae to welcome him.

The first time the Crusaders won Super 12 Todd took the cup to Shinae's school where the kids all posed with it for photographs. "I liked it a little bit when Dad came to school," says Shinae. "I was proud."

Ethan, unselfconscious as only a six-year-old can be, reels off a stream of memories and anecdotes.

"When I first started rugby, at training I was wearing my sneakers.

Dad's going to get me steel sprigs for my rugby boots. I've got plastic ones now, but I want steels. Dad has big long ones on his boots.

"I play forward, at hooker, for Woodend under-eights. I've had a run with the ball. One time against Kaiapoi a big boy passed the ball to me, and I got a big run. Then they bowled me over.

"When Dad played [for Glenmark] against Woodend, he didn't even tackle his brother [Scott]. He told me that he didn't want to hurt his brother.

"Me and Mum and Shinae we went to Glenmark, and my friend, his name is Jeremy, he goes to Woodend school, he was there. I waved to my Dad, and he didn't even wave to me."

Priscilla: "Well, he was in the middle of a lineout Ethan."

Ethan shrugs and moves on. "When Dad played for Canterbury one time, when he scored he got a sore nose. I saw that on TV. Sometimes Dad gets a bit stroppy in rugby, and he just wants to be the boss.

"When he used to go away with the All Blacks I used to get quite sad. When he gets to the airport everybody hugs him. When we went to the airport once [after the 2000 Super 12 victory] everyone was going 'Toddy, Toddy'.

"I went into the changing room and Rascalman signed my jersey." Who is Rascalman? "It's Justin Marshall." Why is he called Rascalman? "I call him that because he calls me a rascal when he sees me."

There's a last, wonderfully innocent statement. "Dad doesn't play for the All Blacks any more, but he's got a French jersey and an Australian jersey and a Canterbury one, and when he dies he's going to give them to me."

In a largely successful effort to let her and the children lead a private life Priscilla has chosen not to put the family in the media spotlight. It's certainly not for lack of opportunity.

"I know they have to do a job, but as it's gone on, and they know that I don't want to do photos, and I don't want to do interviews, they've left me alone.

"When Todd was made All Black captain I had a woman ring up from a magazine, and I said, 'No thanks.' A couple of years ago I would have felt I had to do it, but I stick up for myself a bit more now."

There have been some weird media moments. Just weeks after Todd became All Black captain the *New Zealand Woman's Weekly* ran a front page story headlined: "NZ's reluctant sex symbol."

Priscilla was embarrassed, but not by quotes in the story in which various women reckoned Todd was "cute" and "gorgeous." What she found uncomfortable was that friends might have thought she or Todd had anything to do with the feature.

"The first we knew about it was when Toddy was on the front of the magazine. The thing that was embarrassing was that people thought we'd done an article for the magazine.

"The quotes were from things that had been said years ago. It was run without anyone saying anything to us at all. We didn't say one word.

"I guess in New Zealand, sports stars are the nearest thing we've got to film stars, and that's what it comes down to.

"I had a guy ring me from a Sunday newspaper, and he said, 'I don't normally do stories like this, but this story is on my desk, and I have to follow it up.' I said, 'What is it?' He said, 'Well, ah, could you just possibly tell me if, ah, you and your husband's marriage has split up.'

"I just started laughing. So he said, 'Aw, so it's not true?' I said, 'I'm not even going to comment.' He asked if I wanted to put a disclaimer in the paper, but I said, 'No thanks.'

"The twaddle that goes on, it doesn't make me angry, it's so ridiculous you laugh at it. You can never stop things like that, it happens to all of them."

The media pressures on her husband when he became All Black captain staggered Priscilla. "I was starting to get a bit niggly about it, and then he showed me the written list of telephone interviews he was expected to do in one day. I think there were something like 25 of them. After that I was a lot more understanding."

Privately the Blackadders have family and friends they socialise with but you don't see them out a lot together in public. In Canterbury Todd is such a well-known figure that even going to the movies can end up more like a signing session.

"I can't remember the last time we went to the pictures together. I end up walking about 20 paces in front of him. That's one thing where sometimes I think, when rugby's over we can be a normal family.

Sometimes I look at my friends, and I think they can go out anonymously, Mum, Dad and the kids. I pretty much still can, because I've kept myself out of the media."

The bolthole for them as a couple remains Collingwood. "We're just locals there. When we're with our friends up there, we're just part of the crowd. One of my girlfriends never ever talks about rugby. She treats him as my husband, not Todd Blackadder, the rugby player."

The marriage remains an oasis of normality for Todd, who says simply that, "I'm very lucky that I've got someone like Priscilla." Priscilla is strong in the difficult times and says, "I just think that I've met some wonderful people, and had some amazing experiences, that I would never have had if I wasn't married to Todd."

13. Life and the game

"You learn a lot about yourself"

As he nears the end of his playing career at the higher levels, Todd Blackadder is a man who believes that "what rugby has given me is immense, more than I could ever repay." Without rugby, he says, "I may never have ever been out of the South Island. I may have been a dairy farmer all my life. Not that there's anything wrong with that, but I've had a chance to do so many other things.

"I'm very lucky. That's why when I finish playing I'll always give something back to the game I love, because it's given so much to me.

"As a relatively shy guy, without a great deal of formal education, rugby, and what goes with it, has helped me learn so much about myself."

People who see him handling a television interview with apparent ease in recent years might be amazed if they saw a tape of his first television interview, with TVNZ's Jane Dent before he travelled to Scotland with the New Zealand sevens team in 1993. "It was such a shocker they just cut it up, and they showed clips of the *Black Adder* TV programme through it.

"Rugby's given me a chance to travel the world, to meet some amazing people, and to have some great experiences. Some of those experiences might be just sitting back and having a beer with some mates. But there are other things that a lot of people would never get the chance to do.

"That's why I'd like to do something for New Zealand rugby, in the future, at whatever level I can."

For Blackadder there's been the absolute pleasure of getting to know men like Colin Meads and Sir Brian Lochore. "When you meet people like them they have such a mana and integrity that they're everything you expected them to be.

"If you talk to a guy like John Sturgeon, on the West Coast, who used to be the All Black manager, you see why he would have been a great manager. He's just got everyone's best interests at heart.

"There are some bloody nice people in the game of rugby. At times after-match functions can be a bit boring, but there are also good people."

Rugby opened the door to Buckingham Palace. "In 1997 [with the All Blacks] we went to the palace and shook hands with the Queen. Those are things that you just can't do, you can only dream about them.

"We formed up in a big square, and Sean Fitzpatrick went round with her and introduced us individually. Then Princess Anne came along, and we were all standing there with a cup of tea and a sandwich. It was one of those life experiences that was nice to have."

Blackadder is a great believer in making time on rugby tours to see some of the country being visited. "You've got to enjoy it. When you go to those places it'd be so easy to sit in your hotel. But you could sit in your room and watch videos at home. There's no point in being in a country, and the only countryside you see is the rugby ground.

"A city is a city to me, a Big Mac tastes the same anywhere you go. But I love the countryside. France was beautiful, and while you think of Germany as a very industrial nation, and parts of it are, there's some beautiful countryside, forests, and great little villages.

"I found Sicily intriguing. You almost had the feeling that you should pay someone to walk down the street. There's a hint of *The Godfather* about it.

"In a team you get a lot of privileges. If you get invited to a place, you should make sure you go. The All Blacks went to one of the best wineries in France, and we all got a few bottles each that you might not be able to buy on the open market.

"On tour you have to make time for other things. With the All Blacks and the Crusaders for example your liaison officer might jack something up. I've been on some amazing safaris in South Africa. We went to the Folies in Paris. In Argentina they roasted whole lambs on spits for us, and served up steaks that were about a foot across.

"Most of the Canterbury boys are always on for something. Razor Robertson likes to hunt out a bit of water, and go surfing. Most of the time overseas with the Crusaders there's nobody around in the hotel. They're all out doing things.

"Last year with the All Blacks we went out scuba diving with the sharks off the coast of Durban. [All Black trainer] Mike [Motsy] Anthony and Greg Somerville and I went.

"They have these inflatable boats with two outboards. Because they're on an open coast they take these boats down and drop them off the trailers on the sand. You've got to push them out.

"On the way out, with breakers up to six metres high, the guys running the boats have to be pretty skilled. They've got to work their way out, which is exciting. We all love going hard and fast.

"We were on the way out there and they had these buoys that were a couple of kilometres off the coast. I was sitting beside Motsy and we were in wet suits. I had to squeeze into mine.

"They put all the gear on the boats. We were getting out there, and I could see my tank, but I couldn't see any mask. One of the guys had forgotten it.

"Motsy was getting seasick, and he started to sweat. We were bouncing all the way out there. I said, 'I think my mask has gone.' So we got one off another boat, and then we were all sitting there. We were all going to dive together.

"I grabbed the mask, went to put it on, and by this time sweat was just dripping off Motsy's nose. My mask went 'ping' and the old rubber strap broke. We then had to wait another 10 minutes, which must have felt like a lifetime for him.

"Finally we got down, and that was really exciting. We were only a couple of metres from big reef sharks skipping around.

"With the Crusaders we went down to a boat club in Durban, and some went out swimming, some played volleyball, some sunbathed.

"I went fishing. There was me, and Slade McFarland, and Ron Cribb. We were out there for four hours. Half an hour after we started Ron got seasick. Now anyone who knows Ron knows he's one of the cheekiest guys you'd ever meet.

"Slade and I just loved seeing Ron uncomfortable, and we just had him on the whole time. In the end he was starting to crack, saying 'Let's go, let's just bloody go.' We were both offering helpful tips like, 'We've heard you've got to have a swim first,' but he wouldn't get in.

"When we were going out past a container ship there was this huge fin sticking out of the water. We got up close, and that was how whales sleep, upside down with their tails sticking out of the water. We thought it might have been trapped by a chain or a rope, but it was just sleeping."

If the Crusaders have offered fun off the field, there have, obviously, been big victories on the paddock. Blackadder suggests an integral part of the Canterbury success is the structure of the whole organisation, and the people who run it.

"They've had the right guys in the right places. If you look at the mixture, in the teams they have the Marshalls, the Mehrtens, the Thornes, hard-working guys, who know the traditions and know what gives a Canterbury flavour.

"Every campaign we have our goals, our themes, but we've always had a feet on the ground philosophy. It goes through to the coaches we've had. They're very down-to-earth, straight-up guys, who talk from the heart, Wayne Smith, Robbie Deans, Steve Hansen, Vance Stewart and Alistair Hopkinson. It also coincides with the whole management staff.

"The whole staff are excellent. Mike Anthony is the best trainer in New Zealand by far. When you look at Canterbury over the years, he's had a huge role to play in the success of Canterbury.

"He got a team of amateurs when he started, and even in 1996 while we weren't geared to the new era, we were the fittest side. He then took us right to the pinnacle of winning an NPC and three Super 12s.

"A lot of credit has to go to him. He's a hard taskmaster, he runs the crap out of you, and he makes sure that you do the training. In our most successful years we've always been able to win the games in the last 20 minutes.

"I'd be very surprised if the other sides have worked harder than we have, both in pre-season and all through the competition phase.

"He has such a mixture and variety. Motsy went through finding his feet with the rest of us. He's about the same age as the players, in fact when he started he was still the Shirley senior team's fullback.

"He always says that he was given nothing, and he made athletes out of us. I have him on about how we created him, and made him into what he is. He's just a champion guy.

"You don't want to be late for one of Motsy's sessions. Because he pushes hard, and he wants it so badly, he takes it personally. He passionate about it, so it's more then just getting the guys fit.

"It's like that with our physios, we've had Steve Cope and now Steve Muir, who go the extra mile, as does old Possum, Errol Collins, our masseur. He's a great guy.

"It goes right up to the management. [Canterbury's chief executive] Steve Tew obviously runs the union very well, and he's on the sideline at games, and he turns up to our trainings.

"I'm always asked to the meetings they have. They do ask for the team's input, and they do listen. They don't just run with something without talking to the players. It feels good to be inside an efficient organisation.

"Little things matter, like Steve running the drinks trolley on the plane when we came back from the 1998 Super 12 final. The guys notice things like that. We have to do the business side, when it's negotiations, and that sort of stuff, but he's always been very fair with me, and I know that the guys like him."

The most unsung heroes, in Blackadder's mind, are the partners of the players. "Cathy and Vance Stewart were the people who started involving the partners so much. Penny Deans does it a lot too. Cathy and Penny have put hours into organising things. When we're away they usually get the partners together, and they go to restaurants, or to somebody's house, so there's support for each other.

"Once the season starts players never have a weekend off for months on end to spend with their partners. It's tough going for the girls at times.

"They're on an emotional roller coaster too. It's not much fun turning on the TV, or listening to the radio, and your husband is being bagged. When you get home from training, you're bloody tired, because anything to do with rugby training is physically draining.

"I firmly believe the partners put just as much into the success of the side as anyone."

Blackadder doesn't see Canterbury rugby suffering the massive slump that Auckland did in the late 1990s. "When you see the new wave come through, the Richie McCaws, the Sam Broomhalls, the Ben Hursts, in the pre-season Shield games in 2001, there's an amazing depth in Canterbury."

New All Black Chris Jack is one Canterbury player Blackadder thinks has the potential to be a great player on the world stage. "The second and third years will show whether he has the goods, but I firmly believe he will see it through.

"He's got every asset you would want in a lock. He's big, he's tall, he's athletic, he's young, he's fit, he's strong, and I'm pleased they're holding him back a wee bit.

"At the moment Troy Flavell and Norm Maxwell are playing very well for the All Blacks, and they're looking good for the future too. Troy can do things no other lock in world rugby can do. When you're playing with him you notice these wee things.

"All Black selectors tend to stick with the incumbents, but I'd like to see them give some of the younger guys a go, to give Chris Jack a taste of test rugby, from the first to the 80th minute, so he can actually grow in confidence. At the 2003 World Cup Chris Jack will be in the prime of his life.

"A few years ago because I was a bit sensitive to it, I'd notice it when John Hart would say, 'He's a very good player, but I don't know if he can make the step up [to test rugby].' That puts doubts in your mind. But then you get a chance, and you find that you love it. You could have made the step up a couple of years before if you were given the opportunity."

The amount of talent within the Canterbury ranks, says

Blackadder, does lead to some difficult calls.

"Ben Blair, for example, is such an awesome player, and where does he fit in? Does he stay? Does he sit in the reserves? Or does he make another career move? He could talk to a coach, but coaches want their teams to win, and what a coach wants for the team may not be the best option for Ben Blair.

"It's a fine, narrow line for players and coaches to walk, because both are ultimately judged on performances. It'd be very rare for a coach to say that a player should go to another province to get a real shot at things.

"Ben's got the whole world at his feet, but who does he talk to? Who does he trust? Sometimes you can't see for looking. When a younger guy has a contract in front of them, he does need an agent. I don't believe you can go into contract negotiations for yourself.

"But a lot of players put a lot of trust in agents, and really all some agents want is a percentage. Some of the contracts I've been shown have agents getting 10 to 15 per cent of a player's earnings for all the time the contracts are in force.

"What has the agent done to deserve that? They haven't done the hard work, all they've done is to sign up a bit of paper. My advice is that a young player should make a one-off payment for a contract. He should never be giving up earnings over three years.

"There are a lot of promises made by agents about speaking engagements, but the first thing you want to be doing is playing. As a player the last thing you want to be doing is running round trying to do speaking engagements.

"New Zealand rugby needs people who the players can talk to, someone who, if the need arises, can speak for him. Take a player who is being asked to play while he's injured. It's far easier for someone else to talk to a coach and say, 'Look, this guy is stuffed, he needs a chance to get over his injury.' It's hard for a guy to walk up to a coach and say he needs a break.

"We've got this thing in New Zealand that we don't like to admit you need recovery time. It's the 'big boys don't cry' syndrome."

Blackadder is firmly of the belief that club rugby remains vital to the health of the game here. "What happened to me was that you played club rugby, and if you were good enough you were selected in a sub-union side, you had a trial and if you were fortunate, you were picked for Canterbury.

"Players now are coming through, we've all seen them, at 19, 20, or 21, and they're almost instant stars. Some are getting selected, straight out of high school, for the rugby academies. They're not coming out of club rugby any more.

"The whole structure of club rugby is changing, with the club players getting younger and younger. When I used to play for Belfast, I really enjoyed marking All Blacks.

"A few years ago the NZRU made the mistake of playing New Zealand A as well as the All Blacks. I think it's good for those guys who are one layer down from the All Blacks to be made to play club rugby. To be shared around the clubs, not to all go to one club, so they pass on and share their knowledge with other players.

"The detrimental thing for club rugby with professionalism is the way they tag and earmark players now. How many top players these days will finish their careers, and be able to say, 'I was a good club man.' By going back and playing club rugby, if you play well, you're earning respect.

"Some of the best rugby moments in my career have been winning club championships. Not only for Collingwood in senior B, but also for Glenmark. To be able to say we were the best club in North Canterbury actually means something.

"I think young players should be playing the wily old foxes at club rugby. It's good for professional players to be involved with the good old club guy who does it for the love of the game.

"The young guys coming through are given the best coaches, the top trainers, and they're going to turn out as technically very good players.

"But some guys don't turn up on time for training. This is your job, your livelihood, and you have to think that this is just for a short time.

"Ten years of your life is nothing. It goes that fast, and the reality is that they are going to have to go out and get jobs, and the skills they can learn during rugby, like being punctual, all these little things will help them in later life.

"You can't play rugby forever, and there will never be enough commentating jobs, or enough management, or coaching jobs for all the ex-players.

"It's good money, and I don't believe young players are overpaid, but they've got to be level-headed, they've got to seek a bit of help, and make sure they've got the right people around them so they're not wasting their money. It's not a retirement fund, you can't retire at 29.

"New Zealand rugby's leaders have a responsibility to make sure that these guys come out with some life skills. The cold hard reality is that one day their rugby will be over. With the demands on players now the shelf life for a player is going to be a lot shorter.

"So guys like me that have been through both systems can see you've got to make ground rules. Without taking the fun away, you have to make it a working environment so they're responsible for their actions. So that when they come out of playing rugby, they're better off for the experience.

"If we don't do that then you're basically doing them an injustice. You hear about it with American football, where all these guys come out, and they should be millionaires, and they've got nothing, because they've got gambling problems, or they haven't been able to manage their money, or they've got relationship problems.

"It's tough to have a relationship now for these guys. I'm lucky, I've got a good lady in Priscilla. But it's certainly not a glamorous life for the wives. The team has got demands, and very rarely do you get a weekend off.

"The time you do have off is mostly during the day, during the week, when your partner is working, for example, and then after the game you're tired, or trying to relieve some pressure by sticking your head in a jug. As a young man now you've got to cope with these things."

Blackadder is also concerned that we're categorising our top players at too young an age, which means a whole layer of talented players may miss out because they're late developers.

"A couple of years ago when the Super 12 regions all had an under-21 team they moved the age up to 23. Why not just make it the next-best players? Have a Crusaders B team. If the Colts are good enough, they'll be in that team anyway.

"They can still earmark young players, by having an under-23 tournament, and they'll have a broader base of players. I worry about the fact that they've changed from the under-21 to the under-23 teams. If you're over 23, with the basic structure New Zealand has at the moment, how will they ever know if you're good enough to make a Crusaders team, for example?

"Tight forwards can only hit their peak when they're in their late 20s, but the way we're heading a player like Dave Hewett, whose rugby matured late, could miss out altogether.

"I think the role of club rugby becomes even more important today. A prime example is Leighton Croft, a Glenmark forward I've been playing club rugby with. He's not playing under-23 Crusaders, he's just playing club rugby, and he's playing for North Canterbury and Country. He was given a chance with the initial Canterbury NPC squad and he stepped up and played bloody well.

"It would be so easy to say that perhaps he wasn't good enough, when you've never taken the chain off his collar, and given him a shot.

"If you never give a guy like that a run amongst the so-called elite players, how are you going to know how good he is, and how is he going to know? We've got to create an environment in which everybody is going to get a chance.

"Club players have to go into a game knowing that if they play well enough for their club they have a chance of making a representative team.

"Not only are they playing for sheer pride in a good club environment, but they work hard during the week, and then they play in the weekend, knowing that if they break their arm they could be out of a job.

"That's what they're putting on the line, and that's something you can't take lightly. So when a representative player, or an All Black, comes back you've got an obligation, not only for your club, and yourself, but for your mates.

"It'd be so easy to overlook the club players, and only pick your academy players. It's not too bad in Canterbury, but when I talk to people in some parts of New Zealand, guys never play for their clubs, and to me that's sad."

Blackadder cites a prime example of someone who hasn't had the chance to get his rugby thinking straight before he was playing at Super 12 level. He doesn't want to name the player because he believes his mentors have let him down.

"I don't think he's let himself down. But I've seen in two on ones how he goes himself. He came on the scene, and he was brilliant, he was tagged early on his career, he was on the front page of magazines.

"What made me feel almost sick last year was watching a game where the team he was in did a great move, there was a two on one, and he went himself. He took that try for himself, and this is an environment we are creating a little bit. If he was in a Canterbury team we would have kicked his arse."

The attitude that makes a successful team, Blackadder believes, is selflessness. "That's a vital part of the game. You've got to have a team of players who do things for the team. We've had guys like Steve Lancaster, who has been like a backbone to the team. Because he hasn't always had the chance to get out and play he's had the time to come up with ideas, and he's been there at every training. Then, when Steve had to play, he played bloody well. When Norm Maxwell was right again, old Lancs had to go back to the bench.

"The things that make you a good side are hard work, selflessness, sacrificial acts on the field. What happens is they start coming out in everyone's play.

"In the years when we've been really successful we've done a lot of camps, where we've put people out of their comfort zones, and what's come through are some core values.

"Not just from me, but from all the senior players. As things move on players have left, but we keep reinforcing the values, which all revolve around teamwork.

"A team is made up of team-mates, and if you're good mates you go out and die for each other.

"If you don't know the guy very well, or don't respect him, or don't think he's earned it, if he's a really brilliant guy, but misses 10 tackles, then you think, 'Hang on mate, I'm sticking my butt on the line for you.'

"Sheer brilliance alone is not enough. The biggest thing you've got to earn, whether it's club rugby, or test rugby, is respect. I know what it's like to be last. I know what it's like to be at Lancaster Park when there were 500 people there. Then you play a final, and people can't get tickets to get into the ground.

"The thing I used to grin about when people say teams or players are lucky. There's no luck. It's hard work, that's all it is.

"This year in the Crusaders would have been a great year for things to hit the fan, and fingers to be pointed. But the team stuck together really well. You didn't hear one guy bagging his team-mates. We've gone through the cycles. We've been at the bottom, had success, and now we're shit-kickers again.

"Where we've suffered is that because we've been a successful side for a lot of years, many of our players have gone into the All Blacks. That means for Super 12 we haven't had the time to prepare, and we've had to gloss over things we should have been working on. It's as simple as that.

"In the past it might have taken three or four days to go through our values. For 2001 we did it in about 90 minutes."

Blackadder hopes lessons learned from the load he carried last year will be noted, and might help Anton Oliver in the future.

"What's been so refreshing for me, after being dropped, was to go back and play club footy again. I'd always played loose forward, and to go back and play there again I've enjoyed it so much.

"I feel mentally and physically fresh again. When you're mentally tired you don't know it yourself, because you're too jaded to analyse yourself. But when I had a good rest, I could look back on Super 12 and see how mentally exhausted I was.

"I didn't even want to pick up the phone. I didn't want to talk to anyone. At times I just wanted to sit and watch telly. That's why jet-boating is such a great escape for me.

"Sometimes I'll go up the river with Priscilla and the kids, and it's also a great chance for me to spend some time with Dad, who really introduced me to jet-boating. I enjoy getting away with him, and a couple of guys a bit older than me, Neville and Steve, just to have a quiet beer and a yarn and really unwind.

"One thing I hope, looking back on my experiences, is that they don't fall into the same trap with Anton, and ask too much of him. With the Crusaders not doing so well, you live and die with your team, and it wears you down.

"They've got enough able-bodied captains in Otago in Taine Randell and Kelvin Middleton. If they make Anton the Otago captain, and Anton doesn't do so well, does that mean that his captaincy is not up to scratch? Will he be criticised? I believe to get the best out of Anton leave him as an All Black captain only. Let him be refreshed all the time.

"In the Otago scene he's a natural leader, and he's going to have an input anyway. He's always going to lead in that front row to the best of his endeavours. But don't put added pressure on him all the time."

If there was anything that rankled from his year as a test captain for Blackadder it was that "in a few of the magazines, when I started talking about pride in the jersey and in the team, they started taking the piss out of it. The more times you use it, it does dilute it a bit, but the fact is I was bloody proud of the All Blacks, and I still am.

"Then you see the media start to take the piss out of your words, because you're saying what you believe in. To them it becomes boring after a while, even though what you're talking about are your core values."

If there's a final message he would like to pass on it would be that New Zealanders could afford to borrow just a little of the Australian attitude, and be more positive.

"You don't have to come from a wealthy family to have good manners. The biggest impression you can make on someone is when you first talk to them. Most job interviews are about the person more than the qualification.

"If you go, 'Hello, I'm Todd Blackadder, very pleased to meet you' then straight away the person has an impression that this guy has good manners and is positive.

"On the other hand, 'G'day, here's my CV' can give the impression you're cocky and you don't care. Whether it's in rugby or in general life, it'll be hard. On the other hand, if you're polite, and you're very positive, then all these things are going to brush off on people.

"If someone's doing well, and having a good go, we need to not slam them down. If someone's not doing well at school, we tend to think they're not going to make it in life. But if you look at some of the most successful businessmen they weren't that well educated but they learned a lot of life-skills.

"All I'm trying to say is that you can do anything if you put your mind to it.

"You don't have to be making the rep teams from the time you're nine to make it. You don't have to make the New Zealand Colts. You just have to have a burning desire and a bit of a chance, and a bit of luck on your side. Even the most talented need a little bit of luck. Some things have to fall your way.

"I'd like to think that I'm a good listener. You don't learn a lot when you're talking. You can learn a lot from body language, whether they like something, or don't like something. I'd like to think I've always been sensitive to people. It takes nothing to be sensitive to someone. I've got friends of various ages. Most of my friends aren't necessarily my age.

"I worked for an older guy when I was growing up. You learn a lot from listening to people. You may pick up something that is valuable, and you'll never forget it. We've all listened to speeches and not remembered a thing, but if you're interested in something you'll learn."

And finally, what does he think a young rugby player should aim for in a career?

"I believe you want to be able to walk out of the game knowing you've met a lot of good mates, had a lot of great experiences, and you've made friends for life."

Todd Blackadder

Born: 20-09-1971 at Rangiora
Height: 1.93m
Weight: 114kg
Educated at: Rangiora High School
Position: Lock
NPC team: Canterbury
Super 12 team: Crusaders

First Class Rugby

(to August 31, 2001)

Team	Period	Games	Tries	Cons	Pens	Drops	Points
Canterbury	1991-2001	120	36	-	-	-	176
New Zealand	1995-2000	25	3	-	-	-	15
New Zealand A	1999	4	-	-	-	-	-
New Zealand XV	1993	1	1	-	-	-	5
NZ Trials	1993-98	5	-	-	-	-	-
NZ Colts	1991-92	7	1	-	-	-	5
NZ Development	1994	4	-	-	-	-	-
Divisional XV	1991	2	1	-	-	-	4
Nelson Bays	1990	9	-	-	-	-	-
Nelson Bays-Marlborough	1990	1	-	-	-	-	-
Canterbury Country	1994	1	1	-	-	-	5
Invitation XV	1996	1	-	-	-	-	-
Crusaders	1996-2001	71	6	-	-	-	30
TOTALS		**251**	**49**	**-**	**-**	**-**	**240**